JOOLZ GUIDES

RATHER SPLENDID
LONDON
WALKS

Quirky and Informative Walks Through the
World's Greatest Capital City
by JULIAN McDONNELL

Hardie Grant

QUADRILLE

CONTENTS

INTRODUCTION

Pip pip, tally ho! Welcome to *Rather Splendid London Walks* from Joolz Guides, in which I wander around London telling you fascinating facts!

In this book of 20 walks I will show you some of the fun, interesting, weird and ridiculous things I've noticed on my travels around London.

From an early age I've always wandered aimlessly around the streets of London in a friendless, pitiful manner. Back in my punk days it was the backstreets of Soho, trying to pick up bits of cast-off material to sew onto my psychedelic patchwork trousers! Sometimes my dad would take me and my sister, Lil' Lost Lou, along the Thames riverbank to hunt for treasure such as old coins and clay pipes.

For years I wanted to be a TV presenter. I tried endlessly to convince the TV companies that I was entertaining and decided to make my own videos to demonstrate my amazing abilities. Armed with my philosophy degree from Manchester University, I started making films about London (since that was at least something I was reasonably knowledgeable about, and where I've always lived) and put them on YouTube until I had enough to send off to the TV people. (You see, whenever I checked the job vacancies in the newspaper there were never any 'philosophers required'!)

I suppose I'm just a nostalgic nerd who likes pointing out weird facts and reminiscing about bygone days. Be it a house where Bob Marley recorded a video, an odd green hut where Frank Sinatra bought a sandwich, or an alley where a king threw up – there are nuggets of information and relics around every corner that can turn a seemingly ordinary street into a time machine of intriguing mystery and wonder. Amazingly, it turned out I wasn't the only one who liked this sort of thing and gradually people started asking for more – until I ended up on a mission from God to cover as much of London as I could before I shuffle off this mortal coil!

With the help of Lil' Lost Lou, my trusty sidekick Simon, Kai, Nick, Tom, Laura and a whole bunch of other friends who have all helped over the years, I've aimed to create a wistful, nostalgic record of London, with all its history, culture and weird bits and bobs, as well as trying to be amusing… with a bit of *Columbo* and *The Sweeney* thrown in!

Don't forget to check out the corresponding videos too (see **joolzguides.com** or use the handy QR codes at the start of each walk), but there is plenty of extra stuff in this book that you won't find in the films!

So, it's best walking trousers on, tally ho, and the last one down the pub is a rotten egg!

JOOLZ'S STREET FURNITURE CHALLENGE

Here's a little treasure hunt game for you to play as you walk around with the kids, or just on your own.

What I love about wandering around London is that even if you're walking down a pretty nondescript street in an unglamorous area, there are often many fun little things to make it more interesting.

Score yourself points by seeing how many of these you can spot whilst walking around. And since I'm such a big David Bowie fan, you get a bonus point for spotting anything to do with David Bowie. It's my game, my rules!!!!

Don't forget to share your scores and photos on social media (with the hashtag #JoolzGuidesStreetChallenge).

Good luck!!!!!

Now is your chance for ultimate glory –
The gauntlet has been thrown down.
A stink pipe, a post box, an old coal
hole cover
Are all 'Joolz' in London's old crown.
There's nothing to win;
It's all just for fun,
So earn points and do not delay.
Anything dated or Bowie-related –
We're all heroes, just for one day.

FOUNTAINS AND CATTLE TROUGHS

In the 1850s, with the population of London increasing, it was very hard to find free, clean, uncontaminated drinking water. So in 1859

Samuel Gurney, a Member of Parliament, set up the first free drinking fountain in the railings at the corner of Giltspur Street and Holborn Viaduct. Until then many people preferred drinking beer from the pub, because it was safer! The drinking fountain became so popular that 7,000 people were using it per day, and dozens more were then installed by the Metropolitan Free Drinking Fountain Association. They were often installed near pubs, to encourage people to drink less alcohol. Here the church was more than happy to help in that regard!

In 1867 it was decided that animals also needed a place to get refreshment – so cattle troughs were added, which you can still see dotted around London like sad, abandoned ghosts of the past. Sometimes people use them as flower beds, but often you just walk past them without noticing. I particularly like how many of the drinking fountains were erected in memory of somebody I haven't heard of – probably important people in their time, or much loved.

Once they added cattle troughs the organisation installing them became the snappily titled Metropolitan Drinking Fountain and Cattle Trough Association.

If you spot any of these give yourself **2 points**!!

But if you spot a cattle trough or fountain which actually works and is still in use then it's **4 points**!!!!

Drinking fountain

Cattle trough

Fire insurance plaque

Edward VIII post box

Penfold post box

Gas lamp

Cannon bollard

Old street signs

FIRE INSURANCE PLAQUES

I love spotting these!!

Back in the 18th century, insurance companies had their own fire brigades. If your house was burning down they would only put out the fire if you could prove you were insured by them. Otherwise they'd just let you burn! Those were harsh times.

The first company to do this was the Sun Fire Office – after various mergers and name changes they still exist today as RSA (Royal and Sun Alliance) – and if you were insured by them you got a fire insurance plaque with a nice sun on it. As other companies came into existence they had their own plaques, which you also still see occasionally. Be careful when you're looking for plaques, though, because the residents in the houses don't like people staring at them and taking photos for too long… So don't be surprised if someone yells at you!

Sometimes people buy them in jumble sales and put up fake ones, but that's okay by me.

If you see a fire insurance plaque you score **4 points**!!!!

POST BOXES

Here's another slight obsession of mine!

When you see a post box they usually have 'E II R' written on them, meaning 'Elizabeth Regina the Second' (in Latin '*Regina*' means 'Queen' and '*Rex*' means 'King'), indicating that it was placed there in the time of Queen Elizabeth II.

You don't get any points for spotting an ordinary one like this, but you sometimes see other ones: Victoria, Edward VII, George V (which just appears as 'GR'), George VI and – for the most points of all – Edward VIII!!!

Before post boxes, you had to take your letter down to the local postmaster; but in 1852 the novelist Anthony Trollope, who worked for the Post Office, came up with the idea of post boxes. Originally they were painted green, so as not to be too conspicuous, but the problem was that they blended in too well in the countryside and people couldn't see them! So from 1874 they decided to paint them red.

The earliest ones will have 'VR' on them and sometimes you see nice square ones recessed into walls or enveloped by tree trunks. However, my favourites are the Edward VIII boxes. There aren't many of them because he wasn't King for very long, and when you spot one it is often rather bafflingly neglected and shabby-looking.

So if you manage to spot a post box that isn't Elizabeth II you can have **2 points**!!

But if you spot one which is Edward VIII you get a whopping **10 points**!!!!!!!!!!

GAS LAMPS

Royal insignias appear on other items, too. Street lamps often have them, especially the old gas ones.

There are quite a lot of gas lamps around St James's Park, as well as around Middle Temple and Inner Temple. If you walk around those areas at night, you'll feel like you are in a film about Jack the Ripper, or something written by Charles Dickens. You can tell them by their flickering pilot lights or little round timer mechanisms. Sometimes you even see a man up a ladder repairing them or winding up the timer.

The first street lamps appeared in 1807 along Pall Mall, transforming city life for thousands of Londoners. However, Westminster Council are now, as usual, seeking to remove all the charm of London by converting the gas lamps to electricity! This would entirely remove the romance from a cold winter evening's stroll, but it would make an authentic gas lamp harder to spot!

If you see a gas lamp you get **1 point**!

If you see a gas lamp with the initials of a monarch on it you score **2 points**!!

(But if there's a whole row of gas lamps you can only get points for one of them – otherwise it gets a bit silly…)

CANNON BOLLARDS

During the second half of the 18th century, when enemy ships were captured they would be stripped of all useful materials. However, sometimes the cannon were the wrong size to be used on British ships, which meant they had to find another use for them – so they stuffed them into the ground as bollards. After the Napoleonic Wars ended in 1815 there were even more French cannon lying around. You can still spot original ones here and there, with cannonballs stuck in their muzzles.

I think they look rather splendid, but it's amazing to think they have actually killed

people! You get big ones, small ones, some as big as your head. Some are even planted muzzle-first into the ground.

But beware of replicas! After they ran out of cannon they decided they liked the shape, so they continued with a similar design, resembling a cannon with a ball sticking out of the end.

If you see a cannon bollard you get **2 points**!!

If you see one missing its ball you can have **4 points**!!!!

OLD STREET SIGNS

What a nerd I am! I can't help it, but looking at street signs can actually be interesting!

Normally you will see a sign along the lines of:

Chalk Farm Road NW1
London Borough of Camden

Sometimes, however, you will see a street sign that just refers to 'NW' instead of 'NW1', or 'WC' instead of 'WC2', and so on. If it's missing the number at the end it usually means that it's a sign from before 1917, because it was only in 1917 that the numerical subdivisions were introduced for the postcodes.

So if you see 'Villiers Street WC' it doesn't mean there's a toilet there; it just means the sign is over 100 years old.

Now, let's say you see this sign:

Chalk Farm Road
Borough of St Pancras

Parish boundary marker

Wooden brick paving

Milestone

Stink pipe

Torch snuffer-outer

Stretcher railings

Coal hole cover

Cabmen's shelter

You can be sure that this is a sign from before 1965, because in 1965 many of the London boroughs became amalgamated to make bigger ones. So, for example, the boroughs of St Pancras, Hampstead and Holborn got incorporated into the new London Borough of Camden.

It's harder for you to know which of these are old and new boroughs – but that's all part of the nerdy Joolz Guides challenge!

Oh, also… Sometimes you see old ancient stone street signs, some of which date back as far as the 17th century!!

A pre-1917 sign scores **2 points**!!

A pre-1965 (but post-1917) sign scores **1 point**!

An old stone sign scores **4 points**!!!!

PARISH BOUNDARY MARKERS

During the Middle Ages, England was divided up into parishes, which were areas falling under the clerical jurisdiction of the parish priest. Towards the 19th century they started becoming more like local borough councils, used as convenient administrative bodies – for example, determining where you were allowed to gather firewood or graze your cattle.

In order to know where one parish ended and another began, they used to mark the boundaries with a plaque or a stone – and a lot of them survive today. You often see a boundary stone just poking up in the middle of a park, or by a canal, and it will have the initials of the parish on it. Don't mistake

parish boundary markers for milestones, though, because those are different!

If you spot a parish boundary marker you score **2 points**!!

WOODEN BRICK PAVING

In Victorian times people started to complain about the noise that horses and carriages were making on cobblestones.

One solution was to introduce paving made from wooden blocks. However, after a while they realised that wood got a bit smelly and damp – and was hard to clean – so more modern materials grew in popularity. The old wooden brick paving was removed and mostly used as domestic firewood, but if you look carefully you can occasionally spot surviving sections in the streets.

I haven't seen many examples, so…

If you spot any wooden brick paving you score **10 points**!!!!!!!!!!

MILESTONES

Strangely enough, milestones tend to be a lot scarcer than boundary markers, even though everyone has heard of them. After the invention of the motor car, road signs caused milestones to die out, but you can still find some glorious examples around.

I particularly like the stone ones that tell you something like '4 miles to the Post Office'. In 1767 mileposts became compulsory on all big roads – not only for informing travellers of distances, but also for calculating postal charges, for helping coaches keep on time, and for charging the right fees for changing horses.

The older ones are made of stone and have sometimes faded, but you also see newer metal ones here and there.

If you see a milestone take **2 points**!!

STINK PIPES

Okay, I think these are my favourite!!! Ever since I first saw one I've been seeing them everywhere – but I think people walk past them without noticing, because they look a bit like lampposts.

Occasionally you will spot a very tall pole with nothing at the top of it, apparently without purpose.

Now, we've all tried to light our own farts… haven't we? Oh well, maybe not (and I don't recommend it!) but back in the 1860s when Sir Joseph Bazalgette designed the London sewers, they discovered that all the farty, smelly poo gas that accumulated underneath the London streets was actually quite dangerous and flammable. Sometimes it would ignite and explode, like the time when they were building the first London Underground line at Farringdon and the poor workmen got covered in poo!

So the best way to avoid this was to send these very tall ventilation pipes from the sewers up into the sky, over the Victorian public's heads – that way they wouldn't have to smell it. Anyway, you still see them rusting away in back streets these days, and when you do it's very pleasing.

If you see a stink pipe you can award yourself **2 points**!!

TORCH SNUFFER-OUTERS

Back in the 18th century, before there were streetlamps, wealthier people might employ someone called a 'link boy' to light their way home. If you had been to the opera or a friend's house one of these boys would hold a flaming torch and walk a few yards in front of you. When you got home, to save on fuel, he would snuff out his torch in one of these funny upside-down trumpet-looking things in the railings outside your house.

Some of the fancier houses had more permanent torches burning outside their properties (in Berkeley Square, for example). You can still see the redundant holders within the ironwork on the railings of some 18th-century houses (they're usually ring-shaped, like a basketball hoop). People often use them as flowerpots or hanging baskets, or to install electric lights inside.

If you spot a torch snuffer take **2 points**!!

STRETCHER RAILINGS

Ever seen these weird railings outside council estates? They are made from wire mesh and have two little indents on each end. They are actually Second World War stretchers!

At the beginning of the war all the railings outside buildings in London were removed and used in the manufacture of munitions and other things to help the war effort. Among the items produced were stretchers for carrying injured people when there was an air raid; 600,000 were manufactured using steel, which could be easily cleaned. The two indents were to enable the stretchers to sit slightly raised from the floor. After the war the authorities were stuck with hundreds of these stretchers, and they didn't have any railings around big buildings…so some smarty-pants said, 'Hey, why don't we use the stretchers as railings?!'

They have been gradually dying out, but there are societies to preserve these rather charming artefacts. Who knows, maybe one of your relatives was actually carried on one of them!

If you spot a stretcher railing you get **2 points**!!

COAL HOLE COVERS

In the days when houses had to be heated by burning coal in the fireplace, people didn't want the coal delivery man to come into their houses with his dirty boots making a mess – so there would be a special coal hole installed outside on the pavement, through which he could just pour the coal directly into the cellar. These holes were covered with a particular sort of lid, and you can still see them outside some Georgian and Victorian properties in London.

What is interesting about them is that you get some beautiful designs. They often carry the date when they were forged and the name of the ironmonger who cast them. They could even serve as a bit of a status symbol if you had a nice fancy one with glass in it or an especially intricate design. Some of them are just very plain. After the Clean Air Act of 1956 coal holes died out – and,

of course, some of these former coal cellars are expensive basement flats these days!

If you see a coal hole cover you get **2 points**!!

CABMEN'S SHELTERS

Ever seen those funny green huts that look a bit like garden sheds in the street?

In the 19th century the drivers of hansom cabs weren't allowed to leave their cabs unattended in the road, which meant they found it hard to stop for refreshments. To alleviate this, the Earl of Shaftesbury helped to establish the Cabmen's Shelter Fund, which eventually built 61 of these huts around London. The charity still exists today, helping to preserve and run the shelters for modern-day taxi drivers; 13 of the huts survive across London and they are now Grade II-listed buildings.

Normally only taxi drivers themselves are allowed inside the shelters. You and I are permitted to buy food or drink to take away – however, if you're lucky, you might get a chance to look inside one during the annual London Open House architecture event.

If you spot a cabmen's shelter you get **3 points**!!!

50 points = Joolz Guides Genius! But anything over 10 in one day is perfectly acceptable.

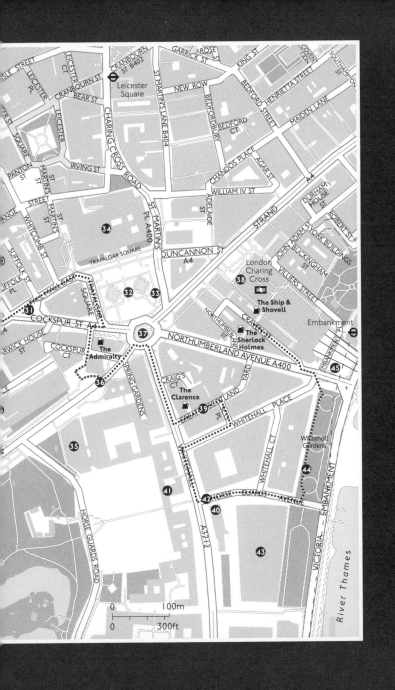

1 A SPLENDID WALK FROM ST JAMES'S TOWARDS WHITEHALL

DISTANCE
5.8 km (3.6 miles)

TIME
2 hours 30 minutes

NEAREST STATION
Green Park

This is an excellent stroll around some of London's oldest shops for discerning gentlemen and ladies, with a few dead people thrown in for good measure!

If you are feeling very posh you can arrange to have afternoon tea at **THE RITZ** ❶, of course, but we are just starting our walk here, a few steps from Green Park tube station. Before crossing the road towards Albemarle Street take note of the window on the corner above the Ritz sign in Arlington Street. In 1921, when Charlie Chaplin returned to his hometown of London for the first time since becoming the biggest film star in the world, he decided to stay at The Ritz. He'd remembered it only just having been built when he was a boy and he'd thought how decadent it was, vowing to stay there one day. On his return he was mobbed by thousands of fans – and he waved to them

from this window. When his grandson, Spencer Chaplin, got in touch to make a Joolz Guides video I arranged for him to wave from this same window. He was thrilled and said it was a very special moment for him, which made me feel very proud. Many celebrities wanted to have dinner with Charlie Chaplin when he stayed here, but he decided to escape through a service lift at the back and travel down to Kennington to see his old house and stomping ground, which he had known as a very impoverished child growing up.

Turn up Albemarle Street and on your left you will see number 50. Since 1768 this has been occupied by a succession of publishers called **JOHN MURRAY** ❷. (After about the tenth John Murray they stopped operating from this address in 2002, but the family still owns the building.) Upstairs there is a very important fireplace, but it isn't really open to the public and not that easy to get in.

By the time the famous poet Lord Byron died in Greece in 1824, his memoirs had been acquired by John Murray from Byron's friend Thomas Moore. Byron was the equivalent of a superstar pop idol today and had been one of the first people we could call a 'celebrity'. He had a portrait of himself printed on the cover of one of his publications, which could be why he was one of the first celebrities to receive fan mail.

Adoring female fans would write to him to say that their breasts were on fire!

> *Why, did my breast with rapture glow?*
> *Thy talents to admire?*
> *Why, as I read, my bosom felt?*
> *Enthusiastic fire.*

This particular fan also wrote about how she trembled as she gazed upon his portrait.

When Byron was at Cambridge University one of the rules was that you couldn't keep cats or dogs as pets, so he decided he'd keep a pet bear instead! He was also famous for sleeping with his half-sister, as well as young boys, and some claim that he invented vampire stories.

In fact, his life was so scandalous that they refused to bury him in Poet's Corner at Westminster Abbey. When John Murray read Byron's memoirs, the publisher was so shocked by all his obscene shenanigans that he decided to burn them in the fireplace upstairs, right here! Such a pity. Just imagine how valuable a copy would be today. It would be a bestseller!

Did I mention Byron was a poet? People seem to forget that fact!

Next, at number 13, is what used to be **THE ALBEMARLE CLUB** ❸, one of the first to admit both men and women. It was here that Oscar Wilde's troubles started when the Marquess of Queensberry (who created the rules of boxing) barged in and demanded to speak with Oscar, who was a member here. Oscar had been seeing rather a lot of the Marquess's son, Lord Alfred Douglas, with whom he was having an affair, and the Marquess wasn't best pleased! Of course, the Marquess wasn't granted entrance, and Oscar wasn't there anyway, so he left a card reading: 'For Oscar Wilde, posing Somdomite' (he meant to write 'sodomite', but the silly bugger couldn't spell). When Oscar returned he was horribly offended and decided to sue the Marquess for libel, but unfortunately it totally backfired. Oscar ended up being convicted of gross indecency and was imprisoned, which was his ultimate downfall.

A little further along is one of London's oldest existing hotels, **BROWN'S** ❹, opened in 1837 (the same year as Queen Victoria's coronation) and it's famous for Alexander Graham Bell making the first phone call in London – the phone is still there! Brown's became popular with monarchs in exile, such as George II of Greece, and many other celebrities including Agatha Christie, Theodore Roosevelt and J.M. Barrie. Rudyard Kipling was said to have finally finished *The Jungle Book* here. Apparently it took him many years… (yeah – well, I'm a slow reader myself!).

Okay, we've nearly finished with this street. But lo! What is this tremendous building?! It's **THE ROYAL INSTITUTION** ❺, which was founded in 1799 to encourage the application of science in practical life. In 1825 Michael Faraday (who invented the rotary engine here) delivered the first Christmas Lecture, and the Christmas Lectures have been held annually ever since, most recently delivered by the likes of Professor Brian Cox. Did you know that ten elements have been discovered here? (I think it's pretty cool, anyway.) In fact, the institution became so popular that they had to make this London's first one-way street!

Turn right at the end of Albemarle Street into Grafton Street, and then left into New Bond Street past **WINSTON CHURCHILL AND FRANKLIN D. ROOSEVELT** 6, remembering to get a selfie. A lot of people don't realise that Roosevelt was disabled, because he never wanted to be photographed in his wheelchair, so it's interesting to note the braces on his ankles on this sculpture. It was actually placed here to commemorate 50 years since the end of the Second World War, but I imagine if he was alive he would have asked them to omit the leg braces!

Turn right into Clifford Street and walk to the end. This is Savile Row.

Savile Row is famous for its bespoke tailoring and has counted amongst its customers James Bond, Withnail (from *Withnail and I*) and many members of the royal family. **HENRY POOLE & CO** 7 is where the tuxedo was invented, after James Potter from New York came to visit the Prince of Wales. He didn't know what to wear and Henry Poole is said to have suggested one of their new jackets, which they had just made for the prince (basically by cutting the tails off a tailcoat). Potter loved the idea and ended up wearing it at his club in New

York – the Tuxedo Club – whose members adopted it as their attire. That's why Americans call it a tuxedo but we Brits call it a dinner jacket. Henry Poole & Co also make uniforms for guards of the royal household, which can cost something like £25,000, last time I asked!

Just a few doors down is **HUNTSMAN** 8, which was the location of Kingsman tailors in the *Kingsman* films.

If you're playing the **STREET FURNITURE CHALLENGE** you can probably spot a few torch snuffers outside a couple of the houses here!

Still further along, at number 3, is where **APPLE RECORDS** used to be 9. I'm always annoyed that they put a blue plaque on the wall here, because I used to enjoy knowing that this was where the Beatles played live for the last time, on the roof (the police closed them down after 40 minutes). Somehow, knowing that doesn't feel as cool ever since they put up the plaque telling everybody!

Savile Row is also where the Japanese get their word for a suit. In the 19th century the Japanese ambassador was visiting London and had a suit made here. When he returned to Japan he was the envy of all his friends, who asked where he got this garment from. He replied 'Savile Row'; someone heard this as 'sebiro', which is now the Japanese word for a suit!

Now turn right down Burlington Gardens.

On your left is a building that is now part of **THE ROYAL ACADEMY OF ARTS** 10, an institution that also includes the big 17th-century Burlington House just behind it.

Originally the Burlington Gardens building was the headquarters of the University of London, which is why it has all these great thinkers and philosophers adorning it. No women, mind you, because obviously women couldn't think in those days.

By 1819 Burlington House was owned by Lord Cavendish, who grew tired of people throwing oyster shells over his garden wall. Oysters were quite a cheap snack in those days – kind of like going for a kebab! In order to prevent this littering, Lord Cavendish ordered a covered shopping arcade to be built, which turned out to be one of the first of its sort in the world. This is **BURLINGTON ARCADE** ⓫, to your left off Burlington Gardens. As you walk through you will see the rather colourful beadles who have policed the arcade since its inception. They look absolutely splendid in their cloaks and top hats and were originally selected from Lord Cavendish's old regiment, the Tenth Hussars, so that his wife could shop in the street without fear of being molested. Some rather curious rules still remain today if you're walking through the arcade: no running, shouting or piddling in the shallow end, no opening of umbrellas and, most famously, no whistling! This is because the upper storeys were occupied by prostitutes and their pimps, and pickpockets would patrol the arcade. In order to communicate and send warnings that the beadle was about, they would whistle to each other!

By the way, many people think they're being very clever deliberately whistling when walking through, but you will still be reprimanded – and it's quite embarrassing, too, when they come to feel your collar! That said, there is one man who is allowed to whistle, apparently. In the 1980s a gentleman was doing his Christmas shopping and whistling a tune to himself when he received a tap on the shoulder.

'Do you mind not whistling, sir,' said the beadle. But when the man turned around the beadle was taken aback. 'I'm so sorry, Mr McCartney,' said the beadle to the Beatle. 'I didn't realise it was you. Please go right ahead!' So, by precedent, Paul McCartney is the only person who is allowed to whistle here… Don't believe me? It must be true – a bloke told me down the pub!!!

I must say, some of the shops along here are a little out of my price range, but one place I'm definitely going to come to is Swaine Adeney Brigg. They are very modest in here and don't tend to show off about all the fabulous commissions they've had over the years, but if you want a bespoke hat made they will make it for you exactly how you want it. They even made the *Peaky Blinders* caps, and Indiana Jones's famous Stetson (except it's not called a Stetson: he actually wears a 'Poet' or 'Crusader', like that of Oscar Wilde!).

Look out also for Hancocks. In 1856 the design of the Victoria Cross, the highest military award for gallantry in the British armed forces, was approved and Queen Victoria granted Hancocks a royal warrant to make them, something which they still do today. The Victoria Cross was introduced during the Crimean War and all of them are said to be cast from Russian cannon seized at Sevastopol – although some have later claimed the cannon were actually Chinese. Victoria Crosses are very rare and have been known to fetch up to £400,000 at auction, since only 1,358 have ever been awarded and only 15 of them since the Second World War.

You now find yourself on Piccadilly and it would be remiss of you not to cross over to the left to take a look in **FORTNUM & MASON** 12, where my mum buys our Easter eggs every year. (The secret is to wait until they are reduced after Easter!) Make sure you use the side entrance, on Duke Street St James's, to see the nice staircase.

William Fortnum was a footman in the royal household of Queen Anne; because of her desire to have fresh candles every day, Mr Fortnum was allowed to keep the old ones, even if they weren't finished. Being an enterprising fellow, in 1707 he convinced his landlord, Hugh Mason, to open a business with him selling candles. Eventually this grew into the huge store it is today. They claim to have invented the Scotch egg, and were also the first place in London to stock tinned baked beans. Queen Victoria even had hampers sent from here to the soldiers in the Crimean War. More recently, I was thrilled to find that I could buy Pitcairn Island honey here – see my documentary *Take Me To Pitcairn*, my best piece of work! – although I notice that they haven't stocked it for a while.

After you've checked if they have any free food samples in Fortnum's (sometimes you can get free choccies!) head down Piccadilly away from Piccadilly Circus and turn left into **PICCADILLY ARCADE** 13, which is almost directly opposite Burlington Arcade.

I prefer Piccadilly Arcade to Burlington Arcade because I'm more likely to buy something from the shops here (when I'm rich and famous).

At the end of the arcade is an excellent statue of **BEAU BRUMMEL** 14, who was a friend of the Prince Regent (that's Hugh

Laurie in *Blackadder the Third*!) who went on to become King George IV.

Brummel was known as a 'dandy'; a man of quick wit who dressed stylishly. He boasted that it took him five hours to get dressed in the morning and is credited with having been the first to wear properly tightly tailored suits. The Prince was awfully jealous of him because he was much too fat to look as good as Beau Brummel, but he tried to emulate his style, nevertheless. Eventually the two argued and Beau Brummel ended up falling out of favour before dying in France, as a penniless scruff with syphilis. It seems that dying this way was all the rage in the 19th century.

Now turn right into Jermyn Street and left at the end into St James's Street. This is a very historic street, but we will just concentrate on a few of the most interesting places.

At number 28 is **BOODLE'S** 15, originally a gentlemen's club, although they now allow women in as guests. These days women are admitted to most of London's posh clubs, many of which are dotted around St James's. Boodle's was frequented by Ian Fleming, who based James Bond's club, Blades, on this one. In fact, Dukes Bar, just down St James's Place over the road, is where he is said to have invented the famous Vesper Martini cocktail – they aren't cheap, mind you, but they do get you pretty plastered!

Down at number 19 are the premises of **JAMES J. FOX** 16, purveyors of the finest cigars for over 200 years, catering to Oscar Wilde, King George VI and Winston Churchill, amongst others. They're very friendly in here and will be happy for you to look at their little museum downstairs, where you can sit in Winston Churchill's chair. You can even

smoke in here (but it should really be one of their cigars, or that would be a bit cheeky). Churchill used to smoke the Julieta, but it was in this shop that they changed its name to a 'Churchill'.

Some of the oldest shops in London are down towards St James's Palace at the end.

You can drop into **JOHN LOBB** , who made shoes for Princess Diana, Frank Sinatra and Queen Victoria. If you're very lucky they might let you downstairs to see all the elves making shoes. I didn't see Rumpelstiltskin in there when they let me have a look; I did, however, see the prototype Wellington boot which was sent to the Duke of Wellington for approval, before he agreed to have some made to stop his feet getting muddy when on campaign!

Next you have the charming **LOCK & CO. HATTERS** , where they made the Duke of Wellington's plumed hat (the one he wore at Waterloo), Churchill's homburg hats, a special one for Admiral Nelson, which had an eye patch to cover his bad eye – but, most importantly, they made Odd Job's hat for *Goldfinger*!!!

It is also claimed that the bowler hat was invented here. In 1849 Edward Coke wanted something more suitable than his top hat to wear at his Norfolk estate, Holkham Hall. His top hat kept getting knocked off by low-hanging branches, so Thomas and William Bowler, who were working at Lock & Co., came up with what we now know as the bowler. It was sturdy, wind-resistant and protected the head. Later, it was favoured by people going to the Derby horse race, and by railroad workers in America (where they call it a derby); but whilst we regard it as a pretty elegant item today, it was worn by all

and sundry in the 19th century, regardless of class. The most famous wearers of this hat have included Charlie Chaplin, Laurel & Hardy and the great Joolz from Joolz Guides!

Next, on your left, is a very Joolz Guides passageway (except this one doesn't smell of urine), with original 18th-century wood panelling. **PICKERING PLACE** is London's smallest square and famous for being the last place a duel was fought in London. Unfortunately, no one seems to know who fought the duel – but it looks like a splendid spot for it. Notice the lovely gas lamps here, too. If you come at night you will feel like you are in a Charles Dickens story.

You emerge back out from this passageway right next to **BERRY BROS. & RUDD** , London's oldest wine shop. The plaque on the wall tells us that this building also used to house the Texas Legation (sort of like their embassy), before Texas was incorporated into the United States.

In 1698 the royal palace at Whitehall burned down and the royal court moved to St James's Palace. The Widow Bourne (whoever she was) decided to open a coffee shop on this site, called The Coffee Mill. In fact, you can still see the scales that were used to weigh the coffee. Later it became very prestigious to know your own weight, so they installed a seat and started recording the weight of many of their famous patrons. These records still exist in the many volumes of books at the back of the shop which we now know as Berry Bros. & Rudd, including those of Lord Byron, the Aga Khan, and Napoleon III.

By the 19th century they were selling wine and over time counted amongst their royal warrants King George III, Queen Elizabeth II and King Edward VII, for whom they created a special tipple that you can still buy here, called The King's Ginger.

Note the telegram on the wall sent by the White Star Line in April 1912 to notify Berry Bros. & Rudd that the *Titanic* had struck an iceberg. There is no mention of all the people who lost their lives; it simply mentions 'you had 69 cases on board'. I guess they knew their priorities!!

Right opposite is **ST JAMES'S PALACE** ㉑, the last place that King Charles I slept before his execution in 1649. The gatehouse is an original Tudor feature, although parts of the palace were hit by bombs in the Second World War. It was the principal residence of George I and II, but these days it's the home of minor royals.

Gosh, time for a drink, I think. How about the **Red Lion**? Walk up Pall Mall and on your left is an alleyway called Crown Passage.

The Red Lion boasts the second oldest pub licence in the West End, although no one knows who has the oldest… It all sounds a bit dubious, but why not?!

Back in the 18th century, when the original pub was built, many of these little alleys existed in London. So, even though the pub has since been rebuilt, it gives a good idea of what the streets would have been like.

It is said that when King James became King of Scotland and England he demanded that a red lion be placed outside all buildings of public importance. This included pubs, and goes some way to explaining why there are so many pubs called The Red Lion throughout Britain. This one does get rather full up, but I do like these rickety old pubs

PUB

The
Red Lion

for a taste of authenticity. They are also friendly to Joolz Guides, so that is much appreciated! Splendid.

Now turn right out of the pub, back down Crown Passage, and left out into Pall Mall.

In the 17th century a game called *pallamaglio* became popular in England. It was a bit like croquet and required a long thin court to be played on, where you hit a ball through hoops. One such court was here, at the bottom of the Haymarket, north of St James's Park. Samuel Pepys describes seeing the Duke of York playing 'pelemele' here in his diary, and it was also common for people to come and watch King Charles II playing this game, which he had learned while in exile. At some point in the 1600s they started to build houses here, but the street was still called Pall Mall after the game.

These days Pall Mall is famous for housing many of London's gentlemen's clubs, including the Reform Club, the RAC, the Athenaeum and the Travellers Club. (You can only join these clubs if you know people who know people, but even then some of them require you to be proposed by several members.) Many plots and scandals at government level have been hatched in

these clubs, behind a haze of pipe smoke and a rustling *Daily Telegraph*. Some have billiard rooms, swimming pools and hotel rooms, and most will have an excellent restaurant. If you are lucky enough to be invited it's quite a fun experience, though not to everyone's taste! They can definitely be a bit snooty.

All the properties on the south side of Pall Mall lie on land belonging to the Crown Estate, except just one: **NUMBER 79 22**.

King Charles II was quite a character and, like many monarchs, he had many mistresses. His favourite was an actress called Nell Gwynne, who wanted a house near the palace – so he gave her number 79.

'But I want to own it!' she protested.

'Well, there you are,' he replied. 'You've got a 900-year lease!'

But this wasn't good enough for her. Nell said that unless he granted her the freehold of the property there'd be no more rumpy-pumpy! So Charles ended up having to convey the property to her by act of Parliament. It then stayed in her family after she died, before being subsequently sold off.

Now walk down Marlborough Road (more or less opposite Crown Passage), alongside St James's Palace, and onto The Mall.

To the right is Buckingham Palace. Who cares? Not me. We're turning left.

I like to look at all the old gas lamps along here. On most of them it should have the initials of the monarch who was reigning when they were installed. Many of them show GR IV (George Rex IV, i.e. King George IV) but it's fun to spot different ones, such as King William IV.

After the *pallamaglio* court was closed on Pall Mall they started to play on what is now The Mall. Originally it was closed off to traffic, making it easier to visit its many shops – and because it was a very fashionable promenade where people would come to see the King playing *pallamaglio*, the word 'mall' was borrowed by the Americans for what we would now call a shopping mall.

On your right is **ST JAMES'S PARK 23**, which is beautiful at night with all its gas lamps; and in the daytime it's jolly lovely with all the ducks and squirrels.

It was originally laid out by King Henry VIII as a deer park. Later, King James I kept crocodiles, camels, elephants and all sorts of animals here. In fact, on the far side of St James's Park he had an aviary full of birds – hence the name of the street on that side of the park, Birdcage Walk.

King Charles II opened the park up to the public in the 1600s and added the pond, or 'canal', as it was then. One of the reasons why I like Charles II is that he sounds like a fun king who liked people to enjoy themselves. He used to go swimming in this canal and catch ducks here for his supper! In 1664 he was given a gift of some pelicans by the Russian ambassador and if you're here at the right time you can see them being fed. Well, their descendants, perhaps!

Anyway, you can hang out in the park if you like but we're carrying on straight along The Mall.

As you continue you will pass statues of **KING GEORGE VI** and **ELIZABETH, THE QUEEN MOTHER 24**. George VI was the one in the film *The King's Speech*, who famously had a stammer.

The beautiful terrace of houses next to George VI was designed in the 1830s by John Nash, the favourite architect of George IV (the former Prince Regent). George IV was often derided for his profligate attitude towards money, and no doubt the public would have preferred him instead to build more social housing, schools and hospitals. However, much of London as we know it was due to George's obsession with building things, and I think these houses look rather splendid. Today the terrace is occupied by institutions such as the Royal Academy of Engineering and various royal societies, but over the years famous occupants have included Lord Cardigan (he of the Charge of the Light Brigade), Prime Minister Earl Grey (after whom the tea is named) and also a section of MI6.

Soon you will see on your left a flight of stairs and a rather imposing monument with **FREDERICK, DUKE OF YORK** perched on top **25**. If you've ever wondered who the grand old Duke of York was, from the nursery rhyme, it was he. Frederick, the second son of George III, was commander-in-chief during the Napoleonic Wars. That said, he is more famous for his hopeless campaigns during an earlier war, which inspired the nursery rhyme:

> *The grand old Duke of York,*
> *He had ten thousand men,*
> *He marched them up to the top of the hill,*
> *And he marched them down again.*

When Frederick died he was horribly in debt. Since his brother had also spent all his money on tailors, architecture and parties, the only way to pay for Frederick to have a statue was to dock the wages of every soldier in the army! Understandably, this didn't go down too well; they started joking

that he needed to be placed so high up that he could escape his creditors – and some even called him the stinky duke, saying at least they couldn't smell him when he was all the way up there! (Rather childish, really…)

At the top of the steps, to the left, is the **NAZI DOG MEMORIAL 26**.

Beneath a tree behind the railings you should see a cute little tombstone which reads *'Ein treuer Begleiter'* ('A loyal companion'). Number 9 Carlton House Terrace, just next door, used to be the German Embassy before the Second World War, where the German Ambassador, Leopold von Hoesch, had a little dog called Giro. Sadly, Giro bit through some cables in the garden and died, so von Hoesch buried him here. However, it's a bit unfair to call it the Nazi memorial, because von Hoesch wasn't really a Nazi. In fact, he was rather popular amongst the Brits and broadly a good egg, but the Nazis hated him. When he died in 1936 his coffin was carried down these very steps, draped in a swastika flag, and hoisted onto a gun carriage with the King's guards flanking it, before being transported to Dover and then across to Dresden – where none of the Nazi party attended his funeral! The British Movietone footage of this is available on YouTube and it is most remarkable to see a swastika being paraded through London. Of course, this was before 'shit got real'. After von Hoesch died he was replaced by Joachim von Ribbentrop, who was a different kettle of fish altogether. Once von Ribbentrop moved in, things changed and Albert Speer (Hitler's architect) designed a new staircase at the Embassy, which was built with marble donated by Mussolini. I've even heard an apocryphal tale about some builders doing renovations at the property in the 1980s, who discovered a huge mosaic swastika. Apparently, they just left it there and it's still hidden under a carpet. It must be true! This bloke told me down the pub!

Now head up into Waterloo Place, past all the statues. On the right you should see **CAPTAIN SCOTT** **27**, the great British hero famous for his failed attempt to become the first man to reach the South Pole. We do like a plucky underdog. Sadly, he arrived to find the Norwegian flag already flying. He had been beaten by his adversary Roald Amundsen, who had no qualms about eating his dogs. Scott thought that extremely un-British and would never undertake such barbarism – but as a result, he and his team were found dead, frozen in their tents. Amundsen must have regretted being the first, because Captain Scott is far more famous now, and if you ask most people they probably think Scott got there first, anyway!

The two splendid buildings facing each other are the **ATHENAEUM CLUB** **28** and the **INSTITUTE OF DIRECTORS** **29** (formerly the United Service Club). The Duke of Wellington was a member of both clubs. If you look on the kerb you will see, on either side of the road, a stack of blocks placed here 'by desire of the Duke of Wellington'. He used to ride everywhere and didn't want to have to leap to the ground from his horse, so this made it easier when he was visiting his clubs. The Duke of Wellington was one of the first people to popularise the wearing of trousers. Indeed, he was ejected from one of his clubs for doing so! Only knee breeches were allowed at that time. (Next time I go to my club I shall arrive without any trousers, since they're so touchy about it, and see if they let me in!)

Now let's turn right into Pall Mall and head towards Trafalgar Square.

Up the road to your left you will see the **THEATRE ROYAL HAYMARKET** **30**. Have you ever wondered why actors wish each other luck by saying 'break a leg'? It's because of Samuel Foote, the dramatist and manager of this theatre in the 18th century, when the theatre didn't yet have a licence to stage plays (although he got around this by holding musical concerts and offering the plays gratis). One day he was out riding with the Duke of York and Albany (the brother of King George III), who had challenged him to a riding contest, when Foote was thrown off his horse and broke his leg. The Duke was horrified, as he had provided Foote with a lame horse, and apologized, saying, 'I'm so sorry. Whatever can I do to make this up to you?' Foote replied, 'Well, I'd love a licence for my theatre to stage plays!' This was immediately granted, so ever since, breaking your leg in the theatrical world has been regarded as good luck!

Keep going past the statue of **KING GEORGE III** **31**. They called him Mad King George, although he was, in reality, a very good king who oversaw great advancements in science and exploration. It was sad that he was afflicted with either porphyria or possibly a mental health disorder in later life, which caused him and his family great suffering. The film *The Madness of King George* tells the story of his decline. They originally wanted to call it *The Madness of George III* (the title of the Alan Bennett play from which it was adapted) but the distributors thought this might cause confusion for Americans who would wonder if they had seen parts I and II! It's true! I didn't make that up!

We have now reached **TRAFALGAR SQUARE** **32**, named after Admiral Nelson's victory over the French, and designed by John Nash. As I have mentioned, King

George IV had spent rather a lot of money and although a statue of him was eventually erected here after he died, one of the other plinths, which was intended for his brother King William IV, remained empty for over 150 years. It was only in 2003 that they decided to start using it for contemporary art which is replaced every so often, and it is now referred to as 'the fourth plinth'. (I think it looks a bit odd, personally. I'd prefer a statue of John Thaw from *The Sweeney*.)

On the southeast corner of the square is what some people call **THE SMALLEST POLICE STATION IN LONDON** 33. It looks like a small circular turret of a castle with a lamp on top.

Since Trafalgar Square opened it has become a place for people to congregate when protesting against something. The first Bloody Sunday riots culminated here in 1887 and later the general strike and the poll tax marches ended up here. It has been a focal point for festivities, too, such as New Year's Eve and the celebration of England's mighty Lionesses in the UEFA Women's Euros 2022!

In order to keep an eye on all the potential troublemakers at these events, it was decided to place a policeman in this little box, with slits as windows, so he could look out and call for reinforcements if things got funky. He had a hotline to Scotland Yard – the light on top would flash to indicate help was on its way. Some people will tell you that the lamp on top came from Lord Nelson's flagship, HMS *Victory*, but that is what is officially known as 'bollocks'.

By the way, I highly recommend you visit the **NATIONAL GALLERY** 34. It has some excellent paintings inside which you will recognise as they are really famous ones. It's also absolutely free, like many of London's museums. One story I heard was that when Walt Disney was in London he was just coming out of the National Gallery when he saw a man outside drawing on the pavement in chalk, and this gave him the idea for Bert's character in *Mary Poppins*. Lucky he didn't come these days, otherwise Bert would have been an unconvincing floating Yoda!! I mean, I can understand one floating person as a street entertainer, but must there really be five in a row?

When I was a child my mum used to let me paddle in the fountains, but of course that isn't allowed any more. In fact, all the fun things, like feeding the pigeons, have been banned by the powers that be. However, you can still get a photo on the famous lions sculpted by Edwin Landseer – but I expect they'll ban that soon too, so better be quick! When you do, remember to take a look at the paws, because they aren't actually lions' paws.

Edwin Landseer was a famous painter of animals and when Queen Victoria asked him to sculpt these lions it took him rather a long time. In fact, it took him so long that the dead lion which had been brought to his studio from London Zoo started to decompose. By the time he came round to doing the paws it had become so bad that it had to be removed, so Landseer ended up using his pet cat as a model! Which means if you look at the lions in Trafalgar Square they actually have cats' paws, with fully retractable claws! What's the difference? They're both cats, I guess.

On the south-facing bronze relief at the foot of the column is quite a rare sight. If you look carefully you should be able to see a man with short curly hair carrying a gun, next to a dying Nelson. It is thought that this is George Ryan, an African sailor who fought for Britain at the Battle of Trafalgar. A sculpture of a Black man in central London in the 21st century is pretty rare, let alone in the 19th century!

Now head past the Admiralty pub and down back onto The Mall. Everything around here has nautical connections. Ahead of you is a statue of Captain Cook (the famous explorer) and on top of all the lampposts you can see cute little ships. Some bloke down the pub with one eye and a wooden tooth told me that these are Nelson's fleet sailing down The Mall, while he looks on from his column, but this sounds decidedly fishy to me.

Quite near here is what used to be the Admiralty building. The stone bunker you can see to the right of Captain Cook is the **ADMIRALTY CITADEL** 35, still used by the Ministry of Defence as an admiralty communications centre. The same very knowledgeable bloke in the pub also claimed that there is a tunnel leading from here all the way to Buckingham Palace, and that Churchill used it as part of the Cabinet War Rooms. In the summer it is usually covered with ivy, acting as excellent camouflage. In fact, during the Second World War they decided it was necessary to disguise it from the air as well, so they grew a lawn on the roof to make it indistinguishable from the park. It's still there today and every so often someone can be spotted carrying a lawnmower up the ladder to the roof.

Now walk under **ADMIRALTY ARCH** 36 and look for the small nose poking out of the wall. Many rumours abound about whose nose it could be. For a while it was popular belief that it was supposed to be Napoleon's nose, placed there so that the cavalry could tweak it when they rode past. Some suggested it was Wellington's nose, as

he was known to have quite a large conk! It's definitely not mine, as it's too small.

In fact it was placed there by an artist called Rick Buckley as an art installation in 1997. He placed many of them around London and it was said that if you found them all you would come into great fortune! These days only seven of them remain and have become known as The Seven Noses of Soho. My friend and sometime cameraman, Kai, made a film about them and, in so doing, necessarily found them all – but hadn't found fortune at the time of going to press. The original idea of the noses was to protest against the prevalence of CCTV cameras in London – some of the highest numbers in the world. The artist was trying to accuse the authorities of being nosey parkers! (I have also seen a couple of ears on buildings, by Tim Fishlock, but I think that was just for fun.)

Admiralty Arch itself is being turned into a hotel, which will have a spectacular view down The Mall. In general I'm not in favour of big corporations taking over iconic buildings, but in this case I think it would be marvellous to stay in such a hotel, especially as most people wouldn't have been able to enter the building before. (I expect they'll have a bar which one can visit, although at the time of writing it hadn't yet opened.)

Now you find yourself on the south side of Trafalgar Square at the top of Whitehall. You should be able to see an equestrian statue of **KING CHARLES I** 37. Charles was very short, but the sculptor tried to make him appear taller than he was. I think he only succeeded in making Charles look out of proportion. The statue was originally placed in Covent Garden – but after the beheading of Charles I in 1649 the statue was ordered to be taken down, and it was given to a metalsmith called John Rivet for dismantling. However, cunning Cockney as he was, Rivet hid the statue in his garden and instead made lots of money selling cutlery and key rings allegedly from 'the melted down statue of King Charles'!

Later on, when his son Charles II was reinstated after the revolution, it was sold back to the King. Delighted to have a statue of his dad back, Charles II had it erected it here, facing down Whitehall. It is the point from which all distances to London are measured in Britain, and they say it's officially the centre of London.

In case you've ever wondered why this area is called Charing Cross, it's because on this spot before the Civil War stood the Charing Cross. It was the last of 12 stone crosses erected between Lincoln and London along the route of the 1290 funeral cortège of Eleanor of Castile, the wife of King Edward I (that's Patrick McGoohan in *Braveheart*!). Each time they rested they built a cross.

Back then London was much smaller and this area was a hamlet called Charing (after the Anglo-Saxon word *cierring*, meaning a bend in the river). Anyway, Oliver Cromwell, who was a terrible bore, had this cross taken down. He wasn't too keen on pubs or theatres, either. No wonder he didn't last very long. Today you can see a replica of the original cross outside **CHARING CROSS STATION 38**.

Now let's walk down Whitehall and turn left at the **Clarence**, into **GREAT SCOTLAND YARD 39**. You might see some police horses here because, as you can tell from the name, it's where the Metropolitan Police were based for many years. 'Great Scott, Holmes!!!' 'Great Scott, Marty!'

What Dr Watson and Dr Emmett Brown are actually saying is 'Great Scotland Yard!'

You'll see many government buildings here. The Ministry of Agriculture, the Ministry of Silly Walks and of course the Ministry of Magic! It is in this street that Harry Potter enters the Ministry via a telephone box in the film of *The Order of the Phoenix* (but the box isn't here in real life – it was just for the film). Ron Weasley can also be seen keeping a lookout on the corner in *The Deathly Hallows Part I*, before dragging Mafalda Hopkirk in through the large gate.

Turn right into Scotland Place and right again into Whitehall Place, before continuing down Whitehall.

In the 13th century the Archbishop of York bought a property here so he could be near the Palace of Westminster, which was where the kings of England had resided since 1049. Later on Henry VIII acquired it and expanded it into Whitehall Palace, which then became the new residence for the monarch – indeed, this is where Henry VIII died.

Having failed to learn a lesson about playing with matches in 1666, somebody rather carelessly burnt down Whitehall Palace in 1698. The only part which survives is the **BANQUETING HOUSE 40**, right opposite the guards of the Household Cavalry. It's totally changed since those days, though.

It was outside the Banqueting House that King Charles I was executed on 30 January 1649. They had erected a scaffold outside in the street, and Charles stepped out of a first-floor window of this very building and onto the scaffold. The story goes that he had asked for an extra shirt to wear because it was so cold that he didn't want people to think he was shivering with fear.

Then he uttered the words, 'I shall go from a corruptible to an incorruptible crown' – and the axe fell. Members of the crowd came forward to dip their handkerchiefs into the blood as a memento, while the King's head was held aloft to the words 'Behold the head of a traitor!'

I read somewhere that prior to chopping off his head, the executioner asked forgiveness of the King for the duty he had to perform, to which Charles replied: 'No, I don't forgive you.' Fair enough, I suppose.

The guards on horseback you can see at the entrance of the **HOUSEHOLD CAVALRY MUSEUM** **41** are part of the King's official bodyguard. This used to be the entrance route to the Palace of Whitehall and then later to St James's Palace, which is why it is still guarded by the King's bodyguard. You can walk through to Horse Guards Parade, where they hold events like Trooping the Colour or (during the Olympics) beach volleyball! However, if you want to ride through here you must be a member of the royal family. (But Prince William, who I know is reading this, probably already knew that!)

If you are here around 4 p.m. you can watch an inspection of the guards. This all began in 1894, when Queen Victoria caught them drinking and playing cards when they should have been on duty. To punish them she ordered an inspection every day at 4 p.m. for the next hundred years! Even though 100 years has elapsed they decided to keep doing it, as it's nice for tourists. In fact, even I like watching it and also getting a photo with the guards – but don't be a smart arse! There's always someone who thinks it's funny

to try and distract the guards or make them laugh. Although they are trained not to react to this tomfoolery there are some pretty scary armed police nearby who you wouldn't want to mess with!! Besides anything else, it's disrespectful and Joolz Guides doesn't approve of horseplay.

Incidentally, tour guides will tell you that the black mark on the number 11 of the Horse Guards Clock is to commemorate the time of day when King Charles I was executed. This is one thing that *wasn't* told to me by my reliable man down the pub, but it does seem to have passed into common London lore. If I had to guess, I would probably assign it a low probability rating, otherwise known as bollocks. It just looks like a black smudge to me. I think a king's memorial would be handled with slightly more accuracy and care, frankly, but you can believe it if it floats your boat!

Now let's turn off Whitehall, down Horse Guards Avenue towards the river. Just behind the **STATUE OF THE DUKE OF DEVONSHIRE** **42** is where Harry Potter enters the public lavatory in *The Deathly Hallows Part I*.

Continue along Horse Guards Avenue and you will see on your right the **MINISTRY OF DEFENCE** **43**. However, the thing that I find more interesting is just at the end, when you get to the green opening. Right next to the building you will see an oddly isolated flight of stairs leading nowhere. This is a remnant of the old Whitehall Palace that burnt down in 1698 and was put here at the behest of Queen Mary (as in William and Mary) so she could step down from her apartments to a royal barge waiting for her on the river. The river no longer flows this far (see **York House Watergate in Walk 2**), and apart from the Banqueting House

36

36

37

43

Sherlock Holmes

Ship and Shovell

and Henry VIII's secret wine cellar beneath the Ministry of Defence (which we aren't allowed to see), this is all that's left of the once magnificent palace.

I'm getting tired now and I fancy a pint, too. Let's just nip through the little garden on the other side of Horse Guards Avenue from the Whitehall Palace stairs. It's called **WHITEHALL GARDENS** 🕘 and it's all part of the land reclaimed by Sir Joseph Bazalgette when he built London's sewers and took the river back 50 yards or so in Victorian times. Actually, there's a memorial to him at the end of the garden just across the busy road near Hungerford Bridge. We'll discuss him in the next walk.

Now head up towards the Playhouse Theatre. You'll notice on your right a beautiful **CABMEN'S SHELTER** 🕘 – the green hut selling coffee and tea. There are 13 such shelters remaining around London and they are Grade II-listed buildings (see the **STREET FURNITURE CHALLENGE**, page 7). Back in the 19th century the drivers of hansom cabs weren't allowed to leave their cabs unattended in the road, which meant they found it hard to nip into a café for refreshments. So in 1875 the Earl of Shaftesbury (a thoroughly decent chap), along with some others, set up the Cabmen's Shelter Fund. The fund built 61 of these huts around London so that cab drivers could enjoy 'good and wholesome refreshments at moderate prices'. You can still see the handrail around the edge which was used for tying your horse onto. In fact, until as late as 1976 taxi drivers were still required to carry a bale of hay for the horse!

The only people who are allowed inside for a drink are taxi drivers, though ordinary folk can buy a takeaway. It won't be a gourmet coffee like Quentin Tarantino makes for The Wolf in *Pulp Fiction*, but it's a very charming experience. I do have a bone to pick with them, though. I heard that both Winston Churchill and Frank Sinatra were granted access to the shelter in Kensington – and neither of them drove a cab, to the best of my knowledge!

Now walk up Craven Street. It looks like a fairly unassuming road, but in fact it was in this street that Charles Dickens got his idea for Jacob Marley's face appearing as a door knocker in *A Christmas Carol*. Most of the characterful old grotesque door knockers seem to have disappeared now, but it could have been a memory Dickens had as a child. It was just close to here, at a place called Hungerford Stairs (demolished when they built Charing Cross Station), that a twelve-year-old Dickens worked in a factory, putting labels on shoe polish. He hated the job – and the people – but it was here that he met a fellow called Bob Fagin, whom he rather liked… so he named one of his villains after him! That's gratitude for you!

Not only was Craven Street home to Herman Melville and Benjamin Franklin (whose house you can visit for a fun dressing-up experience) but it was also where my dad asked my mum to marry him! Now that definitely calls for a drink.

There are many choices. You could try the **Sherlock Holmes**, so called because they have a recreation of Holmes's study upstairs, which was originally built for the Festival of Britain in 1951. It's quite nice to stand outside in the summer, as there is a bit of space for drinkers, but I fancy a pint at the **Ship and Shovell**. It used to be 'Shovel' with one 'l', because local coal hauliers used to drink here (as well as at the Coal

Hole on the Strand) but was later changed to 'Shovell' after Sir Cloudesley Shovell, a 17th-century sea admiral. Before they built the train station there was a porthole in the south wall so that dockers could keep an eye on ships that might need their assistance.

Mine's a large one. Cheers!

PUB

The Ship and Shovell

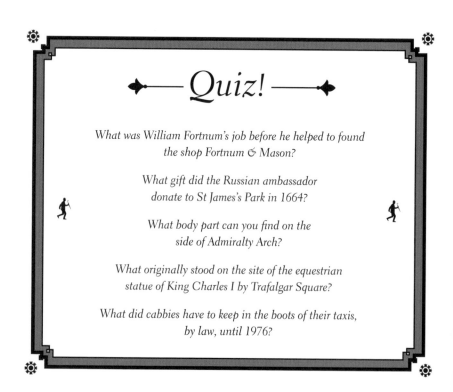

✦ — *Quiz!* — ✦

What was William Fortnum's job before he helped to found the shop Fortnum & Mason?

What gift did the Russian ambassador donate to St James's Park in 1664?

What body part can you find on the side of Admiralty Arch?

What originally stood on the site of the equestrian statue of King Charles I by Trafalgar Square?

What did cabbies have to keep in the boots of their taxis, by law, until 1976?

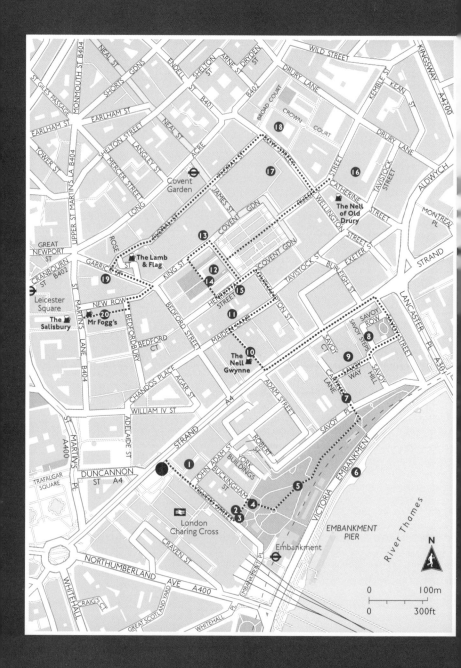

2

2 A TREMENDOUS RAMBLE FROM CHARING CROSS TO COVENT GARDEN

DISTANCE
2.3 km (1.4 miles)

TIME
1 hour

NEAREST STATION
Charing Cross

Let's start outside Charing Cross Station at the top of Villiers Street. I've already mentioned the stone cross outside the station (see **Walk 1**), which is a replica of the one that originally stood on the south side of Trafalgar Square.

I don't know why I like Villiers Street so much. I suppose I like to imagine how it was before they built the station, with those Dickensian steps leading down to the river and all the dockers carrying sacks of grain and coal up and down.

Just on the left is a little alley that smells of urine, with a sign indicating it is **YORK PLACE** ❶, but with the rather curious addition 'Formerly Of Alley'. Back in the 13th century this whole area was owned by the Bishops of Norwich, but it later became known as York Place when it was granted

to the Archbishop of York. Indeed, at the bottom of Villiers Street was York House, which was one of many splendid houses along the riverbank – the most beautiful in London, it was said.

In the 1620s the estate came into the hands of George Villiers, the Duke of Buckingham, who was the 'favourite' of King James I, which basically means they were lovers! George Villiers wasn't very popular and, in fact, fans of Alexandre Dumas might recognise his name from *The Three Musketeers*, in which he is murdered in a pub in Portsmouth by John Felton. This actually happened in real life. Eventually the estate passed into the hands of his son, the Second Duke of Buckingham – also called George Villiers – who was rather a spendthrift and ended up having to sell it. However, one condition of the sale was that George Villiers, Duke of Buckingham, be remembered in all the street names around the area. That is why you are now standing on Villiers Street, which lies parallel to Buckingham Street, around the corner from George Court. John Adam Street used to be called Duke Street, so we had:

George Court
Villiers Street
Duke Street
Buckingham Street

All that was missing was 'of', to complete 'George Villiers, Duke of Buckingham'. It was therefore decided to name this little urine-stained passageway Of Alley. They later changed it back to York Place but, rather pleasingly, decided to add the reminder of its former name. Hence 'York Place Formerly Of Alley'.

(It should be called Piss Alley, if you ask me!)

Carry on down Villiers Street and on the left, before Embankment tube station, you will see **GORDON'S WINE BAR** ❷, thought to be London's oldest. If you want to get a seat in its cavernous depths you need to be there before people leave work, which, in London, can be any time! Fine wines, cheeses and a tolerably convivial atmosphere make this one of London's most charming and characterful wine bars. (It might be my imagination, but on Sunday afternoons it seems to be full of people on internet dates! You can have fun trying to spot them.)

My favourite thing about Gordon's is how it came into being. Before the river was embanked in the 1860s it used to be a warehouse where stevedores and dockers could unload their cargo easily, but after it became landlocked they ended up converting the building into

accommodation. Rudyard Kipling was one of the tenants here, before moving to a house next door to my dad in India in the 1920s! (Daddykins was only five back then.)

Anyway, back in 1364 King Edward III was terribly embarrassed because he was unable to pay back a loan granted to him by the Worshipful Company of Vintners (wine merchants). In order to make it up to them he granted a Royal Charter enabling them to set up and sell wines anywhere without a licence. These people became known as Free Vintners.

Skip forward five centuries to 1890 and a fellow called Angus Gordon comes along and opens up a wine bar here. The council approach him to ask for his licence and he replies: 'I don't need one. Look, see?! I'm a member of the Worshipful Company of Vintners!' Of course, they had to let him go ahead and didn't imagine any other cheeky rascals would try the same thing – but they did! A chap called John Davy used this right in 1965 to open the Boot & Flogger in Borough, but they soon put an end to it after this. So Angus Gordon and John Davy are known as the last of the Free Vintners.

Look out also for the **OLD STREET SIGN** ❸ from before 1917, next to the modern street sign.

Go down the steps and through the outdoor drinking area for the wine bar and on your right you'll see an opening to a park.

The magnificent structure before you is **YORK HOUSE WATERGATE** ❹. It is a wonderful example of the beautiful watergates that existed along this section of the river when it was lined with glorious palaces and mansions. York House stood on the Strand (which means 'shore of the river') and would have backed onto the river here. The gate itself was built in 1626 and you can even see the Duke of Buckingham's coat of arms at the top of it, but after the 1860s the gate became redundant.

If you had been standing on this spot 200 years ago you would have been standing in the river. You see, back then the River Thames was virtually an open sewer. The summer of 1858 was absolutely boiling and became known as 'The Great Stink'. All the untreated human excrement and detritus on the riverbank started to smell so bad that people living nearby couldn't take it any longer. They even had to douse their curtains in disinfectant to stave off the pungent stench. After much prevaricating, the government eventually had to do something – as they themselves were right on the river and couldn't even sit in Parliament. It was time to act, and I don't mean dropping toast to see if it landed butter-side up!

They got hold of an engineer called Joseph Bazalgette, who had an excellent beard, like Lemmy from Motorhead. He had the idea of narrowing the river, causing it to flow more quickly, thereby carrying off all the effluence and poos. He then set about one of the biggest engineering projects in London's history, by building the sewers that we still use today. He knew that the population would increase in the future, so he had the foresight to make the system's capacity six times greater than was needed at the time… and lucky for us that he did! No wonder they gave him a knighthood.

So now we have the lovely **VICTORIA EMBANKMENT GARDENS ❺**, a delightful place to read your book and imagine the likes of George Villiers stepping out of his house through the Watergate and straight onto a boat up the river of poo.

It's fair to assume that, had Parliament been on Primrose Hill, we would probably still be without sewers, as they only decided to act once it started to affect their work.

Carry on through Victoria Embankment Gardens and you will see various sculptures. There's 'Rabbie' Burns, Scotland's most famous poet, who wrote 'Auld Lang Syne' (which means 'for the sake of old times', in case you wondered) and also a soldier on a camel. This is to commemorate the Imperial Camel Corps, who served in Palestine, Egypt and Sinai during the First World War. Just beyond it, outside the park next to the river, you should just be able to see a large stone obelisk known as **CLEOPATRA'S NEEDLE ❻**. It doesn't actually have much to do with Cleopatra, although she would have seen it in her lifetime. It was first erected in Heliopolis around 1450 BC, where it stood for over a thousand years, but was then taken to Alexandria – where it stood for a while but then fell over and lay in the sand, rather neglected, for a few hundred years. With France and Britain constantly competing for artefacts from ancient Egypt, Muhammad Ali (not that one!), the Viceroy of Egypt, decided to gift it to the British in 1819 to commemorate the victory over Napoleon at Waterloo. It remained in Alexandria until 1877, when a plan was hatched to transport it to London. Lugging something that big such a distance was not easy: they had to build a special capsule, inside which the obelisk was placed, and then towed it behind a ship all the way to Britain. The ship hit a storm in the Bay of Biscay and a tremendous effort was made to save the obelisk, with many men losing their lives. When the obelisk eventually arrived in 1878, to the

①

②

④

⑥

Camel benches

⑦

cheers of onlookers, the names of these men were inscribed on the pedestal and two sphinxes were placed either side to guard it – although they are pretty useless guards! They're pointing in the wrong direction and should be facing away from it!

Beneath the marble pedestal the Victorians buried a time capsule containing an array of items of the time. Cigars, coins, a picture of Queen Victoria, bibles, a map of London, Bradshaw's railway guide (which Michael Portillo is always going on about) and photographs of the 12 most beautiful women of the age! I wonder who they could have been. No date has been set for it to be opened, so maybe we'll never find out. We're lucky it's still there, actually, as in 1917 it was hit by a bomb during an air raid. You can still see the evidence of shrapnel on the pedestal.

While you're here, look out for the splendid ornamental street furniture, by George John Vulliamy, who was responsible for the beautiful fish lampposts and the sphinxes. In keeping with the Egyptian theme, he also designed the charming camel benches (further along the embankment).

We've strayed outside the park and onto the river, but now I want to head back through the gardens and up **CARTING LANE** **7**. As you exit there's a nice information board with a picture of what the area looked like when the Watergate was still in use.

Now, because I'm juvenile, I like to call this 'Farting Lane'. As you walk up you will see a lamppost on your left with a rather thick shaft. (No sniggering at the back, please!)

Well, after the installation of the London sewers there was a tendency for the sulphurous, farty gases to explode occasionally, causing much alarm among pedestrians. Enter Joseph Webb, an enterprising gentleman from Birmingham, who patented the sewer gas lamp. This utilised the smelly poo gas from the sewers to light the street by burning it off. They became quite popular, making him rather rich. However, they weren't without their problems and kept having a lot of smelly leaks until eventually they fell out of favour. This one, however, is the last of its kind in London and the sign next to it states that it continues to run off 'residual bio-gas'. (So next time you let one fly in a lift or a classroom and everyone looks at you, you can simply state that it's nothing to worry about, it's just residual bio-gas!)

Now carry on up Carting Lane and you'll see a little road to the right called Savoy Way, leading to Savoy Hill. At the end of that you'll see a little chapel and a dead-end street called **SAVOY STEPS** **8**. This is where Bob Dylan stood with all his word cards in the promotional film for 'Subterranean Homesick Blues', which is often regarded as one of the first ever pop videos. He had been staying at the Savoy Hotel during his 1965 tour of Britain and it was supposed to be used as a trailer for the documentary *Don't Look Back*. If you're with a couple of friends you can recreate the video with someone acting as Allen Ginsberg, Bob Dylan's friend and famous New York poet, in the background.

Turn left at the end of Savoy Hill to return up to the Strand.

Turn left again and you'll come to the **SAVOY HOTEL** **9**. Many people like to book afternoon tea here as it's rather marvellous, like many of the big London hotels. However, if you book a table for 13 you might find that you have an extra guest joining you: Kaspar the cat!

Back in 1898 a fellow called Woolf Joel had organised a dinner for 15 people, but a couple of people dropped out, leaving him with only 13. At dinner there was much conversation about superstition and the number 13, as it was commonly held that the first person to leave a dinner party of 'unlucky thirteen' would be the first to die. Joel thought this was poppycock and said: 'Don't worry, chaps. There's really nothing to worry about, and to prove it I will be the first one to leave.'

Anyway, two weeks later he went home to South Africa and was shot dead! This alarmed all the guests and staff at the Savoy, so in future when 13 guests were dining they would supply a member of staff to be the 14th. However, having a stranger at the table became unpopular; so instead, they had a cat carved out of wood. Nowadays, if you are a party of 13 you can request to have the pleasure of Kaspar the cat at your table – he will be given a napkin and served all the same dishes as everyone else!

The little street leading to the entrance of the Savoy Hotel is one of the only places in the UK where we drive on the right. This is so that when people arrive at the adjacent Savoy Theatre the taxi driver, who sits on the right, can lean back and open the door for the passengers to step straight out in front of the theatre, instead of the driver having to get out and walk around the cab.

In fact, when they manufacture the London black taxis they have to ensure that they can turn around in the road quickly and easily, so they are given a much smaller turning

PUB

The Nell Gwynne

circle than most cars. The official test for conditions of carriage is whether they can get around the fountain here outside the Savoy.

Now cross the Strand, heading in the direction of Trafalgar Square. After the Vaudeville Theatre turn right up another urine-stained alley, called **BULL INN COURT 10**.

There's a rather small, characterful pub here called the **Nell Gwynne**, named after King Charles II's favourite mistress. She's remembered a lot around here, as she used to sell oranges in Covent Garden before becoming an actress, and the pub still attracts many people in the theatrical profession today. Be careful when going down the incredibly cramped and steep flight of steps to the tiny, low-ceilinged toilet! Tricky after a few pints!

Also, beware of the ghost! In 1897 actor William Terriss was stabbed at the stage door of the Adelphi theatre, just around the corner. In a very thespian manner, with his dying breath, he vowed: 'I shall return, dahhhhling!!!' His ghost has been spotted haunting Covent Garden station and this piss-stained alley ever since. (I can think of nicer places to frequent for all eternity, but each to his own. Actors, eh?)

Speaking of actors, in Maiden Lane, at the top end of the alley, is **RULES ⑪** – London's oldest restaurant, founded in 1798. People often ask me what constitutes 'English food', apart from fish and chips. Well, this is it. Lots of game bird: pheasant, grouse, partridge and the sort of thing that might be served in *Downton Abbey* (which has been filmed here) or *Brideshead Revisited*. James Bond visited in the film *Spectre*, and it has also played host to many cabinet members, Buster Keaton, Laurence Olivier, Charles Dickens, Harrison Ford and Paul Newman. More importantly, it was here that King Edward VII had his clandestine meetings with Lily Langtry, the American actress and socialite, when he was the Prince of Wales. (What is it with English royalty and actresses? There was Nell Gwynne, Lily Langtry and now Meghan Markle!) The prince – 'Bertie', as he was known – was already married to Princess Alexandra, but he was a well-known philanderer (and food-lover). He would wobble up a specially created secret staircase and through a concealed door here to meet his 'secret' lover, Lily Langtry, whom everybody knew about!

Now continue past Rules to the end of Maiden Lane and up Southampton Street, until you reach Covent Garden. This was once a big fruit, veg and flower market, but these days it's full of rather expensive boutiques. It's called Covent Garden because in the 13th century the whole area as far as the Strand was walled off and belonged to the monks of Westminster Abbey, whose orchards and vegetable gardens were here. Hence the *Convent* Garden, later known as Covent Garden. Unsurprisingly, it was seized by Henry VIII during the Dissolution of the

MAIDEN LANE

Monasteries and later given to the Earls of Bedford (which is why you can see Bedford Street close by).

ST PAUL'S CHURCH ⑫ is known as the Actors' Church, with memorials to many theatrical people inside, including Charlie Chaplin and Thomas Arne, who wrote 'Rule, Britannia!'. It's probably better known as being the backdrop for 'the best street performers' pitch in the world' – or so I was told by one of the performers, Lucky Rich, who also happens to hold the record as the most tattooed person in history! He was an excellent performer when I saw him, and I heard it said that he also held the record for taking the most money after a juggling show here. This is also where the first ever Punch and Judy show was staged, in 1662. The standard of entertainers varies: there are some great ones and some not so great. Eddie Izzard started out here doing a knife-throwing act! I feel I should also mention some of my favourite performers from the past here. Many will remember Pepe with his red hat, one of the greatest clowns I've ever seen, and also Dr Stoo (Stewart Harvey Wilson), whom I watched for many years whilst working for Hamleys' Covent Garden branch. Quite the most inspirational and talented character I've ever met, and if you ever wondered why I wear a bowler hat, it's because he did! (You can see him hanging around behind Chris Tucker in *The Fifth Element*.)

You'll probably also recognise the West Piazza from the beginning of *My Fair Lady* – although that was actually a film set in which they recreated the whole market, but got it back to front! **RUSSELL HOUSE** 🕐 on King Street, the oldest building in Covent Garden (built in 1716), is on the wrong side in the film and I've heard it suggested that they used the Hogarth print called *Morning* as reference. Hogarth's prints were taken from etchings, which would come out back to front when reeled off…

In the 1960s Russell House was home to The Middle Earth Club, where David Bowie performed in the mime show *Pierrot in Turquoise* long before he became famous. Loads of bands played here: The Who, Pink Floyd, T-Rex and many more. In fact, it was here that Tony Visconti first saw Marc Bolan from T-Rex and made him into a star – also resulting in his introduction to Bowie, a legendary partnership!

Walk down King Street and just before number 9 take the turning through the gate into the churchyard.

If you're a fan of *The Sweeney*, like me, you might like to seek out actor John Thaw's memorial bench, or just enjoy eating your sandwiches in the pleasant garden.

St Paul's Church, consecrated in 1633, was designed by Inigo Jones. The only problem is that the entrance is on the wrong side. Jones wanted a grand entrance on the piazza, but that would have meant the altar (traditionally on the east side of the church) would block the entrance. You can see on the piazza (behind the street entertainers) that the entrance is blocked up.

These days the churchyard is a nice garden but in the 18th century there were graves here (and there still are, actually, but without gravestones). In order to prevent 'resurrection men', or grave robbers, from digging people up, they had to install a **NIGHT WATCHMAN'S HUT** 🕐. The blue hut with windows on either side was where the watchman (in the days before we had actual police!) would sit and keep an eye out. Otherwise your corpse could end up being sold for medical experiments!

Now exit via the opposite gate to the one you came in through, and turn left into Henrietta Street, where Jane Austen used to live.

The recruitment centre for the Royal Air Force used to be based at **4 HENRIETTA STREET** 🕐. It was here that T. E. Lawrence (Lawrence of Arabia), who was quite a national hero after the First World War, came to try and join up in 1922 under the name of John Ross. However, the fellow who wrote the *Biggles* books, Captain W. E. Johns, turned him away! (I mean, why on earth did he try to join with a different name?)

A few hours later Lawrence returned with a messenger from the Air Ministry, who told Johns in no uncertain terms: 'Don't you know who this is?!! Get him into the Force at once, or you'll get your bowler hat!' I guess that meant 'You'll get fired.' It could have all been avoided if Lawrence had just said who he was in the first place. No need to be a dick about it!

One can while away the hours watching the performers and musicians on the various pitches around the market, or visit the London Transport Museum, which is pretty cool. Look out for the magicians' corner at the bottom of James Street, where you can see rather amusing magic shows. To be honest, Covent Garden is not what it used to be, and a lot of the characterful shops have been replaced with swanky expensive brands – but luckily the entertainers are clinging on, which makes it a happy place.

The beautiful covered part of the market in the centre was built in 1830; before that there was a massive square, which you can see in Hogarth's paintings and etchings. It's amazing to think that the council once wanted to smash the whole thing down to make way for a heliport and dual carriage motorway from Trafalgar Square to Holborn!! Lucky that the Covent Garden Area Trust exists to prevent too many liberties being taken.

As you walk through the market, look for the lovely old wooden boards on the walls with archaic rules and regulations – for example: 'No one may throw any root vegetable, fruit, stone or other missile.' Some of the rules which were established by Acts of Parliament still haven't been repealed because the politicians are rather too busy to worry about people throwing peaches.

On the north-east corner of the piazza, which is now occupied by the entrance to the Royal Opera House, stood a notorious pub called the Shakespeare's Head tavern, where the sandwich was invented.

In the 18th and 19th centuries the upper classes would hobnob with creative types at the Beefsteak Club, which met here regularly. On one occasion in 1762 John Montagu, the fourth Earl of Sandwich, was on quite a winning streak at the card table when his tummy started rumbling. Not wishing to leave the gambling table, he called for a quick snack to be brought

to him. When asked what he'd like, he just said, 'Oh, I don't know, just bring me a piece of meat between two slices of bread.' His companions saw what he was eating and all said, 'I say, we'll have what Sandwich is having!!' And ever since then he has been credited with inventing the snack that bears his name. (I seriously doubt he was the first person ever to do it, but we do like to claim things like this.)

The head waiter at the Shakespeare's Head tavern was Jack Harris, who was also a pimp. In Georgian London Covent Garden was awash with brothels, coffee houses, poets, pickpockets and prostitutes; and there was a book called *Harris's List of Covent Garden Ladies*, which was published for 40 years. For two shillings and sixpence you got an annual list of 150 prostitutes, detailing their physical attributes, sexual preferences, prices and the depths to which each was prepared to plunge. Other publications included *The Wandering Whore* (1660–1) and *A Catalogue of Jilts, Cracks & Prostitutes, Nightwalkers, Whores, She-friends, Kind Women and Other of the Linnen-lifting Tribe* (1691). Here's a random selection of entries:

> *Mrs. Forbes — Very much pitted with the pox but has played with her own sex in bed where she is as lascivious as a goat.*
>
> *Mary Holland — Tall, graceful, comely and shy of favours but could be mollified at the cost of £20.*
>
> *Her sister, Elizabeth, on the other hand, was less expensive, being indifferent to money but a supper and two guineas would have tempted her!*

Makes you proud to be British.

Now leave the piazza and go up Russell Street until you see **THE THEATRE ROYAL DRURY LANE** .

In 1709 a dramatist called John Dennis had written a play which was being performed here, called *Appius and Virginia*, in which they needed to stage a thunderstorm – so he developed a method of rattling metal balls around in a bowl in order to imitate the sound of thunder. It was very effective, but unfortunately his play was pretty hopeless and the theatre dropped it after a short run. However, nearby there was a production of *Macbeth* which also needed a thunderstorm and they decided to use this same technique.

John Dennis was furious! 'Damn their eyes!' he ejaculated. 'They won't let my play run but they steal my thunder!' And ever since then we have used this convenient phrase. (Just as a side note, you might think it rather amusing that he ejaculated, but this was a common term in the olden days. If you read Sherlock Holmes you'll notice he ejaculates numerous times!!!).

Another man who may have ejaculated around here was that randy old bugger, King Charles II. When his mistress, Nell Gwynne, was performing at the theatre here he would wait for her in the pub over the road. She could escape from the theatre through a secret tunnel which went underneath the road, leading to the pub, so that no one would see them meeting up. The pub now bears her name: the **Nell of Old Drury**.

Now head back the way you came, towards Covent Garden, but turn right up Bow Street.

On your left is the **ROYAL OPERA HOUSE** , which has a lovely balcony that you can now visit for a selfie overlooking Covent Garden. They also have some costumes worn by famous ballerinas like Margot Fonteyn, and they do tours of the whole building if you are interested.

In 1837 the manager, William Macready, adapted a process of mixing hydrogen, oxygen and the chemical quicklime for indoor use. Shining a spotlight through this haze, he created a wonderful effect on stage – and that's why today we talk about famous people being 'in the limelight'!

Opposite the Opera House is what used to be **BOW STREET MAGISTRATES' COURT** , where the writer Henry Fielding sat as a magistrate. It was his idea in 1749 to create London's first police force, which originally constituted six officers who became known as the Bow Street Runners. Before then, law enforcement was in the hands of private citizens, who could be quite corrupt and weren't regulated by the state. Basically you'd shout 'Stop, thief!' and everyone would chase the miscreant down the street like in the movies, until a part-time constable or night watchman could make an arrest. The Bow Street Runners were replaced by the

9

12

13

14

17

Lamb & Flag

Metropolitan Police in 1829, formed by Sir Robert Peel, who was the Home Secretary and later Prime Minister. That's why we call policemen 'bobbies' – 'Bob' being short for 'Robert'. (Some people call them 'Peelers', too, while others call them all sorts of names which can't be printed here!)

Now turn down Floral Street and walk all the way to the other end. I much prefer these little alleys and back streets. It gives one more of a sense of what it must have been like in times gone by.

Before you reach the end of Floral Street you will see an alleyway on your left called Rose Alley. This leads to the **Lamb and Flag**, which claims to be the oldest pub in Covent Garden and one of the oldest in London. It was quite a rough area in the 18th century and the room upstairs was known as the Bucket of Blood because of the bare-knuckle fist fights that it hosted. It's now called the Dryden Room, after John Dryden the poet, who was beaten up in the alleyway by thugs hired by the Earl of Rochester. (The Earl of Rochester was a most interesting character, whose life was portrayed by Johnny Depp in the film *The Libertine*.) Dryden had written a poem called 'An Essay Upon Satire', in which he criticised King Charles II and his mistresses, as well as the Earl of Rochester. Rochester, also a poet, was on good terms with the King, who tolerated and even enjoyed his bawdy, honest writing – but he was quite a hell-raiser and knew how to drink, smoke and catch syphilis. (You should read some of his poetry, it's absolutely filthy!)

Dryden offered money to find out who had hired the thugs, but no one came forward. I suspect John Wilmot, the Earl of Rochester,

would have been an interesting dinner guest – but you'd probably prefer your daughter to marry Dryden.

On Garrick Street, at the end of Floral Street, is the **GARRICK CLUB 19**, founded in 1831 and named after the famous actor David Garrick. It's unlikely you'll be able to go in unless you are friends with a member. It's popular with actors and people in creative professions, although when Charlie Chaplin went there he reported having a rather dull evening, even though he was surrounded by celebrities like H. G. Wells and Noël Coward. He just wanted to go off exploring London on his own.

The club became very wealthy after A.A. Milne (who wrote *Winnie-the-Pooh*) included them in his will. When Disney wanted the rights to *Winnie-the-Pooh* they had to pay the club $40 million!

At present they do not accept women as members, but Cherie Blair (Tony Blair's wife), amongst others, is working to get that changed. (I'm not sure I would want to join a club that would have me as a member!)

Turn left on Garrick Street, then turn right into New Row and then left into Bedfordbury. You should see another smelly alleyway on your right, called **GOODWIN'S COURT 20**.

This court dates back to the 17th century and is very popular for film productions. It's the street where Meryl Streep's character lives in *Mary Poppins Returns*, and it looks like it's been lifted from the world of Charles Dickens. Well, one side does, anyway! The beautiful old bow windows and original gas lamps give it a very authentic feel. In fact, even Joolz Guides has filmed down here when talking about Harry Potter. Some tour guides suggest that J.K. Rowling was inspired by Goodwin's Court, and that when they were building the sets for the films they based them on this view. Well, tour guides say a lot of things but the bloke down the pub never mentioned it, so who knows? Let's go! It smells of wee!

Time for a drink, I think – and what better venue than the only pub where my mum and dad ever had a drink together in London! **The Salisbury**, just across St Martin's Lane, has a wonderful Victorian interior that hasn't been ruined by refurbishment and has a few little hidden corners, where you can whisper behind your hand about other patrons.

The Salisbury used to be popular with actors. I saw an interview where Sean Connery talked about how he used to hang out here with other unknown actors before he was famous. It was here that serial killer Dennis Nilsen met Andrew Ho, a Hong Kong student whom he tried to murder. Ho managed to escape and the police questioned Nilsen; but Ho didn't press charges, leaving Nilsen free to murder another dozen men or so. If that's a bit gory for you, there's always **Mr Fogg's** over the road. If it's a Thursday night you might even catch Tom Carradine's Cockney Sing Along in Mr Fogg's (if he's still doing it when you're reading this, that is!).

Down the hatch.

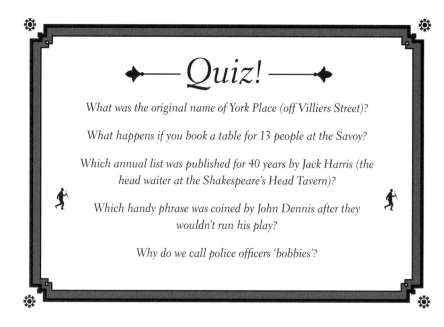

Quiz!

What was the original name of York Place (off Villiers Street)?

What happens if you book a table for 13 people at the Savoy?

Which annual list was published for 40 years by Jack Harris (the head waiter at the Shakespeare's Head Tavern)?

Which handy phrase was coined by John Dennis after they wouldn't run his play?

Why do we call police officers 'bobbies'?

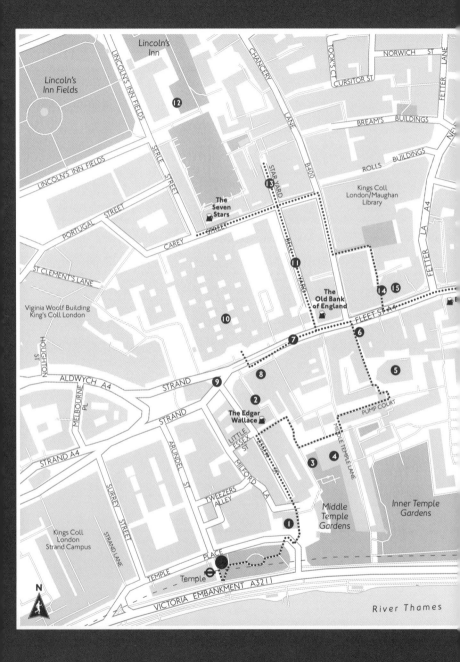

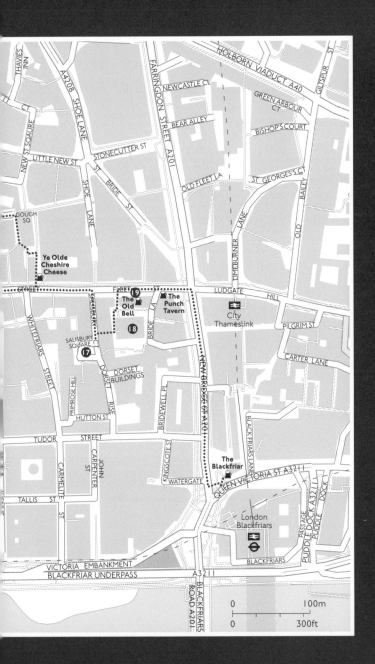

3

3 A TIP-TOP TURN THROUGH TEMPLE AND FLEET STREET TO BLACKFRIARS

DISTANCE
3.4 km (2.1 miles)

TIME
1 hour 30 minutes

NEAREST STATION
Temple

We also start here in Walk 14, but we are going the other way in this one – and can I just say it's better to do this walk on a weekday, or some of the pubs, Inns of Court and other places will be closed!!

What ho, young fellow mi'lad. Let's walk through this little garden outside the station.

At the end of the garden you will see a magnificent house called **TWO TEMPLE PLACE** ❶ with my favourite weathervane on top. I'm obsessed with weathervanes and you can see many of these around London. This one is the *Santa María*, the ship which brought Christopher Columbus to America in 1492. The reason it's there is because the house was built by William Waldorf Astor, the richest man in the world (founder of the Waldorf Astoria in America, and hence the Waldorf salad!)

In 1891 he emigrated to London so that his children would be in less danger of being kidnapped. (Quite why he felt they'd be any safer in England is beyond me! He obviously had a high opinion of us!) So he had this excellent house built. It's usually closed to the public but if you're lucky they might be holding an exhibition there; it's always worth checking because you'll get to see the tremendous interior with its grand staircase and frescoes. The stairs have carvings of characters from *The Three Musketeers* and there are friezes depicting *The Last of the Mohicans*, Shakespearian characters, English monarchs and all sorts of people who don't seem to go together. I find it quite fun trying to guess who each one is, or which frieze is depicting which Shakespeare play. Oh, and don't forget to look at the secret hidden door upstairs, which looks like something from a Sherlock Holmes story! Once a year we have something called Open House London and buildings like these open their doors to public.

Just past Two Temple Place you will see a red telephone box and a passage leading to the left. Head up here and straight up the steps ahead of you, into Essex Street.

Soon you'll see one of my favourite pubs, the **Edgar Wallace**. Edgar Wallace was a journalist, novelist and poet, but became most famous for having written *King Kong*. He was rather prolific and you can see a lot of his books adorning the shelves inside. The pub itself has very unusual decor with vintage adverts on the walls for things like washing powder and cigarettes. In fact, I think my dad is in one of them and I keep meaning to give them one with me in it!!!

After a quick sharpener, carry on to the right into **DEVEREUX COURT** ❷ where, if you're on a serious pub crawl, you could stop at the Devereux, named after Robert Devereux, second Earl of Essex, who was one of Queen Elizabeth's favourites (which seems to mean 'her bit on the side').

After a good old bit of plotting against the Queen, Devereux was placed under house arrest in Essex House, a grand building that stood here until the 17th century. Eventually he had his head chopped off and a builder called Nicholas If-Jesus-Christ-had-not-died-for-thee-thou-hadst-been-damned Barbon knocked his house down for redevelopment.

Strange times, those, when you consider that Elizabeth was 53 when she started her affair with Essex (who was in his teens!) and knew him all his life!

Next to you there is a gate leading to a courtyard, but before going through, glance up to the left and you will see a chance to earn points: two plaques!!

On the left is an anchor, which demarcates the boundary of the parish of St Clement Danes (we'll be walking past the church later); St Clement was martyred by having an anchor tied around his ankles and being thrown into the sea. The one on the right, by contrast, is not a boundary marker – it is a property marker. This is the symbol for the Duchy of Lancaster, which is the private portfolio of land and property of the British sovereign in their role as the Duke of Lancaster. During the reign of Queen Elizabeth II she would sometimes be introduced as 'The Duke of Lancaster', which sounded a bit odd.

Now go through the gate and find yourself in the charming and relaxing **MIDDLE TEMPLE GARDENS** ❸.

Amidst the hustle and bustle of busy London streets lie these little oases of calm where one can escape the mayhem of the city. Middle Temple and Inner Temple are two of the four Inns of Court. When you qualify as a barrister you must join one of these inns. Don't ask me how it is decided which one you join – 'Dammit, Jim, I'm a tour guide, not a lawyer!!!' – but I like to think the Hogwarts Sorting Hat places you in either Middle Temple, Inner Temple, Lincoln's Inn or Gray's Inn.

Originally these grounds were the headquarters of the Knights Templar who, in the 12th century, set out to protect pilgrims visiting Jerusalem. They were also known as the Knights of the Order of Solomon's Temple, hence Knights Templar. What actually happened was that they became rather wealthy throughout Europe, with their secret dealings and transactions, much to the annoyance of the Pope and the King of France (who was skint). So in the end they were disbanded and their possessions were confiscated. These grounds (or inns and hostels, as they were) ended up being leased to a bunch of lawyers who were looking for somewhere to set up their practices. Later on King James I granted the whole area to them in perpetuity and they've been here ever since! Just try shifting them…not a chance!

Now, because the two inns are right next to each other, the way to tell which side you are on is to look at the insignias. You can see the emblems everywhere – on top of lampposts, on water pipes, and above doors. Of course, my favourite way to tell is to look at the weathervanes. If you see a lamb and flag then you are in Middle Temple, whereas if you see Pegasus (the flying horse) you are in Inner Temple.

The large building with the lamb and flag weathervane is **MIDDLE TEMPLE HALL**

4, completed in 1572. Sometimes, if you're cheeky, they'll let you look inside – otherwise, you'll just have to see it in my video! It has the best example of a Tudor hammer beam ceiling in London, and a table made from timbers of Sir Francis Drake's ship the *Golden Hinde*. When I was a boy my dad, who was a barrister (among other things), took me for lunch there and it was like being in a Harry Potter film. All the judges sit on 'Top Table', while all the barristers and solicitors occupy the other tables – at least, that's how it was when I went! You don't have to be a lawyer to go there, though. You can book lunch there yourself if they have room, but you have to dress up smartly!!!

Most interestingly, we know that William Shakespeare himself performed in this very hall on 2 February 1602, in the cast of *Twelfth Night*! We do not know a huge amount about the movements of Shakespeare, so I find this fact particularly pleasing.

Now walk past the hall and turn left up Middle Temple Lane and then right through a little tunnel to **TEMPLE CHURCH 5**.

On your way you will see lots of authentic gas lamps, which give the whole area a Victorian atmosphere; if you come at night you really feel like Ebenezer Scrooge or David Copperfield. It is unsurprising that they often use this area for filming – you might recognise it from *Mary Poppins Returns*, where the lamplighters do their dance and the BMX bikes ride down this street.

What's that? It's not as good as the original? Well, of course it isn't! The original is practically perfect in every way, but the sequel is perfectly tolerable and Emily Blunt is very good, at least.

Because the church is round, my dad used to tell me that this is where King Arthur met with the Knights of the Round Table. I believed him, because of all the creepy effigies of knights on the floor. However, whilst it's a fun story to tell children, when I grew up I decided this can be confidently placed in a box on my shelf marked 'Bollocks'.

The church was consecrated in 1185 by Heraclius, who was archdeacon of Jerusalem. Some of it was damaged by the Luftwaffe, but the Norman gate still survives intact. The knights were pretty powerful and important, and the head clergyman here still has the unique title of the Reverend and Valiant Master of the Temple. In medieval times he could sit in Parliament as First Baron of the Realm.

There are possibly over 100 knights buried beneath the church; one of the effigies inside is of William Marshal, the most famous knight of his age. Numerous theories have been proposed as to why some of them have crossed legs – but a bloke in the pub told me that it's just a decision by one of the medieval sculptors to give them the appearance of marching into battle.

Just behind where the Royal Courts of Justice stand today (coming up soon) there was a jousting pitch where William Marshal once famously unhorsed Richard the Lionheart. Along with some of the other knights you see here, Marshal was involved in meetings between King John (of Robin Hood fame) and the rich, powerful barons who were aggrieved at the amount of power the king displayed. William Marshal acted as a mediator and swore on behalf of King John that the barons' grievances would

be met. This is what ultimately led to the signing of the Magna Carta at Runnymede – our first bill of rights! (I wonder if one of their grievances was having to spend £5 to get into the church?)

Most importantly of course, this is where Tom Hanks comes in *The Da Vinci Code* looking for the grail.

On leaving the church, find your way up the passage past Dr Johnson's Buildings leading to the big gate (look out for any winged horses on the way) and out onto Fleet Street.

Above your head is **PRINCE HENRY'S ROOM 6** at 17 Fleet Street, named after the Prince of Wales, who actually would have become King had he not died of typhoid fever aged 18, leading to his brother going on to become King Charles I (who got his head chopped off). It is one of the only buildings in the City of London to survive the Great Fire of 1666 – though it was actually a tavern in those days, frequented by the likes of Samuel Pepys the diarist, who wrote in an entry in 1661:

… to the Fountain tavern and there stayed till 12 at night, drinking and singing, Mr. Symons and one Mr. Agar singing very well. Then Mr. Gauden, being almost drunk, had the wit to be gone; and so I took leave too.

Now, here's some fun with language.

If he had taken his hat too then he would have used one of my favourite linguistic devices: a zeugma! Here are a couple of examples: 'He took his hat and his leave' or 'He left in his car and a temper.' Score yourself some points by creating a zeugma of your own! Feel free to tag me (@joolzguidesofficial) in a photo of yourself on Instagram along with your zeugma! Okay, later perhaps.

Let's carry on past the sculpture with a dragon on top.

This is known as **TEMPLE BAR** ❼. A beautifully ornate gate designed by Sir Christopher Wren originally stood here, but as the street got more congested with traffic it became necessary to remove it. After spending 100 years or so in the park of a stately home in Hertfordshire, it was then sold for £1 and moved to the entrance of Paternoster Square, by St Paul's Cathedral, where you can still see it (although today it doesn't have any traitors' heads on spikes, like it would have done in those days).

The monument that replaced it here was designed by Horace Jones (who also did Tower Bridge) and the dragon indicates that you are approaching the City of London. Not Greater London as we know it, but more like the area defined as Londinium by the Romans, known also as the Square Mile, which had city walls and gates like Ludgate, Newgate and Aldgate.

This is traditionally where the reigning monarch stops to ask permission to enter the City of London; some tour guides will tell you that he cannot enter without the permission of the Lord Mayor. This also belongs in the box marked 'Bollocks'.

In 1066, after William the Conqueror (or 'William the Bastard', as he was known) defeated Harold at the Battle of Hastings, he headed north, sacking various villages. When he reached London he threatened to ransack the city, where a lot of important noblemen

had congregated, but they surrendered peacefully, accepting him as overlord – thus saving him the hassle of getting past the city walls. By way of appreciation, he granted the city something called 'The Conqueror's Charter of William I', recognising the importance of London, which was already a centre of trade and wealth back then. You can still see the charter, which is the oldest document in the archive at the Guildhall, in which William promises to preserve the rights and privileges which they had in the days of Edward the Confessor. That's why even today the City of London has different rules and their own Lord Mayor and police force, who can be recognised by their distinctive helmets.

(It's a little-known fact that when they take their helmets off, their heads are actually the same shape as the helmet! I've even heard that the crack in their bums is horizontal and not vertical, causing a terrible rumbling sound if they slide down a hill!)

So when, for example, Queen Victoria enters the City of London for her jubilee, as depicted on this monument, she stops out of courtesy and requests to enter. The Lord Mayor surrenders his sword but the Queen doesn't take it; she merely touches it, as if to say: 'I know I can enter here and you are beneath me, but thanks for showing me this courtesy.' The monarch has power over the Lord Mayor but simply never uses it.

Before we move on, I should mention that this is also the spot where the Fleet Street Pillory stood. This is one of the places where, in 1703, Daniel Defoe was pilloried for writing a seditious pamphlet defending the freedom of religion. The pillory is the one where your head and wrists are clamped while the crowd throw things at you – not

FLEET STREET

to be confused with the stocks, where you would be seated on the ground with your feet clamped. People would throw all sorts of rotten food and sometimes quite heavy objects, and it was quite usual to have your ears nailed to the pillory, too. However, when Daniel Defoe was pilloried the crowd just threw flowers, as he was so popular.

Continuing along on the left side of Fleet Street, as it becomes the Strand, you will come to **TWININGS** ⑧, where the royal family buy their tea. Thomas Twining started his tea business in 1706, opening London's first tea rooms on this very spot. The sign above the door is the official company logo, which they first hung here in 1787, and it's been here ever since. This makes it the oldest company logo in continuous use on the same location in the whole world!

Inside you can do tea tastings and there is even a small museum at the back, where they have what is claimed to be the first tip jar in the world. Basically, it's a box with 'T.I.P.' on it, which was placed in the tea rooms in order to speed up service. If you put money in the box they would come to you more quickly. I've argued with people over this many times, because it's supposed to stand for 'To Insure Promptness', whilst my friends say that it should be spelt 'Ensure'. However, since Dr Johnson's *Dictionary* was not printed until 1755 it is perfectly possible that spelling was a bit sketchy. I mean, there's

no apostrophe in 'Twinings', either, and I regularly see menus misspelt even today.

Anyway, I like the story, so I'm sticking with it!

Speaking of Dr Johnson, that's a statue of him behind **ST CLEMENT DANES CHURCH** ⑨, which is just further along, on the traffic island. Look at all the shrapnel damage on the walls caused by the bombs during the war. Note also the beautiful lamppost on the traffic island, which doubles up as a ventilation shaft for the public lavatories below.

St Clement Danes (designed by – guess who? – Sir Christopher Wren!) is now the official church of the Royal Air Force, which is why it has statues of characters like Sir Arthur 'Bomber' Harris, who was Air Officer Commanding-in-Chief during the bombing raids by Germany in the Second World War.

It is believed that the Danish King of England, Harold Harefoot (son of Cnut) is buried here, hence the name of the church containing 'Danes'. He was originally buried in Westminster Abbey but when his brother Harthacnut took over as King, he dug up his corpse, chopped off its head and threw him into the River Thames! (And you thought *you* had sibling rivalry!) Then some sympathetic fishermen recovered his bones and buried them here.

If you are here on the hour you might hear the bells playing the nursery rhyme 'Oranges and Lemons'. Quite why the bells of St Clement's say 'Oranges and Lemons' is not entirely clear (and they might even be referring to St Clement's in East Cheap) but a bloke in the pub told me that in the old days, if you wanted to bring goods ashore from the river it would cost more in docking fees if you did it within ye olde City of London. So in order to avoid this expense, many cargo ships would unload a little further up, near the church of St Clement Danes, and a typical cargo would have consisted of oranges and lemons.

> *Oranges and lemons,*
> *Say the bells of St Clement's.*
> *You owe me five farthings,*
> *Say the bells of St Martin's.*
> *When will you pay me?*
> *Say the bells at Old Bailey.*
> *When I grow rich,*
> *Say the bells at Shoreditch.*
> *When will that be?*
> *Say the bells of Stepney.*
> *I do not know,*
> *Says the great bell at Bow.*
> *Here comes a candle to light you to bed,*
> *And here comes a chopper to chop off*
> *your head!*
> *Chip chop chip chop the last man is dead.*

Did you know that William Webb Ellis, who invented rugby, used to be rector of this church? A game originally played by men with funny-shaped balls, if you ask me.

Opposite Twinings are the **ROYAL COURTS OF JUSTICE** ⑩, built in the 1870s after they held a competition for the best design. George Edmund Street won, with the result being this wonderful building, which you can actually go inside. You do have to go through airport-style security and you can't take photos, but you can even see a trial if you like. It won't be a criminal case, though; it will be a civil case like divorce, or George Michael suing his record company, or Johnny Depp's libel case.

There are a total of 19 courts, each of which has its own individual design. When George Edmund Street completed his plans he claimed that his building was absolutely perfect and without rival. However, everyone was shocked and said: 'You can't say that! No one has the right to create absolute perfection except our Lord!' So in the end he decided to include one deliberate aberration, which you can seek out when visiting. Go to the end of the main hall and just before the staircase you will see a column which hasn't been finished. It doesn't reach the ground and serves no purpose.

'There,' said Street. 'My building is perfection except for that column!'

Go up the stairs and you'll see some nice examples of judges' outfits and robes, most of which aren't usually worn in normal court but are from more important ceremonies or cases. They are very expensive, though one of them, frankly, looks like a Santa Claus outfit bought from a fancy dress shop! (They must have seen him coming.)

Hopefully you can get out the back door here and onto Carey Street – if so, skip below to the bit about the Sir Thomas More building.

Otherwise, you'll have to go back out the main door and turn left towards the dragon on Temple Bar and then left at the **Old Bank of England**.

If you're turning this into a pub crawl (and it does make a nice one) you could stop here for a pint. It used to be the Law Courts branch of the Bank of England and still retains the feel of a bank with its high ceiling.

Seven Stars pub cat

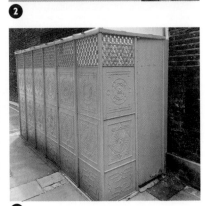

PUB

The Seven Stars

Fancy a pint? Well, the pub we just passed is perfectly tolerable for refreshment. The **Seven Stars** actually refers to the seven provinces of The Netherlands, as this area was commonly frequented by Dutch seamen in the 17th century. If you can squeeze in (it is full of lawyers these days) you might see the pub cat, who is famous for wearing a ruff and looking very cute. The steep climb to the toilet up the rickety old staircase might pose problems for some, but I'm told we're lucky to have a toilet at all. Until not long ago, patrons had to use the public toilets around the corner! I recently had an excellent plate of pasta in here too!

Then turn left up **BELL YARD** ⓫. This is the street where Mrs Lovett had her famous pie shop. She was the girlfriend of Sweeney Todd, the Demon Barber of Fleet Street, who used to slit his customers' throats. It is said that there was a tunnel that led from the basement of his shop to here and that she would chop up the victims and serve them up in her pies!!!

Don't worry, it's probably not true…she used them for bolognese sauce, instead!

At the end of Bell Yard turn left into Carey Street, past the pub and fine selection of telephone boxes, to the next corner.

Here, in the building with Sir Thomas More above the door, is where the bankruptcy court resided. There is an archaic expression, often used in Victorian literature like Dickens and Sherlock Holmes stories, 'to be in queer street' – meaning 'to be bankrupt'. My friend (who is a QC) told me that this is a corruption of 'Carey Street', as people would exit the court here and find themselves in Carey (Queer) Street. Well, who am I to argue? Whenever I've argued with him I've lost.

Turn left out of the pub and you will see what looks like a milestone on your left, probably covered with dog urine or sick. These are actually parish boundary markers, with which I am slightly obsessed. Points, yay!!!

We don't use them so much these days in Britain, as most have been replaced by local borough councils, but a parish was an administrative district which had its own church. The marker on the right reads 'SDW', which stands for St Dunstan-in-the-West (a church that we will come to soon). The other marker is rather worn out, but had the shape of an anchor (which we saw before) and the letters 'SCD', standing for St Clement Danes. So this tells weary travellers that they are passing from the parish of St Clement Danes into that of St Dunstan-in-the-West.

Now for a minor detour. If it's open you can turn left and have a walk around **LINCOLN'S INN** ⓬. This is another one of the Inns of Court and was attended by Margaret Thatcher and Tony Blair. Some of the buildings date back to the 1500s, but many have been restored.

I've had enough of Inns of Court. Let's go back out and turn left and left again into **STAR YARD** **13**, where ahead of you is what looks like an old public lavatory. That's exactly what it is – but this one is a listed building from Victorian times, called a pissoir. Annoyingly, it has been closed for some time, but frankly they should open it up again, because people just urinate around the back of it!

You'll also see London's oldest tailor, Ede & Ravenscroft, which opened in 1689 and counted joint sovereigns William and Mary amongst their customers. This is where you come to buy your lawyer's wig or judge's gown, examples of which you can see in the window.

A judge's full court dress can run into thousands of pounds for breeches, wig, gown, buckles and the rest. I heard a rumour that they even throw in the black cap used for passing the death sentence! Although the UK no longer has capital punishment, the black cap is still a part of a judge's ceremonial dress, and is carried into the High Court. Barristers don't have to spend quite so much, but they must still be dressed properly with their wig and gown. If they are not correctly dressed and they address the court, the judge will say: 'I cannot hear you.' The judge doesn't actually say 'La la la', fingers in ears, but it's a clear message to the barrister to go and dress appropriately. All rather childish, really.

Because of these wigs costing so much money, many barristers try to get them second-hand, or inherit them from their parents. This is actually a preferred option, because no one wants to be seen as a 'wet around the gills' young, new lawyer, for

fear of being targeted by more experienced barristers. It is not uncommon, therefore, to see barristers with very old, nasty, withered wigs which look like dead rats hanging off their heads. It all sounds a bit like being at an English public school (or private school, as they say in America).

Now turn left, up past the Knights Templar pub, and take a quick look at the post box on the corner of Chancery Lane. This has the logo of King Edward VII, which means it was placed there during his reign. I'm a little bit obsessed with these post boxes. I was very upset recently when I walked straight past an Edward VIII post box without filming it, because those ones are very rare, as he wasn't King for very long. Anyway, this one is only Edward VII, but you still score points for spotting anything other than an Elizabeth II post box!

Turn right on Chancery Lane, then cross the road and turn left through a gate, which is Cliffords Inn, and follow this passage round until it comes back to Fleet Street.

Before the end of the passage, just short of Fleet Street, you will see some sloping ledges around knee height on the left-hand wall. These **URINE DEFLECTORS** **14** were often placed on buildings in alleyways to prevent people urinating. Drunken revellers still stagger in here today and relieve themselves against this wall without thinking, only to find their urine dripping back over their trousers off the ledge!

Turn left and you're by the parish church of **ST DUNSTAN-IN-THE-WEST** **15**. There is a statue of Queen Elizabeth I here which was actually carved during her lifetime, so she would have seen it herself. The two figures next to the clock are Gog and

Magog, who have origins in Biblical texts, but more recently came to be regarded as the guardians of the City of London. They're pretty useless, if you ask me. They can barely ring a bell, although they do try every hour.

It was at this church that John Donne was vicar some years after being a member of Lincoln's Inn. He is the one who wrote such lines as 'No man is an island' and 'Never send to know for whom the bell tolls; it tolls for thee.'

On the building next door you will see titles such as *The Dundee Courier* and *People's Journal*. This is a throwback to the days when Fleet Street was awash with journalists and newspaper publishers. You can still see other remnants on various buildings, such as the London News Agency, if you look upwards. If you then look downwards, on the street, various newspapers are also remembered in each of the alleyways which lead off from Fleet Street.

One such newspaper was *The Daily Courant* which, in 1702, became the world's first daily newspaper, so the alleyway claims! It was in this publication in 1785 that there was a report of a man whose throat had been slit, having last been seen talking to a barber. This spawned many legends and stories about Sweeney Todd, the demon barber of Fleet Street, whose shop was at number 186 (where DC Thompson is now based). They make the *Beano* and *Dandy* comics here these days.

Legend has it that Sweeney Todd had a chair which flipped back and dropped the victims through a trapdoor into the basement after he had slit their throats. There was then a tunnel which led under the church to his girlfriend Mrs Lovett's pie shop in Bell Yard, which we just visited.

Inside the window of number 186 you should see an old printing press. Back in 1500 Wynken de Worde, an associate of William Caxton, brought a printing press to Shoe Lane, near here, and this started a trend of printers setting up in this street. This probably explains why many newspaper publishers occupied the area. In fact, 'Fleet Street' became the generic term for the national press – but they all started to leave in the 1980s, after Rupert Murdoch moved to Docklands. If you ever watch the 1970s TV shows *Minder* or *The Sweeney*, they often come to Fleet Street to get information from 'Fleet Street hacks'.

Now keep going and cross over Fetter Lane – or Fewters Lane, as it was called in the 15th century. One of my favourite London historians, John Stowe, writing in the 16th century, described the 'fewters' or 'idle people' lying about in this lane, which is how it got its name. There are many streets in London that had much worse names than this, such as Shite Burn Lane, which became Sherborne Lane after the puritans did away with the more fruity street names. Grope C**t Lane would have been familiar in many towns in England in the Middle Ages, as a place to pick up prostitutes.

If you fancy a tipple there's a nice wine bar over the road called **El Vino**. It has a beautiful interior and you can really imagine the smoky atmosphere of the 1970s in here, with journalists gossiping and drinking sherry. However, if you were a woman back then you were not permitted to approach the bar unless accompanied by a gentleman. Women had to wait in their seats in the back room until they were served. That was until 1982, when two customers, Tess Gill and Anna Coote, took them to the Court of Appeal.

Lord Justice Griffiths said that since this was a place where journalists could pick up the gossip of the day, it put female journalists at a disadvantage if they were not able to pick up the same stories. So El Vino lost the case and now women have to buy their own drinks! Fine by me. I'll have a glass of port! Actually, they also do decent but simple food in here, too. I usually have the fish and chips.

Of course, you might prefer a more traditional pub, which is next on the walk. Keep walking up Fleet Street until you see a sign saying **Ye Olde Cheshire Cheese** and turn left into Wine Office Court.

Although Ye Olde Cheshire Cheese can get very crowded with tourists and after-work drinkers, if you go in the daytime you can get a seat and pretend you are Charles Dickens or Samuel Pepys. This was the first building to reopen after the Great Fire of 1666 and is still one of my favourites. Look out for the archaic sign over the door of the saloon reading 'Gentlemen Only Served In This Bar'. Don't take it seriously – women are allowed in; but they do yell at you if you use your tablet or mobile phone, which is frowned upon. The pub is a labyrinth of passages and tucked-away rooms, and if you go in the winter you will come out smelling of coal because of the open fire. Downstairs used to be a part of the Whitefriars monastery, and it really feels quite monastic down in the crypt below. They even still have one of the wooden beams charred from the Great Fire. And what do you have upstairs from a monastery? A brothel, of course! During renovations the builders chipped off all the old tiles around the fireplace in the upper rooms and they were illustrated with quite explicit pornographic images! You can still see them in the Museum of London, but you might need to arrange an appointment, which

could be a bit embarrassing (and unnecessary, since you can just look online… at the tiles, I mean, not at porn!!).

The stuffed parrot behind the bar was the original Polly the Parrot, and world-famous at one point. Journalists had to mind what they said within earshot because Polly would overhear their gossip and then repeat it at volume, sometimes losing the journalist's exclusive scoop! She was resident in the pub for 40 years from the end of the 19th century and met many celebrities, including Charlie Chaplin, Arthur Conan Doyle and Mark Twain. Other famous patrons of the Cheshire Cheese were Charles Dickens, Benjamin Franklin, Samuel Pepys and Lord Tennyson. In fact, it's fair to assume that anyone who lived in London from 1667 onwards is likely to have drunk here – most famously, of course, Dr Johnson, whose tankard you can still see in the chop room, along with his chair. It was his local, after all, and we shall go to his house next.

Turn right out of the pub and ask for **DR JOHNSON'S HOUSE** **16**, which is through the alleyways, at 17 Gough Square. This is where he spent the best part of 10 years compiling the first extensive English dictionary. It wasn't actually the very first dictionary, as some pretty poor efforts did exist beforehand, and you can see them in the museum here, with definitions which would make Baldrick from *Blackadder* proud. Whereas Baldrick's definition of 'dog' was 'not a cat', the older dictionaries defined it as 'an animal well known'.

The house is a beautiful example of an 18th-century townhouse, and the curator lives in a cute little cottage next door.

Now, at the time of writing there was a deal that if you said 'Pip Pip Tally Ho' on the door they would give you a discount, but it was only a temporary experiment. It might be amusing to try, though, as they are most bemused by the amount of people who say it with much gusto on entering! Inside you can see Dr Johnson's famous gout chair and the authentically preserved interior, along with many of his works. You can even dress up in a funny wig and make lots of *Blackadder* references! My favourite part, though, is the shop, where you can buy postcards with various definitions from his *Dictionary*. For example: 'Oats – a grain, which in England is generally given to horses, but in Scotland supports the people.'

Did you know? Whenever there is a debate in the US Congress over the interpretation of the Founding Fathers' words in the Declaration of Independence, they consult Dr Johnson's *Dictionary* because that was the one used at the time.

Now return to Fleet Street and, heading east towards St Paul's Cathedral, turn right down Salisbury Court to **SALISBURY SQUARE** **17**. Not very much to look at, I agree, but perhaps you can take a seat and contemplate a courtesan's revenge – for this is where the publishers Stockdale's had their printers, T. C. Gillett.

Who cares? Who are they?

Well, back in 1809 Frederick, Duke of York (see **the grand old Duke of York, who we visited in Walk 1**) had been having an affair with one Mary Anne Clarke, whom he had set up in a fancy house. It was quite common amongst his brothers and other royalty to take mistresses, but this developed into a scandal at government level when she started to sell army commissions and promotions at a favourable discount, with the Duke's knowledge.

When the Duke unceremoniously dumped her, Mary Anne Clarke wrote her memoirs. She had 18,000 copies printed up here – and notified the Duke. He was horrified, as there were particularly juicy chapters about him and their affair, so he bought all 18,000 copies and burned them here in the square, in exchange for £10,000, the publishing rights, and a pension for Mary Anne Clarke.

It's a pity no copies survived, although it is said that Stockdale's did suggest one printed book be sealed up with other documents and deposited with Messrs. Drummonds, the bankers of Charing Cross, so that the Duke, having purchased them, would retain the copyright and could suppress any subsequent attempt to publish. Sneaky... Imagine how much it would be worth now!

Now nip back up Salisbury Court and through St Bride's Avenue to the church of **ST BRIDE'S** **18**, designed by... um... who was it now...? Ah yes, Christopher Wren, in 1672.

There's been a church here since possibly the 6th century, when it is said St Bridget founded it, hence the name St Bride's. Several churches followed and after the Great Fire of

1666 Wren built this one, with his tallest ever steeple. My favourite thing about it is that in the early 18th century, on nearby Ludgate Hill, a pastry chef named Mr Rich fell in love with his boss's daughter and was inspired by this church steeple (which he stared at every day through his window) to create a cake for his wedding with many layers – a design that still endures today. The fact that it's also called St Bride's is a pleasing coincidence. They should put a bride and groom on top!

The lightning conductor was placed there after a heated discussion between Benjamin Franklin and King George III. The King thought it should have a blunt end, but Franklin opted for a sharp one, leading to much teasing by the press, who called them the sharp-witted Franklin and the blunt King George.

Inside there is a crypt dating back to Roman times, where you can see many artefacts and remains. It's all a bit creepy, if you ask me.

This whole walk makes for a very good pub crawl and just next to St Bride's is the **Old Bell**, built at Christopher Wren's request for the workers building the church. The pub features in Ralph Rylance's *The Epicure's Almanack* from 1815, which listed over 650 establishments 'where a man might readily regale himself according to the relative state of his appetite and purse'. Rylance says of the Old Bell that 'the beverages are good and the dinner charges are moderate' – although that might well have changed since the 19th century!

Have you ever seen someone at the pub grimace and leave the table, saying 'I'm just off to point Percy at the porcelain', 'I'm going to point Terence at the tiles' or 'I'm off to drain the main vein'? What they are, of course, saying is: 'I'm going to the toilet.'

PUB

The Old Bell

A more polite euphemism is 'I'm going to spend a penny' – and the reason for this is that just next to the Old Bell is **95 FLEET STREET** ⑲, where the world's first modern public lavatories opened in 1852. Following the success of George Jennings' flushable 'monkey closets' at the Great Exhibition of 1851 it was decided to open one here, as they made so much money. The charge was one penny, which is why these days 'to spend a penny' means 'to go to the toilet'. (Don't go in there and urinate today, though. It's a newsagent!)

The area between here and the river had quite a reputation for harbouring criminals in the early 18th century, and indeed it was here that Daniel Defoe hid after writing his sarcastic pamphlet criticising the government whilst the nearby taverns carried 'wanted' posters. This eventually led to him being put in the pillory, as we discovered on page 58.

Now, since this seems to have turned into a pub crawl, you might as well look in at the **Punch Tavern** just before the crossroads. It's a nice Victorian pub, but this would just be a quick stop if 'twere I, because we shall now finish at the **Blackfriar**. Turn right at the crossroads and you'll find it down on the left by Blackfriars Bridge. This is another Victorian pub with an interesting interior.

It was built on the site of the old medieval priory of the Blackfriars, after which the bridge is also named.

Before we go inside, look at the bridge itself: you can see little alcoves where people can sit, which were modelled on pulpits, as a reference to the days when monks frequented this area. The bridge was rebuilt in the mid-19th century and you can still see the remnants of the old bridge alongside it.

In 1982 Roberto Calvi was found hanging beneath the bridge, with $14,000 and five bricks stuffed into his pockets. He was known as 'God's Banker' because he was the chairman of the biggest private bank in Italy, Banco Ambrosiano, which was used by the Vatican. He had gone on the run after an embezzlement charge and although no one was convicted of his murder, many thought the Mafia were involved. Calvi was a member of a masonic lodge called the *Frati Neri*, meaning the Black Friars – which could explain why this location was chosen. By staggering coincidence, his private secretary had jumped out of her window, leaving a suicide note, the day before. Hmmm…

Where were we? Ah yes, the pub!!!

In the summer they have some good outdoor space where you can watch the City workers on their way home, but I'm freezing and knackered, so I'm heading inside. Make mine a pint of Doom Bar. Cheers!!!

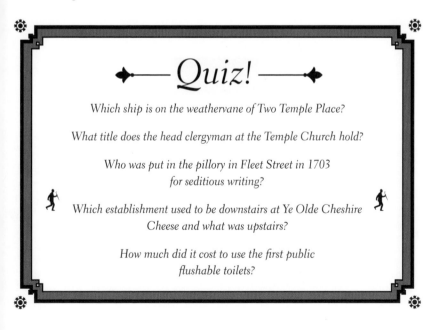

◆ — *Quiz!* — ◆

Which ship is on the weathervane of Two Temple Place?

What title does the head clergyman at the Temple Church hold?

Who was put in the pillory in Fleet Street in 1703 for seditious writing?

Which establishment used to be downstairs at Ye Olde Cheshire Cheese and what was upstairs?

How much did it cost to use the first public flushable toilets?

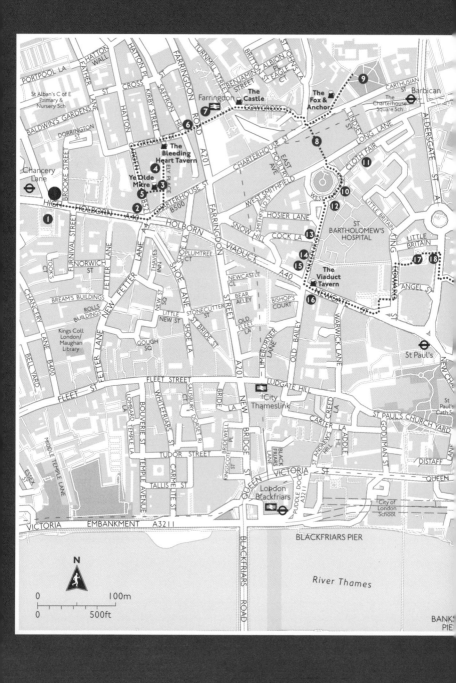

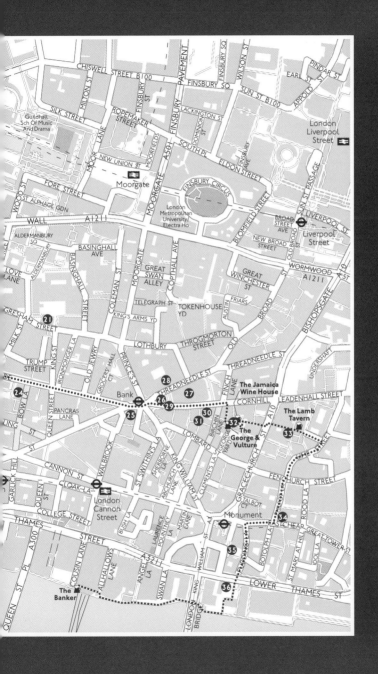

4 A MARVELLOUSLY MEDIEVAL MEANDER FROM CHANCERY LANE TO LONDON BRIDGE

DISTANCE
4.8 km (3 miles)

TIME
2 hours

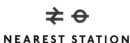

NEAREST STATION
Chancery Lane

Outside Chancery Lane tube station is a set of beautiful old rickety buildings that date from the 16th century and are probably the best example we have of what London looked like before the Great Fire of 1666. This is **STAPLE INN** ❶, which used to be one of the Inns of Chancery but was also where wool was weighed and taxed – a system known as the 'wool staple'. You can go through the little opening and you are transported into a beautiful, serene, Dickensian scene away from the traffic.

Charles Dickens writes of it in *The Mystery of Edwin Drood*:

> *It is one of those nooks, the turning into which out of the clashing street, imparts to the relieved pedestrian the sensation of having put cotton in his ears, and velvet soles on his boots.*

It's now used by the Institute of Actuaries (yawn) and there's a little hall dating from the 16th century with a hammer beam roof in the corner of the quadrangle, which is closed to the public but definitely worth a look if you can wangle your way in somehow. Sometimes they hold industry conferences or after-work drinks there.

Now back on the busy street, walk east along High Holborn towards the **STATUE OF PRINCE ALBERT DOFFING HIS HAT** ❷. People find it a bit peculiar, but he is most likely saluting. Despite not being in the military, he seems to be in some military dress, perhaps carrying out an inspection of his troops and saluting them, as doffing one's hat was the precursor to the salute. After a while, it became too much trouble to remove one's hat, so people just touched the brim, which developed into the salute.

Now cross the road at Holborn Circus and go down Charterhouse Street, before turning left into **ELY PLACE** ③ which, until recently, wasn't a part of London but a part of Cambridgeshire.

Now, if you've got a moment…

In medieval times, bishops held high office and would attend Parliament, which meant that many of them had a London residence. One of the these was the Bishop of Ely, whose London residence, the Palace of Ely, was on these grounds. Ely is a city in Cambridgeshire, and this area around Ely Place was legally part of the diocese of Ely, even though it was in London. It was therefore known as an enclave or 'liberty', where the usual laws and taxes of London didn't apply. I've heard it said that criminals on the run from the City of London authorities often sought sanctuary here, but a bloke in the pub told me that this isn't strictly true. However, they do still have their own beadles to keep an eye on the place, as it is a private road (although you can still walk down it).

What I like about it is that Shakespeare knew this area and included it in two of his plays. John of Gaunt, who delivers his famous speech ('This royal throne of kings, this sceptred isle, This earth of Majesty, this seat of Mars… This England') in *Richard II*, lived here in real life and would have known the place to be covered with strawberry fields.

'My lord of Ely!' says Gloucester in *Richard III*. 'When I was last in Holborn, I saw good strawberries in your garden there. I do beseech you send for some of them.' These days they still do a strawberry fair every so often, but the strawberry fields have long since evaporated.

Hidden away at the end of the street is the only surviving part of the bishop's palace, which is the **CHURCH OF ST ETHELDREDA** ④, the oldest Catholic church in England. It was built in the late 13th century and is one of the few buildings still standing in London from the reign of King Edward I. (Edward Longshanks, as he was known; you might remember him as being the mean king in *Braveheart* who has Mel Gibson executed.) If you have a bad throat you might want to come here when they do the 'Blessing of the throats', as St Etheldreda is one of the patron saints of throats. (Who knew?!!)

Some of the roof got damaged in the Second World War, but the crypt is largely unchanged and was used by Sir Christopher Hatton as a tavern (more about him on page 76), and then Oliver Cromwell used it as a prison during the revolution.

The royal coat of arms in the vestibule is interesting. After King Henry VIII created the Church of England it became customary to place these in all churches to remind worshippers that there was a new sheriff in town. The Pope was no longer head of the Church – the King was top dog. That said, St Etheldreda's has now reverted to being Catholic, so perhaps they should remove it.

Inside the church, in a box by the altar, is the 'uncorrupted hand' of St Etheldreda, while on the wall are effigies of various martyrs who were executed for their Catholicism. Take note of John Houghton at the end on the left, as we will talk about him later.

On leaving the church, turn right and then right again up an alleyway with urine trails on the ground leading to **Ye Olde Mitre**, which always smells of toast. (I seem to have a thing for these alleys.)

This is one of my favourite pubs and one of London's oldest. Please note the spelling and pronunciation. It is not pronounced 'yee': it is pronounced 'the'. Although it looks like a letter 'Y' it is actually an archaic character used for the sound 'th', called a thorn, and if you hear anyone referring to it as 'yee', their example is not to be followed by learned men or women.

Inside the door, encased behind glass in the corner, is an old tree stump. Back in Queen Elizabeth I's day this used to be a cherry tree, and she was even known to have danced the maypole around it, but it also served another purpose. Her 'favourite', Sir Christopher Hatton (otherwise known as 'her bit on the side'), was looking for a place to stay in London when he came to visit her on a booty call, so she suggested taking up rooms here at the Palace of Ely. However, the pleasingly named Bishop Cox protested. 'No, you don't!' he said. 'Those are my servants' quarters!'

To which the Queen replied: 'Proud Prelate, I understand you are backward in complying with your agreement; but, I would have you to know, that I who made you what you are, can unmake you; and if you do not forthwith fulfil your engagement, by God, I will immediately unfrock you!'

So he said, 'All right, you miserable cow,' and let the rooms to Hatton for ten quid, ten bales of hay and one red rose per year!

The grounds were then divided up, with the cherry tree marking the boundary. Anything east of the tree was the bishop's and anything west was Sir Christopher Hatton's grounds. That's why the street we will soon come to is called Hatton Garden.

If you've seen the film *Snatch*, this is also where Doug The Head conducts his dodgy business from. It makes sense, because when you walk to the end of the passageway you find yourself in Hatton Garden, with its history of independent jewellers and 'high end pieces at affordable prices'. (Depends what you find affordable!)

Keep walking until you come to the corner, where **88–90 HATTON GARDEN 5**, formerly Hatton Garden Safe Deposit Ltd, was the scene of the largest jewellery heist in British criminal history. Over the Easter bank holiday weekend of 2015, some brazen fellows went down a lift shaft next door and drilled a hole into the wall of the vault, making off with £200 million worth of other people's valuables. At first the police thought that it must have been committed by someone very agile, like a child or an athlete, because the hole was so narrow. However, the culprits were soon arrested and turned out to be a group of elderly men, some in their seventies!

The event was soon turned into various films

and when Michael Caine was researching the role of Brian Reader, the ringleader, he approached Mr Reader's daughter for help – but she protested, saying that Michael Caine was far too common to play her dad! (Caine did point out that he was an actor and, as such, could do a number of accents.)

Turn right down Greville Street and past the **Bleeding Heart Tavern**.

It is claimed (although to be fair to him, the bloke in the pub didn't say this) that in the 17th century Lady Elizabeth Hatton was brutally murdered and her body was found here, torn limb from limb with her heart still pumping blood. She was the wife of Sir William Hatton (descendent of Sir Christopher Hatton, who owned the surrounding estate). Later stories, for example in *Bentley's Miscellany*, have Lady Hatton selling her soul to the devil in exchange for a position in high society and a house in Holborn. On her housewarming night she dances with the devil and he rips out her heart, which is found still beating the next morning. This is, of course, bollocks, but if you look down Bleeding Heart Yard there does seem to be a red splat on the ground, for some reason. The name is more likely to be a remnant of an old pub sign relating to St Mary of the Bleeding Heart, which stood here. The sign had five swords stabbing her heart, but if Londoners can make a gruesome story benefit them, somehow they will.

Further down you will see **SAFFRON HILL** ❻, which is where Fagin lives with his gang of pickpockets in *Oliver Twist*. It looks vastly different these days, but would have been a real slum in Victorian times. The Artful Dodger takes Oliver to nearby Clerkenwell Green, where he gets caught stealing a gentleman's handkerchief.

The road sign for Saffron Hill tells you that you are in the Borough of Holborn. 'Holborn' comes from the Old English 'hollow', meaning 'valley', and 'bourne', meaning 'brook'. If you look ahead of you down the hill, you'll see Farringdon Road – but this wasn't always a road. Back in the 18th century this was the River Fleet (after which Fleet Street is named). There are many underground rivers in London, such as the Tyburn, the Westbourne and this one, the Fleet, which rises in Hampstead Heath and enters the Thames at Blackfriars.

So 'Holborn' probably referred to the river in the valley. If you put your ear to the drain on Saffron Hill you should be able to hear it flowing, although it has been culverted and now forms part of the sewer.

Cross over the street and towards **FARRINGDON STATION** ❼, taking note of the beautiful Victorian viaduct as you cross.

Farringdon Station was opened in 1863 as the terminus of the Metropolitan Railway, which was the first underground passenger railway in the world. It ran from Paddington to Farringdon and at one point, when they were digging the tunnels, the sewer close by exploded, showering the workers with faeces. Just thought I'd mention it.

What I like about this stretch of the London Underground is the sense of space above your head when you are on the platform. Since the tunnelling shield hadn't yet come into use, they used the old 'cut and cover' technique, which meant the tunnels were not all that deep, and at some stations (Baker Street, for example) you can still see the vents where the steam could escape. The trains on the Metropolitan and Circle lines are much more accommodating for the taller gentleman like myself, too!

Ye Olde Mitre

9

9

11

12

So if you're ever wondering why the London Underground is so crowded, it's because it was the first one built in the world and they can't expand it without closing down the whole thing for months on end.

Oh, go on then, we can have another drink if you insist.

In front of you is the **Castle**, where they do a tolerably good Scotch egg and pint of ale. Despite what you might think, the three golden balls hanging outside do not mean that the landlord has three testicles. This is actually the sign for a pawnbroker. You will have also seen them in Hatton Garden, where people can deposit an item in exchange for a loan. So why is it outside a pub?

Well, when King George IV used to visit (that's the son of the mad one), he was very keen on gambling on the cockfights that took place here. As he was quite a spendthrift and always running out of money, he ended up lending the barman his pocket watch in exchange for a loan – and in order to legalise this process he thought he'd better grant him a pawnbroker's licence, too. I don't think the current landlord still holds the licence, but there are many pictures of King George inside, along with the cockfights.

Once refreshed, continue up Cowcross Street toward **SMITHFIELD MEAT MARKET 8**.

The reason it's called Cowcross Street is that in bygone days farmers would bring their cattle up to the market for slaughter and have to cross over the River Fleet with their cows first.

At the time of writing, Smithfield remains the oldest meat market in London. It was established 1000 years ago as a livestock market called 'Smooth Field', just outside the city gates. With any luck you'll still be able to witness it as a meat market, because there are plans to move the market out and, from 2025, house the Museum of London here instead. It will certainly be a nice location for the museum, inside this wonderful structure designed by Sir Horace Jones in the 1860s. He was a very busy man, as he also designed Tower Bridge and Leadenhall Market.

Oh, by the way, don't forget to look at the weathervane on top of the Rookery Hotel in Cowcross Street. In years to come, people will wonder why it features a cow or bull, but you will know!

Before going through the market, let's just nip up Charterhouse Street to **CHARTERHOUSE SQUARE 9**.

On your way you'll notice the **Fox and Anchor**, a beautiful pub which also has fine rooms upstairs available for temporary hire. I usually take a sausage roll in here (heated, with mustard on the side) but they have a lovely Victorian dining area towards the back. It's one of the only pubs in London where you can get a pint of beer at 6 a.m.,

PUB

The Fox and Anchor

because it traditionally caters for the market traders, who usually start around 4 a.m.

Continue into Charterhouse Square and spare a thought for the 50,000 plague victims who are lying beneath your feet, for this was London's largest plague pit during the Black Death of the 14th century.

Despite all the death associated with it, I like this square for its variety of architectural styles. On your left is a medieval gate and monastery wall; behind that is a Tudor mansion; next, you have Georgian houses; and opposite, you have the Art Deco Florin Court, which you might recognise as Hercule Poirot's home in the TV series. There are also some 20th-century eyesores, not to mention the Brutalist 1960s Barbican estate looming in the distance.

In the 14th century a chap called Walter Manny asked permission from Pope Clement VI to open a Carthusian monastery here, and you can still see the chequered wall and medieval gate, which is all that survives today. You see, when King Henry VIII came along and closed all the monasteries, the head friar

here, John Houghton, whose effigy we saw in St Etheldreda's Church, refused to swear to the act of succession. As punishment he was hung, drawn and quartered and a quarter of his body, containing his arm, was nailed to the top of this very gate!

Meanwhile, they used the old bricks from the monastery to build the Tudor mansion behind, which is very impressive and fun. If you want to go inside you can arrange a private tour or go on Open House days (or, alternatively, just watch the excellent video on my YouTube channel!).

This is where Queen Elizabeth I held her first court as Queen. She had been staying in Hatfield House when she was told: 'Your sister's died. You'd better go to the Tower of London to prepare to be crowned.' But she said: 'No way! That's where people get their heads chopped off. I'm going to Charterhouse!'

Later on, in 1611, the richest commoner in England, Thomas Sutton, started a charity alms house here for old men who had fallen on hard times, as well as a school for poor boys. (Sutton was responsible for military supplies, which loosely made him an arms dealer of sorts! So he was an arms dealer who opened an alms house…well, kind of…). The charity still exists today; the gentlemen living here are known as 'brothers' and get to swan around the beautiful buildings. To become a brother, you must be unmarried and not own your own house or have vast savings. Women can also become brothers (but not sisters). The women staying here are referred to as 'lady-brothers'.

In case you're wondering why you can see dogs on the weathervanes, staircases and all over the place, they are talbots. Talbots are extinct now, but they feature on the Sutton family crest.

There's a nice museum here, which is free to enter – and don't forget to look at the chapel, with Thomas Sutton's wonderful tomb and graffiti from schoolboys of years gone by.

Did you know that this is where the throw-in rule was invented in football? The boys in the school used to play football in the cloisters and when the ball went out through a window, one lad was sent to retrieve it and had to throw it back in through the window over their heads.

Now retrace your steps back to Smithfield and walk through to West Smithfield.

Aptly enough for a meat market, this is where, in the 18th and 19th centuries, you could come and *sell your wife*. Yes, you read that right! It wasn't an uncommon practice in those days; if you've ever read *The Mayor of Casterbridge* by Thomas Hardy, you'll remember he sells his wife at the beginning of the book and regrets it for the rest of the novel.

The fact is that it was quite an expensive and laborious process to get a divorce, and usually only posh people had the time or money. So local magistrates started turning a blind eye to wife-selling. It would usually be with the consent of the wife herself, too, so it wasn't quite as barbaric as it sounds. That said, she was brought down with a halter around her neck and then handed over to the highest bidder at the auction. Then a town crier would walk through the square ringing a big bell, shouting, 'Oyez, oyez! Hear ye! Mr Jones has sold his wife for five shillings and a pickled egg,' etc. The reason it was done here

was so that there could be as many witnesses as possible, because it wasn't a strictly legal process, so it needed some sort of ratification.

I heard the most recent wife-selling incident took place in 1911 in Leeds. I believe the unhappy bride sold for £10!

'Aye… that'll do.'

The ramps you can see going down in the middle of the square are where James Bond drives down to visit M in *Skyfall* after MI6 gets blown up; and on your left is a street called Cloth Fair, with the oldest house in London (number 41), dating from 1598 (although it doesn't look it, since it's been renovated). They wanted to knock it down but John Betjeman, who lived next door, started a petition to save it and won!

The name 'Cloth Fair' comes from the Bartholomew Fair, held here every year from 1133 to 1855, where cloth was sold by the yard and other goods were traded. It was traditionally declared open by the Lord Mayor, who would cut the first piece of cloth, and that's why we cut a ribbon these days when opening a new building. (Well, that's what I heard, and it's good enough for me…)

This square is one of my favourite places in London because it has so much historical and cultural importance. I couldn't possibly describe everything, so I'm just concentrating on my favourites. You can read more elsewhere about the Peasants' Revolt and how Wat Tyler met with King Richard II in 1381 and was stabbed by the Lord Mayor, but this isn't a history book!

More Joolz-style is the plaque for **WILLIAM WALLACE** (10), otherwise known as Mel Gibson in *Braveheart*, on the south side of the square. He was hung, drawn and quartered here in 1305; in fact, his execution was particularly brutal because he really pissed off King Edward I. First, he was dragged here from the Tower of London, behind a horse. Then, after hanging until he was almost dead, he was let down and castrated. Next, his balls were stuck in his mouth and his intestines were cut out and burned in front of him. I expect that would have been enough to polish most people off, but he was then beheaded and his limbs were sent to four corners of the kingdom, while his head was put on a spike on London Bridge.

Harsh times, those.

Look to your left from the plaque.

ST BARTHOLOMEW THE GREAT ⑪ is the oldest church in London and also probably my favourite. It was built in 1123 by Rahere, the jester of King Henry I, as a part of a priory and it used to reach as far as what now seems like a gatehouse. Other bumbling oafs will claim that Queen 'Bloody' Mary would sit at a window in this gatehouse while watching Protestants being burned in the square, but this is bollocks because it was built in 1595, after she died. However, when they were digging here they did find a layer of thick ash under the square, from the Protestant-burning days of Queen Mary.

In the 18th century they decided to build a concrete Georgian façade over the gatehouse and for many years it was used as a shop. Everyone forgot about it until a Zeppelin dropped a bomb in 1917, shattering the façade and revealing the pretty Tudor building beneath. Since then it has been restored and you can walk through it to the church itself, which still evokes the medieval era.

Since Covid-19 they seem to have scrapped the entrance fee, but you can still leave a donation if you like, and it's definitely worth it. This is where Hugh Grant gets punched in the face by Duckface in *Four Weddings and a Funeral*. They also filmed *Robin Hood: Prince of Thieves*, *Shakespeare in Love* and *Another Country* here – but most importantly, it's where Miss Piggy gets married to Kermit the Frog in *Muppets Most Wanted*! (Or so I read.)

As you walk around and read the depressing inscriptions on the tombs, eager to remind you of your mortality, check out the weeping memorial of Edward Cooke. His tears were quite a phenomenon for some years, with people flocking to see the miracle. Sadly, however, once they installed the Victorian heating system, his tears dried up. (Perhaps he's crying on the inside.)

You will also see a horrible gold statue of St Bartholomew, sculpted by Damien Hirst. The reason he is holding his own skin is that St Bartholomew was martyred by being flayed alive.

Opposite him is Rahere's tomb itself. I often feel it should read 'Here Rahere Here'. When they disinterred him the 19th century, to restore his tomb, a local stole one of his sandals and they resealed his tomb without recovering it! Now he haunts the church with one sandal, looking for the other. I mean, who steals a dead man's shoe!!?

Now leave the church and walk straight ahead.

Curve round past **ST BART'S HOSPITAL** ⑫ and you should see a statue above the gate of King Henry VIII – the only statue of him in London. When he knocked down all the monasteries he cut the funding for the

hospital that formed part of the priory here, which really wasn't cricket, especially as they were doing such good for the sick and poor. In the end he agreed to re-found the hospital in 1546, and subsequently endowed it with property to provide ongoing funds. It's the oldest hospital in England that still occupies its original position. My sister thinks Henry's statue looks like her, but she doesn't wear such a big codpiece.

Just inside the King Henry VIII entrance there's a little museum on the left, which is definitely worth a look! You can see W.G. Grace's cricket bat (he was a doctor – who knew?) as well as a selection of scary Victorian medical devices, including a particularly painful set of male catheters! The best thing, however, is the amazing mural on the staircase of the North Wing, painted by Hogarth. Don't miss it. Occasionally they also have concerts upstairs in the Grand Hall, which is a beautiful space.

Next door you might recognise the location from BBC TV's *Sherlock*, where (spoiler alert) he jumps off the building. Watson is around the other side of the building, in the middle of the street, so he doesn't actually see him hit the pavement…

You can contemplate all this while eating a toasted sandwich from Beppe's Café opposite. It has been there since 1932 and is one of a few original classic cafés left in London, with beautiful green tiles and original features. These days you might call it a builders' café or greasy spoon, but it's better than that. (They don't even stir the tea with the same knife that they used to flip the bacon! What's the world coming to?)

Further along Giltspur Street you will see a boy with his cock out in **COCK LANE** ⓭.

COCK LANE

In medieval times this was the only street where prostitution was permitted, but that isn't the reason for the name. Many streets around here have names pertaining to livestock because of the market.

The statue is known as the Golden Boy of Pye Corner and was placed here after the Great Fire of 1666 because this marks the limit of the fire – it didn't reach any further than this.

As usual with major disasters, people wanted to find a scapegoat. At first they all blamed the Dutch, since we had been at war with them. Then a Frenchman called Robert Hubert admitted to starting it himself and was promptly taken off and hanged. It was a bit mean, really, as he was clearly mad and hadn't even arrived in London until after the fire had started. Next they tried to blame the astrologer William Lilly, who had predicted the fire – but he managed to get himself off the hook. In the end they tired of all this finger-pointing and decided to blame 'the sin of gluttony', since the fire started in a pie shop, and placed what they describe as this 'prodigiously fat boy' here. He doesn't seem very fat to me (although his ball sack is quite fat, to be fair).

My favourite story about Cock Lane is a famous hoax that took place in 1762. A fellow called William Kent had moved into number 65 with his dead wife's sister, Fanny.

During this time Kent lent some money to the landlord, Richard Parsons, and got into some arguments over its repayment. After Fanny died of smallpox, Parsons concocted a story about her ghost scaring people and claimed that she had been poisoned, in order to serve Kent right!

Fanny's ghost would appear amidst scratching sounds (which were probably rats in the ceiling, or Parsons' daughter scratching pieces of wood together) and it became quite a *cause célèbre*, attracting many people to séances held at the house, with even Dr Johnson attending one. Charles Dickens wrote about it and Hogarth referenced it in his paintings.

Eventually, it was proven to be a hoax and Parsons was put in the pillory – all so that I could pleasingly refer to it as 'the Ghost of Fanny Scratching in Cock Lane'. (Rather puerile, really… I blame my school, you see.)

Further along Giltspur Street, just after the deer's head, you'll see a **WATCH HOUSE** (14) erected (fnarr, fnarr) in 1791. Before the Metropolitan Police existed, law enforcement was a bit sketchy and you'd have night watchmen to keep an eye on things. Just where the golden boy is there used to be a pub called the Fortune of War, where grave robbers (known as 'resurrection men') would trade newly dug-up corpses with the medical students from St Bart's Hospital, so they could carry out their research. The only corpses you were allowed to dissect were ones who had been sentenced to death – but as these grew fewer, medical students had to seek alternatives, so a watch house was placed here to stop any illicit activity.

At the end of Giltspur Street is the church of **ST SEPULCHRE-WITHOUT-**

NEWGATE (15). I like these odd names. This one actually means 'without' as opposed to 'within', because it stands just outside the city gates. There were many city gates, some of which will be familiar to you: Ludgate, Aldgate, Bishopsgate, Moorgate, Cripplegate, Aldersgate and Newgate. Opposite the church is the **OLD BAILEY CENTRAL CRIMINAL COURT** (16), which was built on the site of the notorious Newgate Prison, which played host to countless familiar names, from Giacomo Casanova to Oscar Wilde.

The road was named Old Bailey because it followed the old fortified wall (otherwise known as a bailey). Famous trials here have included those of Dr Crippen, the Krays, Lord Haw-Haw and Ruth Ellis (the last woman to be hanged in Britain).

Newgate Prison had existed here since the 12th century. It was a pretty foul and loathsome place, full of disease and rats, where even doctors wouldn't want to enter. On execution days, wagons loaded with prisoners would leave here on their way to Tyburn Gallows (Marble Arch today), whilst the great bell of St Sepulchre would toll. (This is the bell from the nursery rhyme 'Oranges and Lemons': 'When will you pay me? Say the bells of Old Bailey.')

After a while they stopped doing the hangings at Tyburn and in the 18th century they started doing them out here in the street. Hundreds of people would come to see the hangings. The last public hanging here, which took place in 1868, was that of Michael Barrett, executed for attempting to rescue prisoners from Clerkenwell Prison. Amazingly, 20,000 people came to watch – and they arrived by the newly built London Underground! You can almost imagine the route they took to Farringdon Station. Then they probably walked down exactly the same street that we just did! Yikes...

Within St Sepulchre's church itself is a really creepy artefact. Inside a glass cabinet on one of the pillars is a small hand bell, which was rung by a bellman outside the condemned prisoners' cells the night before their execution. There was a passage leading under the road from the church and the man would walk through, chanting:

All you that in the condemned hold do lie,
Prepare you, for tomorrow you shall die;
Watch all, and pray, the hour is
drawing near,
That you before the Almighty
must appear;
Examine well yourselves, in time repent,
That you may not to eternal flames
be sent;
And when St Sepulchre's bell
tomorrow tolls,
The Lord have mercy on your souls.

Charming! I mean, the poor prisoner is floundering in his cell, thinking: 'I die in the morning. What I really need is a cretin with a bell keeping me awake!!'

That said, I've heard that those were more religious times and they probably felt they were being helpful, trying to get prisoners to repent before meeting their maker. This custom continued for hundreds of years after Robert Dowe left £50 in his will to keep it going. I guess the money eventually ran out, or it stopped after they knocked down the prison.

Also buried somewhere in the church is the body of Captain John Smith, who rescued Pocahontas and founded Virginia. He has a stained-glass window here, but the sign

reading 'Near this spot lie the remains of John Smith' keeps moving. You can pick it up and place it anywhere you want, so he could be anywhere in the church.

Back across the road is the **Viaduct Tavern**, which is a perfectly tolerable place to have a pint of ale. Traditionally it was a gin palace and you can get a good many gins here, but the food is limited to snacks like toasted sandwiches. The tapestries on the wall featuring women represent commerce, agriculture, science and fine art (and you can also see these women on Holborn Viaduct itself, along the street). If you look carefully you can see a hole in one of the tapestries,

which was caused by a rather overexuberant serviceman celebrating the end of the First World War by firing his gun in here. I don't know what the landlord had to say about it; he was probably too busy celebrating!

If you are good and ask nicely, they might even show you the prison cells beneath the pub. They still have the holes in the ceiling where kind-hearted passers-by could drop food through for the inmates. Don't get locked in, though; apparently there's a ghost!

Now continue up Newgate Street and turn left through the ruins of Christchurch Greyfriars, which was bombed during the Blitz. These days it's a rather lovely garden where you can eat your sandwiches; the only part of the church still standing constitutes one of London's most desirable residences, in my opinion.

Turn up King Edward Street and then turn right into **POSTMAN'S PARK** **17**, named after the headquarters of the General Post Office which stood alongside here in the 19th century. (On Haverstock Hill in north London there is a charming milestone which reads 'Four miles to the Post Office', so if you see it you will know that it's exactly 4 miles to this park.)

The reason for the slight mound is that this garden was originally a burial ground, until London's population increased to the point where they were having to stick bodies on top of each other. Many burial grounds were cleared as larger cemeteries were opened on the edge of London. If you look at the edge of the garden, you'll see all the old gravestones stacked up. I've always felt sorry for the ones who are stacked behind and therefore not visible, but then again, most of the inscriptions have worn away. Fortunately one is still legible, that of Eleanor and William Loveland, which is an excellent name. My good friend's middle name is Loveland, which he hated when we were at school, and by strange coincidence he was also a postman *and* has a daughter called Eleanor.

On one side of the park you will see the Memorial to Heroic Self-Sacrifice. This was initiated at the end of the 19th century by George Frederic Watts, an artist who put up the first of these tablets commemorating people like Thomas Simpson, who died after

rescuing many people at Highgate Ponds when the ice broke, and John Cranmer Cambridge, who drowned near Ostend 'whilst saving the life of a stranger and a foreigner'. I have always wondered if the stranger and the foreigner were the same person, or if the foreigner was also his friend, or just a foreign person. Hmmmm.

They stopped putting up the tablets for 78 years but then in 2009 Leigh Pitt was recognised for having drowned in a canal two years previously, whilst rescuing a 9-year-old. It seems that you don't *have* to drown or be engulfed by the flames of a burning building to be remembered here, but it helps! Like in the case of Alice Ayres, whose name you might recognise from one of my favourite films, *Closer*, when Natalie Portman meets Jude Law here. (Great film!)

Walk through the park and outside, just to the right, you'll see a **POLICE CALL BOX** **18** that resembles a mini TARDIS (Doctor Who's spaceship). Doctor Who actually had one of the other, larger ones which have all but disappeared from London now, although you can still see a replica outside Earl's Court Station. The principle is the same though: the light would flash and a nearby policeman would come and answer the telephone inside the box and be told some instructions by his sergeant. They could also be used by the public to call the police. The larger ones were like mini police stations and could even hold someone under arrest temporarily, but were more often used for filling out forms. Like many charming aspects of British life from the early 20th century, they have died out, what with mobile phones and radios, so if you see one anywhere else it is probably a spaceship from the planet Gallifrey. (TARDIS stands for Time And Relative Dimension In Space, by the way.)

Continue past the police call box and then cross over to hang a left up Gresham Street and walk past the **GOLDSMITHS' HALL** 19. When a jeweller needs to get a piece of gold hallmarked they would originally come to the Goldsmiths' Hall to verify that the item was gold. That is why it's called a hallmark.

It's quite popular to keep bees in the city these days and if you look to your left you'll see some remains of the old city wall, which sadly isn't very impressive at this location. Whenever I point it out to people, their first question is always about the beehives!

'Who owns them?' they ask.

'None of your beeswax,' I reply.

There is more of London Wall further down Noble Street, along with a million other interesting things, but I can't include everything in this walk! That will have to wait.

Just next to the Goldsmiths' Hall is the **WAX CHANDLERS' HALL** 20. Wax chandlers received their royal charter from Richard III and are the twentieth most important of the City of London livery companies. Basically they're the ones who used to make candles and wax writing tablets in the old days. These days they do less candle-making and more civic and promotional stuff, but they've had various incarnations of their hall on this site since 1501.

Keep going and you'll come to the junction of Wood Street, so called because the houses here were built of wood, despite an edict of King Richard I stipulating that they should be made of stone to prevent fire. The church tower you can see on Wood Street is actually a private residence now. It was the church of St Alban, but was destroyed first by

WOOD STREET

the Great Fire of 1666 and then by the Nazis during the Blitz.

Honestly, there are so many churches around here – and there were even more 300 years ago!! If you're on the corner of Wood Street and Gresham Street you should be able to see the church of **ST LAWRENCE JEWRY** 21 (just in front of the Guildhall, which is also worth a look for its architecture, art gallery and access to the remains of London's Roman amphitheatre). In medieval times this area had quite a large Jewish population until King Edward I (Longshanks again!) kicked them all out of England.

If you look at the weathervane you will see that it is in the shape of a gridiron, because St Lawrence was famously martyred by being barbecued on a gridiron. They really did think up some gruesome ends for Christians in those days. Apparently, as the flames engulfed him, he said, 'You can turn me over now, I'm done on this side!'

Now head down Wood Street, past a boring office building that used to be ABC (Another Bloody Church) called St Michael's, beneath which lies **THE BURIED HEAD OF KING JAMES IV OF SCOTLAND** 22.

My favourite London historian, John Stowe, records that after the battle of Flodden Field in 1513 (one of the bloodiest battles between England and Scotland), the body of the dead

King was taken to a monastery in Surrey. It must have stayed there for a while, because some years later some workmen chopped off its head for a laugh, and then Launcelot Young, the master glazier to Queen Elizabeth I, took it to his house in London in Wood Street. It still had its red hair and beard, but when it got too manky he gave it to the vicar of his local church, who buried it with the other bones.

St Michael's church got demolished and they built an office block in its place, so it's quite possible his head is still down there!

Nearby they built a pub called the Red Herring (which makes it sound like a made-up story, even though it's right there in John Stowe's *Survey of London*!) but that's gone, too. I mean, why didn't they call it the King's Head? Some people have no imagination, honestly…

At the other end of Wood Street, on the corner of Cheapside, there's a little garden with a **TREE 23** that seems to have more rights of light than I do! Well, I suppose it is rather old – some say it dates back to the 18th century – and it is known as one of the 'great trees of London', giving it listed status. The buildings next door have a clause in their leases forbidding any building higher than two stories, so that the poor old fellow can get enough light. These days Londoners are very fond of this spot, especially those who fancy a cigarette (or a can of Tennent's) and can sit in what used to be the churchyard of St Peter Cheap whilst contemplating who 'Poor Susan' might have been. She famously features in a poem by William Wordsworth, 'The Reverie of Poor Susan' (not one of his best, in my opinion).

At the corner of Wood Street, when daylight appears,

Hangs a Thrush that sings loud, it has sung for three years:
Poor Susan has passed by the spot, and has heard
In the silence of morning the song of the Bird.

It's amazing that there was yet another church here. You can still see the cross keys in the railings of the churchyard, which represent St Peter's keys to the Kingdom of Heaven.

By the way, Cheapside and St Peter Cheap took their names from the old word meaning 'market'; many of the streets which turn off Cheapside have names pertaining to marketplaces, including Poultry, Grocers' Hall Court and Ironmonger Lane.

Turn left and head towards Bank. The tall church on your right is **ST MARY-LE-BOW 24**, designed by, you guessed it, Christopher Wren. There has been a church here since Saxon times, but the first one got blown over by a hurricane and all that survived was the arched (or bowed) crypt, upon which the Normans then built another church. Anyway, the current one was built after the previous one burnt down, and I'm sure you can see why I believe it was Christopher Wren who started the Great Fire of London!

The famous 'great bell of Bow' (from the 'Oranges and Lemons' nursery rhyme) was cast in the Whitechapel Bell Foundry, as were Big Ben and the Liberty Bell; it rang out the curfew of London. William the Conqueror had ordered a bell to be rung every evening to remind everyone to put out their candles, to prevent any great fires – and since he was French, the word 'curfew' developed from the French *couvre-feu*, literally meaning 'cover fire', or 'put your bloody candles out!'

Traditionally, anyone born within the sound of the Bow Bells is an official Cockney – cor blimey, apples and pears, how's yer father, know what I mean, guv'nor? (Like an East End Londoner who talks a bit like David Beckham or Jason Statham.)

Incidentally, the word Cockney comes from 'cock-aye' meaning a cock's egg, or a malformed egg, from the days when city folk would visit the countryside and the locals would laugh at them because they were ignorant of country ways.

Of course, these days, with all the traffic and tall buildings, you can barely hear the Bow Bells 200 yards away – but in the olden days you could hear them as far away as Highgate Hill. (Perhaps that's why Cockneys are dying out.)

In fact, one person who heard the Bow Bells on Highgate Hill was Dick Whittington, who is well known to British people as the Lord Mayor of London and, more commonly, for the pantomime where his cat kills rats on a ship. In reality we don't know if Dick Whittington had a cat, but he did come to London in the 14th century seeking his fortune, and got a job in a kitchen. When his boss treated him badly he packed his bags – but as he headed back north, he fancied he heard the sound of the Bow Bells ringing out across the fields, saying: 'Turn again, Whittington! Thrice Lord Mayor of London.'

So he turned on his heel just near Archway (near the Whittington Hospital) and did indeed go on to become Lord Mayor of London – four times (see **Walk 5**).

By the way, if you're interested, just a bit further along from here, Grope C**t Lane used to run south from roughly where Tesco

is situated. A suitable name for a street frequented by prostitutes, but the Puritans put an end to that. Hey, I didn't name it!!!!

Now keep going until you get to the big junction ahead and you are at Bank.

The big building with columns on the right is **MANSION HOUSE** 25 , where the Lord Mayor of London lives. He isn't to be confused with the Mayor of London. The *Lord* Mayor wears tremendous robes, gets a grand procession every year, travels in a fancy coach, lives in this wonderful house, gets to sit in the House of Lords, and has great power within the City of London. The *ordinary* Mayor of London is the one we mortals vote for, wears a suit from Marks & Spencer and lives in a flat somewhere, grumbling about transport, police and cycling lanes.

Straight ahead is the statue of the **DUKE OF WELLINGTON** 26 , supposedly cast from cannon captured at the Battle of Waterloo. I don't know what the French government makes of all this stuff we've nicked from them – but then again, Napoleon got his hands on quite a bit of stuff too, so who's counting?

The building with columns behind the statue is the **ROYAL EXCHANGE** 27 and on the roof you can see another one of my favourite weathervanes.

The Royal Exchange was founded in the 16th century by Sir Thomas Gresham as a bourse, or marketplace, where valuable goods and alcohol could be exchanged. Apparently, when he was a baby, Gresham was abandoned by his mother and left inside a basket in a cornfield. He was only discovered because a kind old lady heard a grasshopper chirping nearby, so this became the family crest and now appears on the weathervane.

This is more or less the centre of the financial district, known as the Square Mile, and up until the 1970s it would have been common to see people dressed like Joolz Guides with bowler hats and umbrellas around here. These days people look at you as if you're a freak if you dress like that, though they seem perfectly happy to go around with their bottoms exposed and making all sorts of other peculiar fashion statements!

To the left is the **BANK OF ENGLAND 28**, where you're supposed to be able to take your banknotes and ask for the equivalent in gold bullion. It doesn't work any more, though – I've tried. You might like the museum inside, however.

I'm more interested in these lampposts outside. At the base of each one there's an emblem representing one of the City of London livery companies. Since the 12th century certain guilds became regulated, to maintain high standards and keep their tradesmen in check. When they became big and important enough they would be given a headquarters and special robes, to distinguish them from other guilds. We've already walked past the hall of the Worshipful Company of Wax Chandlers, and there were many others, such as the Worshipful Companies of Vintners, Gardeners, Grocers, Fishmongers, Mercers, etc..

The most important ones became known as the Great Twelve and every year since 1515 they have marched in order of importance in the Lord Mayor's Show. However, the Merchant Taylors and the Skinners were always arguing about who was more important. This went on for

so long that eventually the Lord Mayor decided to alternate them each year between numbers six and seven, which gave rise to a handy phrase. These days you often hear football commentators referring to confusion on the pitch by saying: 'Oh, that was diabolical defending, wasn't it, Clive? The defenders were at sixes and sevens there!'

Now head up Cornhill past the statue of **JAMES GREATHEAD 29** who, despite his name, was not a porn star – although with that beard he might have had a good shout! He was actually very important in the building of the London Underground, having perfected the tunnelling shield, which made progress much quicker.

At **32 CORNHILL 30** there was once a publishing company called Smith, Elder and Co., who were in correspondence with some writers called Messrs Acton, Currer and Ellis Bell. However, when Acton and Currer turned up in person one day, the publishers were astonished to find they were actually blasted *women*!!! They were two of the three Brontë sisters – Anne and Charlotte, no less. The wooden doors on the outside of the building feature some interesting carvings, depicting important events that took place in the vicinity. The bottom one shows the Brontë sisters at a meeting with William Thackeray, during which he quoted some lines from *Jane Eyre* – but Charlotte didn't recognise them as her own!

Shooting off to the right at various intervals are alleys and passages that used to contain many coffee houses. You can still see evidence of them in the labyrinth of passages that would once have been full of errand boys running up and down, because this is where the stock market first started. Stockbrokers were too rowdy and therefore not allowed into the Royal Exchange, so they had to meet in coffee houses, which were the new cool places to hang out. The first recorded exchange in marketable stocks took place in **CHANGE ALLEY** ㉛ at Jonathan's Coffee House in 1698. Messengers would run between here and other coffee houses, such as Garraway's, and more famously, Lloyd's, while great ideas and plots were taking root. Those meeting at Lloyd's eventually needed a larger place to meet, so they moved and grew into what is now Lloyd's of London.

It's easier to find your way if you stick to the main road and then turn right into Ball Court, where you see the sign for **Simpsons Chop House**, and follow it round to **ST MICHAEL'S ALLEY** ㉜, behind the church.

This is where Scrooge's counting-house is located in *A Christmas Carol*. We know this because it's described as being near Cornhill, facing 'the ancient tower of a church, whose gruff old bell was always peeping slily down at Scrooge out of a Gothic window in the wall'.

When Bob Cratchit is allowed to go home he is so happy that he runs down Cornhill and plays in the snow with some children. Meanwhile, 'Scrooge took his melancholy dinner in his usual melancholy tavern' – which would have been Simpsons, as it is so ancient.

By the way, I thoroughly recommend Simpsons for lunch if you want to see how City workers have dined for hundreds of years. It's a very authentic and charming experience. Apparently it's traditional to have an egg served with everything.

'Lamb chop with a sausage. Would you like a fried egg on that? Certainly, Sir.'

PUB

The George and Vulture

Unfortunately, at the time of writing Simpsons was closed due to a dispute with the landlord. I'm hoping that by the time you read this it has reopened. It would be truly shameful to lose this institution, which has been here since 1757.

Dickens also used to come to the **George and Vulture** and has Mr Pickwick lodge here in *The Pickwick Papers*. They do allow women in these days, though I still don't see that many in there when I peek through the window. All these taverns are jolly nice places to eat, but don't tend to be open on weekends, as the whole of the Square Mile seems to go to sleep.

The **Jamaica Wine House** is a pub now, but in 1652 it was the first coffee house to open in London, when it was called the Pasqua Rosée. A good place to slip in for a beer, or stand in the courtyard with all the bankers (who should be at work but always seem to be drinking here during the day!).

In the 18th century this was where sugar plantation owners and slave ship captains did deals over enslaved Africans. They even had adverts on the wall for slaves who had escaped. One such advert was for 'A negro boy named James… Whoever brings him to the Jamaica Coffee House in Cornhill shall have ten shillings reward.'

Follow St Michael's Alley round and go through to the main road, Gracechurch Street.

On the other side of the road is **LEADENHALL MARKET** ㉝. This was designed by Horace Jones (who did Smithfield Market and Tower Bridge). It's lucky that he did such a nice job, because when they were digging here they found one of the largest Roman basilicas in northern Europe and, in their infinite wisdom, decided to build on top of it. That said, Leadenhall Market is very pleasing on the eye and often used in films. Most notably in *Harry Potter and the Philosopher's Stone*, where Harry comes here with Hagrid. They walk up Diagon Alley and into The Leaky Cauldron, which is actually an optician's with a blue curved door in Bull's Head Passage!

In the Middle Ages there was once a wealthy family who lived here and had a big house with a lead roof, hence the name Leadenhall. I rather like how all the businesses have to adhere to the same decor; it keeps it looking charming.

If you're thirsty you could try the **Lamb Tavern** – but try to resist the temptation to start a fight in there, like John Wayne did in the film *Brannigan*!!!

Head out of the market into Lime Street and follow it down to Philpot Lane.

On the corner of Philpot Lane and Eastcheap there is a building that, at time of writing, is a Joe and the Juice. On the white plasterwork just around the top of the ground floor level, you'll see a couple of **NAUGHTY MICE FIGHTING OVER SOME CHEESE** ㉞. They are quite hard to see, so you might have to squint your eyes – this is probably London's smallest memorial.

When they were constructing this building in the 1800s, one of the workers put down his sandwich for a moment – but when he looked again, it had gone. Soon he accused another worker of stealing it and a fight broke out, resulting in him falling to his death!

Not long afterwards, someone nearby spotted the true culprits: a couple of mice who had made off with the sandwich and were still nibbling the cheese! So as a fitting reminder of their unfortunate friend, the builders decided to include two mice on the side of the building.

What? Of course it's true! Honestly, who do you think I am?

Around the corner you should be able to find the **MONUMENT TO THE GREAT FIRE OF LONDON** ㉟, designed by – you guessed it – Christopher Wren, and built on the site of the first church to be destroyed by the Great Fire of 1666. They say that it started in the baker's shop in Pudding Lane and if the Monument were laid flat, the top of the column should arrive at the exact point. Although these days, historians are trying to argue that the fire might not have started there after all... but who cares? I mean, wherever it started has long since disappeared.

You can go up the 311 steps to the top, but it's pretty tiring. At one point it was said to be the best view in London and it's still not bad...if you don't mind big, ugly buildings. It's amazing to think that originally it only had a low railing; people kept jumping off, so they had to add a wire mesh cage. (Well, it seems like a low railing if you're 6'6", like me!)

After you've come back down and been given your certificate it's worth heading down the hill to **ST MAGNUS THE MARTYR** ㊱ designed by – ahem – Christopher Wren. (You're starting to agree with me about him starting the Great Fire now!) This was actually the second church to be destroyed by the fire. Before they rebuilt London Bridge the old medieval bridge, started in 1176 and still standing in 1831, was slightly further east than the current one and came ashore here. You can still see some of the old stones just abandoned here, like Roman ruins. Speaking of which, there is also an ancient wooden pile which was used by the Romans to build their river wall, dating from AD 75!

If you want to see what the medieval London Bridge actually looked like, you can see a wonderful replica model inside the church (although I think they removed the traitors' heads on sticks, as it doesn't seem very religious).

Time for a drink to finish this walk. There are plenty of pubs around here, but I fancy one with a nice view of the river for now. Walk around to the back of the church, onto the riverside path, and head west along the river. You'll go through a couple of tunnels and past several bars which you could stop at if you like. Personally, I like to keep going and get a pint from the **Banker** at the end of Cousin Lane. It commands splendid views of the river. You can even sit on the steps as the tide threatens to wet your shoes. Cheers!

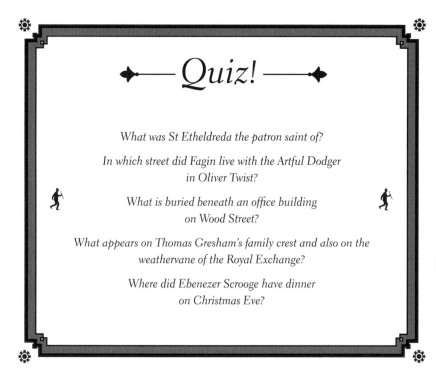

✦—— *Quiz!* ——✦

What was St Etheldreda the patron saint of?

In which street did Fagin live with the Artful Dodger in Oliver Twist?

What is buried beneath an office building on Wood Street?

What appears on Thomas Gresham's family crest and also on the weathervane of the Royal Exchange?

Where did Ebenezer Scrooge have dinner on Christmas Eve?

5

5 A RATHER PLEASANT STROLL THROUGH HIGHGATE AND KENWOOD

DISTANCE
9.2 km (5.7 miles)

TIME
4 hours

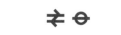

NEAREST STATION
Gospel Oak

We start at Gospel Oak Overground station. If it's more convenient for you to take bus 214, 88 or C11 to Parliament Hill Fields then skip the next section in italics.

Come out of the station and turn left into Gordon House Road. Then turn left into the park and walk straight ahead. You will pass the **PARLIAMENT HILL LIDO ❶** *on your left (where you can have an outdoor swim if it isn't too full) and the running track.*

On your right you pass the mansion blocks where Sir John Betjeman was born, which he described as 'red cliffs' in his poetry.

At the top of the path turn right, and keep going until you see a café on the left. After the café turn left (but not the sharp left), keeping the sort-of bowling green on your right.

Over to your left on the hill you will see the

STONE OF FREE SPEECH ❷. *People say that 200 years ago this was the point where people could gather for religious and political meetings. These days, you still get people meeting there for the equinox, and I must admit it is a rather splendid place to conduct a discussion, I would think.*

Over to your right you should be able to see the park exit in the north-east corner. Exit here.

And welcome to those who took the bus straight here. You missed a pleasant stroll across the park!

Look at the lovely old **GHOST SIGN ❸** for the tea rooms which used to exist here. These days it's Bistro Laz, where I have eaten and it's perfectly good if you're peckish.

There are a few cafés around here where you can buy a snack before your ascent of the hill. Don't worry, it's not too bad, unless you have an aversion to middle-aged men in lycra!

Start walking up Swain's Lane, avoiding any cyclists whizzing past you at Mach 3. It seems to have become a bit of a cycling Mecca because of its gradient, which averages 8 per cent but in some places reaches 20 per cent over 900 metres (1000 yards).

It's called Swain's Lane (after Swine's Lane) because in the 14th century pig herders and other farmers would bring their livestock down this hill on their way to Smithfield meat market in the City.

Beatles fans might like to stop and have their photo taken outside **NUMBER 59** ④ and replicate a moment from the Beatles' 'Mad Day Out', when they went all over London doing a photoshoot with the famous war photographer Don McCullin. Apparently they tried to do the photoshoot by Karl Marx's grave in Highgate Cemetery, but got chucked out.

A bit further along, on the corner of Chester Road, is the beautiful gothic entrance to **HOLLY VILLAGE** ⑤, which looks like it could be Dracula's house. Behind this lugubrious building lie another seven houses built by the second richest woman in England at the time (after Queen Victoria), Baroness Angela Burdett-Coutts. She was the granddaughter of the owner of Coutts Bank. A hard life, but to be fair, she did give a lot of her money away to support homes for the poor, prostitutes and ragged schools. She also helped to found the NSPCC and the RSPCA! In 1872 she was given the Freedom of the City of London, which meant she could walk her sheep over London Bridge if she liked; and if ever she were to be hanged

she could request they used rope made out of silk!!

These days people do actually live here... Imagine bringing your date back on a rainy night with lightning and thunder. (I'd set my ring tone to the sound of a horse rearing up and neighing, just for japes!!)

As you continue up the hill you'll notice **HIGHGATE CEMETERY** ⑥ on your right, the entrance of which is further along, but it already starts to feel a bit spooky at this point. Incidentally, if it's late at night and you see a tall man in a hat jumping out and scaring you before disappearing into a wall, it isn't me! It could be the Highgate Vampire, who has been spotted many times in various guises by passers-by. Some see a phantom gliding into the pond, others see a ghostly cyclist. They're probably just freaked out by all the graves, if you ask me.

Back in the 1800s the churchyards of London were becoming too full, with bodies needing to be buried one on top of the other. Before long it became so bad that Parliament decided seven cemeteries were to be built further outside the city centre to accommodate London's dead. Highgate Cemetery is one of the most well-known, because of all the famous people buried here. If you want to visit the graves you can pay the entrance fee and spend an afternoon walking amongst the 53,000 tombs. There's Douglas Adams, Malcolm McLaren, George Eliot and many more, including Karl Marx, whose tomb is the most famous and imposing. The other side of the road has the older West Cemetery where more notable people are buried, like George Michael and his mum, but you need to do a special tour to access that side. In fact, when it was decided to build the newer East

Cemetery, it was necessary to dig a tunnel under the road so that the coffins could be taken from the chapel in the west side, down in the hydraulic lift, and over to be buried on the east side without taking them outside the consecrated ground, which was seen as a bad omen.

If you're a cheapskate like me, you just turn right into **WATERLOW PARK** **7** and peek over the fence, where you can just about make out Karl Marx's tomb and still take a nice photo for your Instagram if you have a decent lens!

I love Waterlow Park and you get a lovely view of London if you get to the right spot. I always imagine that fairies live in this particular pond and that the trees are possessed by spirits. In the 17th century the Dukes of Lauderdale owned the grand house here, Lauderdale House, which is used for exhibitions and social functions these days. Along with the surrounding gardens, in the 19th century it became the property of philanthropist Sir Sydney Waterlow, who donated it to the public so that people who didn't own any outside space could enjoy the nicely laid-out gardens. I once went to an excellent outdoor performance of Noël Coward's *Private Lives* at Lauderdale House. It was better than most things I've seen in the West End!

After you've sat down and contemplated the changes London has been through over the centuries whilst looking in wonder at the view, it's time to leave the park and you'll find yourself on Highgate Hill.

We aren't going to turn right, because I don't fancy coming back up this hill again – but if you do feel like a quick detour, just nip down the hill where, just before Archway Station, you'll find a statue of a cat inside a cage. This is **DICK WHITTINGTON'S CAT** **8**, marking the point at which he heard the sound of the Bow Bells beckoning him back to London. Having been sold a promise that the streets of London were 'paved with gold', he was astonished to find they were actually paved with dog poo, and the job he got in a kitchen was lousy so he headed back 'oop north'! However, the Bow Bells rang out and, influenced by what I can only imagine were hallucinations from illicit substances he must have taken, he fancied the bells were saying, 'Turn again, Whittington! Thrice Lord Mayor of London.' (See **Walk 4** for more on the Bow Bells.) This was enough to convince him to return. He then got very rich, married his boss's daughter (the saucy swine) and indeed succeeded in becoming Lord Mayor of London, not three but four times! He lent money to the King and fined breweries for serving bad beer. We could do with his sort today!

This road was probably nicer in the 14th century, just being an old dirt track leading up to Highgate Village. (At least, it looks like that in the old Ladybird books we used to get at school.) Of course, the Whittington Hospital and Whittington Stone pub are named after this moment, so try not to ignore the little cat like everyone else – even though there's no evidence he even had a cat! And you can't hear the Bow Bells from here any more, which means you ain't a Cockney if you're born at the Whittington.

But anyway, we're not heading that way; we're turning left out of Waterlow Park and up Highgate Hill.

By the way, it's hard not to visit a few of the wonderfully charming pubs on your way through the village and, in fact, it's the very reason I go to Highgate sometimes. This was the highest point on the sheep herders' trail, so they would often stop here for a bit of refreshment after climbing the hill, which is why there are so many pubs in such a small area.

I can't say for sure whether rock star Adam Ant has ever visited Highgate, but he certainly didn't have anything to do with a paving stone here, which you might find interesting. See if you can spot it as you climb the hill. It says 'Adamant' on it, which always pleased me as a child. It's actually the name of the Aberdeen non-slip paving manufacturers, and comes from the Greek for 'invincible'.

You have the **Angel Inn**, where the Monty Python team drank frequently (there's even a plaque) and where the pub quiz isn't too

PUB

The Prince of Wales

difficult (I've won there occasionally); but further along you have the **Prince of Wales**, which claims to have the hardest pub quiz in London. This is a lovely pub backing onto Pond Square. I'd take a pint here if I were you, and sit out back if it's a nice day.

This part of Highgate has many charity shops and quaint little places, making it feel very much like a village, which is precisely what it was for many years. It lies in the shadow of my old school chapel, which we will come to in a moment.

Next to the Prince of Wales is Highgate Wholefoods, which used to be a Lloyds Bank when I was at school, and one of the smallest banks in London. It's not surprising that they closed, because they say it was the most robbed bank in London.

One of my favourite moments at school (apart from when Kishaw ran into the lunch hall and stole Mr Tweedale's wig from off his head, resulting in the art teacher doing away with his hairpiece for ever more) was when Joe Jenkins was an hour late for triple history one afternoon.

Piggy Palmer said: 'What kind of time do you call this, Jenkins?!'

To which Joe replied: 'Sorry, Sir. I was in the bank at lunchtime when some robbers came in and held it up!' Classic.

Carry on past the zebra crossing and there's a passage to your left leading to Pond Square. Before going down it, look up just above number 67 (which is currently a chocolate shop) and you should see a cute little sign saying **'RAJ TEA ROOMS' 9**.

I'm amazed that this sign still hangs here, but I'm so glad it does. The tea rooms were run by the very eccentric Darcy Brewster (who was the brother of my maths teacher, but they didn't get on). You had to pass through a clothes shop and up the stairs to get there, and it felt like you were trespassing, but once inside it was a cosy, cute café that felt like a front room, where Darcy seemed to let you get away with murder. Kids from the school would smoke dope, drink alcohol and – worse still – fraternise with Channing girls!!! (Channing being the local girls' school.) All that remains is this little sign.

Now head down the passageway.

POND SQUARE 10 used to have a pond in it (I bet you never would have guessed) and now it is one of the most desirable addresses in London. That said, it is haunted…by the ghost of a white plucked chicken!!

In 1626 there was a bloke called Francis Bacon who was Lord High Chancellor to King James I (and some say his lover). He was also a scientist, philosopher and father of empiricism, with a pointy beard and ruff.

Anyway, he got into an argument with his friend Dr Witherborne at the bottom of Highgate Hill. Witherborne wouldn't accept his hypothesis that fresh meat could be preserved if frozen. It was January and the square was covered in snow, so Bacon promptly bought a chicken from an old lady, stuffed it with snow, and buried it in Pond Square. But it was so cold that he caught a chill and had to be taken to Lord Arundel's house nearby, where, for some reason, he was put into a damp bed which made him worse – and he died! (I've no idea why the bed was damp. It seems odd to put a sick man into a damp bed in January! Maybe he was incontinent?)

Anyway, ever since then motorists have reported seeing the ghost of a chicken leaping out in front of them, causing them to have accidents.

So, the frozen chicken was invented in Highgate!

If you walk along South Grove, past Bacon's Lane, you will see Lord Arundel's house – now called **THE OLD HALL 11** and occupied by Terry Gilliam of Monty Python.

Well, butter my cucumber sandwiches, if it isn't time for another drink! Actually, it's very easy for a visit to Highgate to turn into a pub crawl, but right here is the **Flask**,

probably my favourite, as we used to drink here when I was at school… (Well, just after I left, perhaps. Ahem.) It's been here since 1663 when Hampstead, the village close by, was famed for its natural springs with great health benefits and people would come from far and wide to take the waters. The pub got its name because it sold flasks for people to fill up.

The Flask still retains its cosy country tavern ambience and has several little nooks and corners to hide in. Indeed, Dick Turpin, the highwayman, hid here when he was on the run. Other famous customers included Hogarth, who is said to have sketched two men fighting here with tankards, Byron,

Keats, Shelley and Coleridge, whose house is across the road. As I sit in the pub's little committee room, I like to imagine those rumbustious poets enjoying several tankards of ale before staggering over to Coleridge's house to sing merrily outside his window. Legend has it that this room was where the first autopsy was performed in London, with a body freshly taken from the cemetery, and it's also haunted by the ghost of a poor Spanish barmaid, who hanged herself after being spurned by the barman.

(By the way, if you happen to encounter a pub that *doesn't* claim to be haunted, can you let me know, please.)

Highgate seems to be very popular with celebrities, and it's unsurprising because it's really very pleasant. The houses in The Grove, opposite The Flask pub, have been home to Sting, Kate Moss, J.B. Priestley and George Michael. In fact, when George Michael died, the whole of the little garden opposite was turned into a shrine with candles, pictures and messages of condolence on banners – until the neighbours got fed up with it and had it cleared.

We won't go down Highgate West Hill, but take note of the big gated property on the right, just past St Michael's Church. This is **WITANHURST** 12, which we will talk about later!

I like St Michael's because you can see it from far away across the fields. Between the church and the bus stop there is a splendid milestone (see the **STREET FURNITURE CHALLENGE**, pages 11–12). Yay, points!!!! It says that it's five miles to St Giles (near Tottenham Court Road Station).

Now go back up Highgate West Hill to Highgate Village, keeping the Flask on your right, and you'll see the **Gatehouse** on your left.

I used to drink here as it was cheaper than the other pubs and it has a theatre upstairs, but the interior is all modernised. The pub occupies the site of the old toll gate, which is where the name 'Highgate' comes from: the toll gate high up on the hill. The land beyond, along Hampstead Lane and down to East Finchley, was owned by the Bishop of London and you would have to pay a toll here. Although the original building is no longer here, it was the earliest recorded building in Highgate.

I'm obsessed with parish boundary markers, and on the side of the building here you can see the boundaries of St Pancras Parish and the Parish of Hornsey.

Across the road is **HIGHGATE SCHOOL** 13, where I learned how to make smutty remarks and conjugate Latin verbs. It was founded in 1565 by Sir Roger Cholmeley under a charter of Queen Elizabeth I, and I'm not even the most famous product of the school! Sir John Betjeman (who lived opposite, in Byron Cottage on North Hill) was taught here by T.S. Eliot. Another former pupil was Tom Hooper, who directed *The King's Speech* and *Les Misérables* (he was a rotten batsman, by the way). And if you hate maths, you can blame John Venn, who also studied here, for inventing the Venn diagram. It's all changed a bit since I was there. They now accept girls and have a school canteen with gender-neutral toilets, and all pupils are allowed to wear skirts. In my day it was short trousers, school on Saturdays, 'Get your hair cut, McDonnell!' and formal lunch with long tables and benches as far as the eye could see. The headmaster was on 'Top

Table' and rang a bell to announce that we may begin, after saying grace, and it was all a bit like Hogwarts really (except with the Dark Lord Sauron keeping watch).

Regular viewers of my YouTube channel may have seen my film *Take Me To Pitcairn*, which is all about the mutiny on the *Bounty*, about which I have had a small obsession since I was young. It is ironic that I attended this school for so many years and all that time I didn't realise that one of the mutineers is actually buried in the little cemetery behind the chapel. It was Peter Heywood, who was initially condemned to death but was subsequently pardoned (largely because of his posh, rich family, much to the annoyance of Captain Bligh).

Now walk down North Hill, passing a really cool-looking retro petrol station.

Ignore the blue plaque at number 92 for Charles Dickens, stating that he 'stayed here'. I mean, the man has so many plaques! I like him and all, but you don't need to commemorate every bench he sat on or tree he peed behind!

Opposite the house where Dickens tied his shoelace or patted a dog is **HIGHPOINT** **14**, a 1930s building on one of the highest points in London. It was sometimes used in episodes of *Poirot* and, more importantly, was where Emma Peel (played by Diana Rigg) lived in the 1960s TV show *The Avengers*. I only mention this because my dad was also in a couple of episodes of *The Avengers* with the late Honor Blackman!

All this talk of pubs has made me fancy another pint – and where better for that than the **Wrestlers**, which is the oldest pub still in business in Highgate. As far

PUB

The Wrestlers

back as 1547 drunk people have come here to get even more drunk and settle their differences in a fight, which is how it got its name. The fireplace is still original, but is the only part of the pub that survived after the pub burned down in the 1920s. Above the fireplace you'll see a set of what look like deer's antlers and some instructions for the ancient custom of 'swearing on the horns'.

Originally it was a gimmick to attract more customers, but swearing on the horns has become a yearly tradition in the pubs of Highgate. Lord Byron wrote about it in *Childe Harold's Pilgrimage*:

> *And many to the steep of Highgate hie.*
> *Ask ye, Boeotian shades, the reason why?*
> *'Tis to the worship of the solemn Horn,*
> *Grasped in the holy hand of Mystery,*
> *In whose dread name both men and maids are sworn,*
> *And consecrate the oath with draught and dance till morn.*

Worshipping the horn doesn't mean you have a bulge in your trousers. It means that anyone who swears on the horns becomes a 'Freeman of Highgate', which comes with several weird and rather ridiculous privileges. The ceremony consists of a set of silly oaths and issuing of fines for petty offences, like wearing a hat indoors or having a big nose, and afterwards you are issued with a certificate. So, for example, if I (who am now a Freeman of Highgate) am walking through the village and see three pigs in a ditch, I may, without any let or hindrance, kick the middle pig out and take its place. A Freeman may also kiss the prettiest girl in the pub (but if you get a slap, don't blame me!) and if you arrive at the pub with no money you can have a drink for free – but if it is then discovered that you were lying and you did have money, you would have to buy a round of drinks for the whole pub!

If you don't believe me, you can see me doing it in my video about it on YouTube. Look, if Lord Byron did it then it was probably a pretty decadent thing to do, okay?

Anyway, I think this is a perfectly suitable place to finish this walk. If so, cheers. I'll have a pint of ale.

If you don't want to finish yet, let's continue for the second leg of this walk, across Kenwood and into Hampstead Heath.

Having staggered out of the Wrestlers, walk down the hill and turn left up Broadlands Road. There's not much to say about it, but it's a pleasant road which must be nice to live in. This is just to get us to a good start point but towards the end, with the junction of Bishopswood Road, you might wonder what the strange construction is on your left, looking like concrete squash courts. These are **FIVES COURTS** ⑮. Eton Fives is a game played in posh schools where you hit a ball with your hand against the wall. A bit like

squash, with two players on each side and no rackets. It was invented at Eton School, where the boys used to play it in their free time against the side of a church, which is why the Fives courts have a buttress sticking out, making the game harder. You might be surprised to hear that it's a pretty good game! (I was rather good at it, I recall, but never got over the trauma of being beaten by the fifth pair from Ludgrove School, both of whom looked like Harry Potter!)

Carry on to the end of Broadlands Road, into Bishopswood Road past the school playing fields (look out for a stink pipe!) and turn right up Hampstead Lane until you see the entrance to Kenwood next to a red telephone box.

Turn into the park and you'll be presented with another magnificent view of London. Well, I say magnificent, but I must admit the view of St Paul's is slightly tarnished by the buildings behind it. It's true that this is one of the 13 protected vistas in London, meaning that it's forbidden to block the view of St Paul's with any constructions. However, the regulations don't seem to say anything about what you place *behind* St Paul's – and this can still ruin the view, in my opinion.

Now walk through to **KENWOOD HOUSE** ⑯, behind you as you look at the view, and you might be tempted to stop for tea and scones in the quaint café with its lovely garden. Handy place to go to the toilet if you've been drinking a lot!

Outside the house is a steep bank, where you used to be able to sit and watch the Kenwood concerts on a summer's evening without having to pay. However, they've now decided to be mean and extended the official ticketed seating area so that you can't see the performances unless you pay for a ticket. It's still a nice thing to do, though.

You might recognise this spot from the film *Notting Hill*, where Hugh Grant's character overhears Julia Roberts on some headphones, leading to another falling-out between the two.

Don't be fooled by the bridge behind the lake! It's actually a sham, made out of a piece of wood as decoration in the 1780s. One renowned gardener at the time wanted it removed, saying that it was 'below the dignity of Kenwood'; but luckily, the Earl of Mansfield, who owned the property at that time, decided to keep it.

It was here that Dido Elizabeth Belle lived with her great-uncle for 30 years in the late 18th century. You might have seen her represented in the 2013 film *Belle*, starring Gugu Mbatha-Raw. For some time it was thought that Dido was born into slavery in the West Indies after Sir John Lindsay, a British naval officer, discovered an African woman, Maria Belle, being held as a slave on a Spanish ship that they captured. However, it is now thought that she was born free in London in 1761 after Maria moved there. After Maria gave birth to his child, Lindsay left their daughter, Dido, with his uncle, the Earl of Mansfield. At Kenwood House she was raised as 'an educated woman'.

I wonder what happened to her mother in the meantime.

It's amazing to think the whole thing was nearly demolished to make way for luxury flats in 1922, after the Mansfield estate sold it, but fortunately it was saved by none other than the richest man in Ireland!

In the 1920s the house was bought by the Earl of Iveagh (a member of the Guinness family and head of their brewery), who decided, via the Iveagh Bequest Act of 1929, to leave it posthumously as an example of an 18th-century gentleman's home. You can now go inside and see the Rembrandts, Gainsboroughs and Vermeers, among other beautiful artworks. (I always said Guinness was good for you!)

Further along the path, in the little garden area, you'll find a sculpture by the renowned British artist Barbara Hepworth, one of the few female artists to gain international fame between the 1920s and 1970s. She was famous for her modernist sculptures, such as the 'winged figure' outside John Lewis on Oxford Street, which I've always thought was very ugly; but if you are into modern sculpture, you can find another famous one further along and to the left.

With pride of place, like a general on the higher ground surveying the battle beneath, stands a sculpture by Henry Moore, one of our most prominent artists. You've probably seen his sculptures dotted around London and other places. This one is called *Two Piece Reclining Figure No. 5*. (Apparently he was better at creating art than naming it!)

In the distance, on the hill, you can see Witanhurst, which is the second largest private residence in London after Buckingham Palace, with 65 rooms. We saw its gates in Highgate opposite St Michael's Church. It was rebuilt in 1913 by Sir Arthur Crosfield, who made millions out of his soap business. These days it's apparently owned by a Russian billionaire and has a value of over £300 million. (I do remember that when I tried to film nearby, I got yelled at by a scary security guard.)

4

6

8

9

13

14

Now turn around and try to head towards what looks like a little cottage that looks like it belongs in an episode of *Heidi*. It's the **OLD DAIRY** 🔟, built in 1794 by the second Earl of Mansfield for his wife. In those days, Kenwood House was seen as 'the finest country residence in the suburbs of London' and it was very fashionable for aristocratic women to have a hobby like tending a dairy, since that's what Marie Antoinette did; Dido Belle is believed to have supervised an earlier dairy and poultry yard on the site. Originally the dairy supplied milk and cream for the house, with ice kept downstairs. It has been restored in modern times, and on special days you can see cheese being made the old-fashioned way.

Now try to find your way back out to Hampstead Lane, through the little gate and to the right.

Exiting the car park, we want to turn left – but I just want to mention The Bishop's Avenue over on the right, next to more playing fields. This area was once owned by the Bishop of London but was sold in the early 20th century, and is now known as Billionaire's Row. Royal families, business magnates, oil barons and celebrities own houses down here, some of which are worth over £65 million, but many are actually unoccupied. These rather tasteless, tacky mansions are often bought through offshore companies by billionaires as investments, remaining empty a lot of the time. The Sultan of Brunei has a house here, as did Colonel Gaddafi's son, before all his assets were seized.

So, where were we? Yes, left out of the car park and up towards the **Spaniards Inn**, which sits opposite the other one of the Bishop of London's toll gates (we saw one

at the Gatehouse pub in Highgate). This is a listed building, which is why the council haven't been able to knock it down, despite it causing quite a bottleneck where the traffic piles up.

The pub is called the Spaniards after the two Spanish brothers who owned it fought a duel here, in which one of them died and was buried nearby. It was built in 1585 and I fancy popping in for some fish and chips and a pint in their garden.

The Spaniards Inn was commonly frequented by highwaymen and there is evidence in the Old Bailey's records of them being apprehended near here. Legend has it that Dick Turpin, the most famous highwayman of them all, used to drink here when his dad was the landlord – and he still haunts the upstairs room. They used to have his pistols on the wall, but they've been removed, which doesn't bother me too much, since (a) they probably weren't his pistols, and (b) he was a thoroughly nasty individual who, by all accounts, got what he deserved when he was eventually hanged in York.

After a splendid repast, head out and continue along Hampstead Lane. Note the horse trough on the right, which is a relic of Victorian London. There are many of these lying around and, whilst now obsolete, some are used as flowerbeds and other improvisations. It looks like telephone boxes are now going the same way – obsolete relics of a bygone age.

Another ghost who used to be seen along here, and in the beer garden of the Spaniards Inn, was that of a woman in white. It was she who was Bram Stoker's inspiration for the character of Lucy in *Dracula*. In the novel, the 'bloofer lady' was seen abducting small children along here, before sinking her fangs into their necks!

Now, if you like, you can walk straight along Hampstead Lane and pick up **Walk 6** from Jack Straw's Castle; but there's a lot to cover and lots of options, so I think it's nice to turn left into Kenwood and Hampstead Heath just after the zebra crossing, through the gate.

Keep going down the stony path, keeping the wooden fence all covered in ivy on your right.

Don't stray from the path, or you might get eaten by a werewolf.

Continue down the hill through the bushes of holly and undergrowth, and it feels almost like you shouldn't be there, or like you're in a Grimm fairy-tale. At the bottom of the hill there's a tree that has fallen over and a clearing. Beyond that you will see some daylight behind the trees. Yay!

Rummage through the trees and nettles and get onto the main path, out in the open, and turn right.

HAMPSTEAD HEATH

Follow the path and you'll reach a gate, which is the point where you leave Kenwood and enter Hampstead Heath.

Go through the gate and bear slightly to your right (not sharp right) and walk down a narrow foot-trodden path, through the trees and down the hill.

The walk becomes most serene and you might feel like Robin Hood or Puck, picking your way through the trees and bushes. At the bottom of the hill you should see a little **BRIDGE 18**. (The route to it is hard to describe, so you might need to use your phone! Or you can ask a passer-by for the little bridge. If in doubt, look for the Viaduct Bridge on Google Maps, which is very close by.)

I like looking at the names etched into the stone by long-gone Londoners. They're fading away now, but some are from the 1800s. Who knows, two star-crossed lovers on a summer's day writing their names in the 1800s, a weary traveller on his way to the tavern, a tall YouTuber who wears a bowler hat…

You might want to sit on the bench here and contemplate the existence of fairies; or you can just walk to the end of the bridge.

At the other end, look to your left and you'll see the **VIADUCT BRIDGE 19**. We're going

The Spaniards Inn

there in a minute, but if you like, you could take the wooden steps ahead of you and go up the slope to the **HOLLOW TREE 20**, also on Google Maps, which is good for a selfie. It always reminds me of the fairy-tale by Hans Christian Andersen, *The Tinderbox*, when the soldier climbs down into the tree at the request of an old witch and encounters the dogs with eyes as big as saucers. There are lots of squirrels here, too.

Now go back down to the Viaduct Bridge.

It feels like you are in the countryside, to a certain extent. Before the expansion of London, Hampstead and Highgate were just small isolated villages. You can still get a sense of that today.

The Viaduct Bridge was built in the 1840s by Sir Thomas Maryon Wilson, who owned some of the heath. His intention was to build grand villas here, with this as the driveway, but luckily he was forbidden from doing so.

Legend has it that there was a tunnel leading from the Spaniards Inn to this point, through which Dick Turpin used to make good his escape from the authorities.

The whole area is very relaxing and pleasant these days, but back in the 17th century it was rather boggy and unhealthy, with the unglamorous name of Hatchett's Bottom. In 1777 the malaria-ridden swamp was drained and the pond created, allowing them to build the houses nearby in what is now called the Vale of Health, no doubt to attract buyers.

Walk across the bridge, looking at more of the carved initials, and enjoy the view of the pond with lily-pads on it (where I used to think Jeremy Fisher lived).

At the end of the bridge turn right down the steep path, without falling over or getting stung. With the pond still on your right, take the second path on the left (the proper one, with a railing next to it).

Soon you'll come to a big stony path, more like a main thoroughfare almost, with trees lining either side. This leads from Highgate to Hampstead. Cross over this path and, if you look carefully, you should be able to see on your right and your left a little babbling brook.

This is the source of one of London's underground rivers, the Fleet, which I mention in **Walk 4**. It rises here and goes into a little grille and under the ground, but it also forms the ponds here. It then flows into the City beneath Farringdon Road, where it forms part of the sewers, and out into the Thames under Blackfriars Bridge.

Once you've crossed the path, go down into a little dip and then up, and keep going until you come out into a clearing. Keep going straight along the sort-of path, keeping the clearing on your right. In the distance you'll see the Royal Free Hospital. Head in that general direction.

When you come to the ponds, turn left and walk between them.

The pond on the left is the **MIXED BATHING POND 21**. In total there are three bathing ponds on Hampstead Heath: the men's pond, the women's pond and the mixed pond. Most tourists seem to favour the mixed pond, which can get very full in the summertime – and they've even started charging for entry. But you might prefer to try the others, which are further towards Highgate. Don't worry, the water is clean…

enough. From what I can gather, the female bathing pond is in the most beautiful setting, with trees on all sides; but, of course, I am not allowed in to verify this.

There's a whole culture of people who prefer to go in the winter months, when it's empty but totally freezing! My tailor has been going for around 60 years, always at about 7 a.m. on a cold day, and even appeared in a BBC documentary about it. The nutter.

I once saw a couple of men, tackle out, stark naked, playing badminton in the changing area… Just saying.

Keep going straight up the main path to the viewing point at the top of **PARLIAMENT HILL** 22. We've already seen a view of London, and this isn't one of my favourites, but nevertheless it's worth a visit – if only to turn around and enjoy the view in the other direction, which is what I tend to do! I love looking at Highgate from this point, with St Michael's Church proudly reaching towards the sky. I always imagine how little the view must have changed in the last few hundred years, in comparison to how much it has changed if you turn around and look at the vast metropolis. This is a popular place for people to fly kites. I can personally recommend the WORLD smallest KITE (*sic*), which I used to sell and is still available online. Alternatively, in the wintertime, the hill is good for sledging in the snow!

Looking towards the centre of London, below you is the running track and beyond that, to the left, the Parliament Hill Lido – the outdoor swimming pool we passed at the start of this walk. Again, like everything in London, it gets busy in the summer!

Pointing towards the Lido, turn right and go

back almost the way you came, but bearing slightly to the left. You should reach a path that leads out of the heath into the street called Parliament Hill.

One of the first houses on the right is **WHERE GEORGE ORWELL LIVED IN A DINGY FLAT** 23. It looks like a rather splendid house now, but he wasn't very domesticated – perhaps a hangover from his time living as a tramp when he wrote *Down and Out in Paris and London.* On one occasion his wife had left his dinner for him in the oven, only to discover on her return that he had instead eaten the jellied eels she had left out for the cat. Many locations in Hampstead are referenced in his novel *Keep the Aspidistra Flying.*

Keep going straight and you'll come to Hampstead Heath Station, with the lovely ghost sign opposite advertising the LNER railway from King's Cross to Scotland.

You're now in South End Green, which has many cafés and shops – but as this is where we will start **Walk 7**, let's go to the pub.

More or less opposite the station, on South Hill Park, you will have just walked past the **Magdala**, where Ruth Ellis shot her boyfriend in 1955, thereby ending up as the last woman to be hanged in Britain. She had been having a fractious on/off relationship with a playboy racing driver called David Blakely and lost several babies, one of them due to him punching her in the stomach. In the end she got very drunk and asked her friend for a gun (which he stupidly gave her) and shot Blakely in front of everybody, before surrendering to a nearby off-duty policeman. He couldn't believe how little trouble she was. She just said words to the effect of 'I'm glad I killed the bastard, it's a fair cop, guv'nor' and she was taken away to Hampstead police station.

On the day of her trial she bleached her hair peroxide blonde and said little in her defence. Nowadays she might have got a lesser sentence for diminished responsibility, but this was the 1950s.

More recently they made the case into a film starring Rupert Everett and Miranda Richardson, called *Dance with a Stranger* (one of my mum's favourite films).

I do like this pub. I think I'll have some food, actually. Oh, and I'll take a pint of Guinness, too.

Tally ho!!

◆— *Quiz!* —◆

What was Francis Bacon trying to prove that caused him to die after catching a chill in Pond Square?

Name one privilege that a Freeman of Highgate can enjoy after swearing on the horns?

What is the name of the game played in posh schools where you hit a ball with your padded glove?

What is the funny little building opposite the Spaniards Inn that causes a bottleneck in the road?

Who was the last woman to be hanged in Britain?

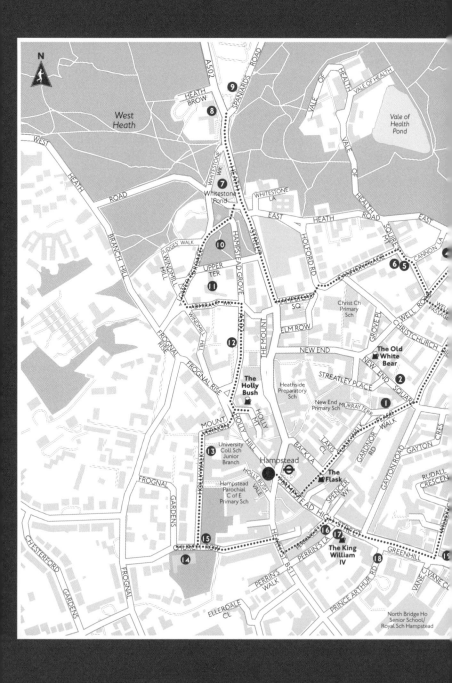

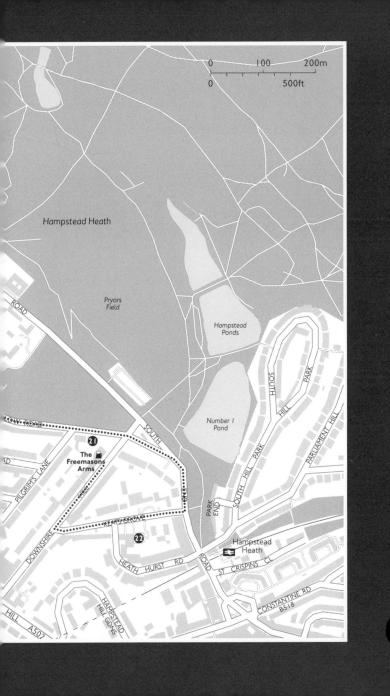

0   100   200m

0   500ft

Hampstead Heath

Pryors
Field

Hampstead
Ponds

Number 1
Pond

ROAD

TOW ROAD

21
The
Freemasons
Arms

PILGRIM'S LANE

SOUTH

WILLOW

SOUTH END

DOWNSHIRE

KEMPLAY GROVE

22

HEATH HURST RD

HAMPSTEAD HILL GDNS

HILL A502

SOUTH HILL PARK

SOUTH HILL PARK

PARLIAMENT HILL

PARK
END

SOUTH HILL PARK

Hampstead
Heath

ROAD

ST CRISPINS CL

CONSTANTINE RD
B518

6

6 A DELIGHTFUL DAWDLE THROUGH HISTORIC HAMPSTEAD

DISTANCE
4.5 km (2.8 miles)

TIME
2 hours

NEAREST STATION
Hampstead

What ho! Welcome to Hampstead, which is rather well-to-do. There isn't even a McDonald's or a KFC! That said, when there was a McDonald's here, they insisted on it being painted black, so it didn't ruin the aesthetic of the area.

Besides being very posh, it is a tremendously beautiful neighbourhood with a very village-like feel. Back in the 1720s Hampstead was just a small village, known for its wells and mineral waters, but by 1760 it had grown into a town with 300 houses and, most importantly, 19 pubs, some of which I'm sure we'll visit! It was said to be so healthy that there wasn't a single recorded death from bubonic plague here.

Walk down the High Street and turn left into Flask Walk, where the parish stocks used to be in the olden days.

This is one of many quaint streets typical of the area, with antique shops and boutiques, unspoiled by traffic, leading to the **Flask**. Personally I'm very fond of this pub, as it's the last place I had a drink with my dad. We had fish and chips, and jolly nice it was, too. In the 18th century people arriving from Highgate, having bought a flask from the *other* Flask pub in Highgate, would fill it up here with the supposedly healthy waters of Hampstead's spring, which we'll come to. Flasks were often dispatched from here to Fleet Street, where they would be sold to city-dwellers seeking cleaner or medicinal water. (The funny thing is, it wasn't even that good for you, but they weren't to know. It certainly helped you go to the toilet!)

Just after the pub is possibly the cutest French restaurant I've ever seen, called La Cage Imaginaire. I've never eaten there, but

I'm always jealous of those people dining whenever I walk past.

Keep going and you'll see on your left another example of the snappy short names the Victorians favoured: **THE WELLS AND CAMPDEN BATHS AND WASH-HOUSES ❶**, built in 1888 for those poorer inhabitants of Hampstead who didn't have running water. It's hard to imagine anyone poor living in Hampstead these days. That said, a little further along is a block of council flats, but I wouldn't like to guess at how many of the occupants these days are actually council tenants. Perhaps I'm being cynical, but many council flats have been bought by the occupants over the years and then sold on. I imagine these ones must be worth a pretty penny.

Next to the council flats, in New End Square, is **BURGH HOUSE ❷**. This was built in 1704 for a Quaker family, but in the 1720s the physician William Gibbons moved in and put his initials on the gates. He was one of the people responsible for promoting the health benefits of Hampstead's waters. Sounds like an old quack to me. These days it's a museum with a lovely quaint café and library containing books about Hampstead's history – and you can even hire it for your wedding, like my friend did. (She then asked me to give a guided tour on a London Routemaster bus for the wedding guests. The first time I ever gave a guided tour of London! Apparently I was okay and didn't spoil the wedding.)

Burgh House has had many residents over the years, including Rudyard Kipling's daughter, who was visited here by Kipling just before he died in 1936; but my favourite was Israel Lewis, an upholsterer, who was fined £5 for creating a dung heap in the garden.

It smelled so much that he was made to remove it. I often find it amusing to think what people have been remembered for. I'm sure he did many great things in his life, but to be remembered for building a dung heap is better than being forgotten, I suppose. As Oscar Wilde said: 'The only thing worse than being talked about is not being talked about!'

Gosh, there are so many little lanes and alleys around here that it's impossible to create a route that doesn't look a bit higgledy-piggledy. If you're on a pub crawl (like I usually seem to be) you could turn left here up New End Square and try the **Old White Bear**, which has finally opened up again after years of being closed. I'm so pleased it wasn't turned into luxury flats! They had me worried for a minute.

However, it's a bit early for a drink, so I'm just carrying on straight up Well Walk (with Burgh House on my left).

But what's this I see? Another pub!

Ah, the **Wells Tavern**, where I indulged in much underage drinking in my youth and once saw Robert Powell playing the fruit machine. A fine actor, great in *The Thirty-Nine Steps* and *Jesus of Nazareth*! It's beautifully located and great for an outdoor beer, although I notice, like many pubs, it seems to be more of a restauranty gastropub these days.

Carry on along Well Walk and you'll soon come to an old drinking fountain called the **CHALYBEATE WELL ❸**, which no longer works, opposite Gainsborough Gardens (named after the Earl of Gainsborough who, in 1698, donated six acres of land here for the benefit of the local poor and weary travellers who might be thirsty).

A clean glass of water in those days was far preferable to the nasty stuff that came out of the Thames, and the natural waters here had become quite popular.

Chalybeate means 'pertaining to minerals and iron salts'. It was thought that the rainwater would pass through the soil acquiring nutrients, before emerging here as a healthy elixir! In 1701 John Duffield, who

PUB

The Wells Tavern

leased the land, wasted no time in building a health spa and pump house, which turned the area into quite a popular destination. But before long, it started to attract undesirables like gamblers, prostitutes, beggars, drunks and…would you believe it…artists! John Constable lived just along Well Walk on the left. Perhaps the final nail in the coffin was when Hampstead Heath Station opened in 1860 attracting… wait for it…Cockneys from the East End on days out! What next, eh? They'd come up to enjoy 'appy 'ampstead, especially when there was a bank holiday fair (which still continues today).

I once went to John le Carré's house in Gainsborough Gardens, but he wasn't at home at the time. Jolly nice it was, though.

Right behind the drinking fountain is a little leafy passage leading up a slope. Follow this passage up to Well Road and turn right.

At the end of the road on the left corner is a huge gothic mansion called **THE LOGS** ❹, Boy George's house (which he reportedly put up for sale in September 2022). This isn't where he famously handcuffed a male escort to the wall and kept him prisoner, having accused him of hacking into his computer. That was at his flat in Shoreditch. George got 15 months for false imprisonment for that!

Now go back the way you came, up Well Road, humming 'Do You Really Want To Hurt Me', and turn right up Cannon Lane (you should see a sign with a hand pointing to Cannon Place).

On your left you will soon see a crooked door in a crooked wall. I don't know if a crooked man lives inside; however, it does have an authentic cannon bollard outside, with its cannonball missing. (See the **STREET FURNITURE CHALLENGE**, page 9.) Points, yay!!!

The cannon is right outside the old **PARISH LOCK-UP** ❺, which was a single small cell where prisoners could be held until further arrangements were made for them. Not many of these remain in London and it could also have been used as a drunk tank, where you might be thrown to sober up if you've been making a nuisance of yourself after drink. It certainly retains the appearance of a small prison on the outside, with its little windows in the huge expanse of brick. It forms part of the garden wall of **CANNON**

HALL **6**, where various magistrates held court, but was closed in 1829 after the formation of the Metropolitan Police. Now it's a private residence (which I hope has some windows on the other side, because it would be a bit gloomy otherwise) – probably worth millions of pounds.

Now, I thought we'd get this hill out of the way at the start of the walk. Don't worry, most of the walk will be downhill afterwards!

Carry on up Cannon Lane until you reach Cannon Place, and what's this? More cannon!! I'm in Joolz Guides heaven!!

This is now prime Hampstead real estate. I ain't got no homies around this part, bruv.

At number 14, immediately on your left, you'll see the main entrance to Cannon Hall. As well as hosting magistrates, it was at one time the house of Daphne du Maurier, who wrote *Jamaica Inn*, *Rebecca*, *Don't Look Now*, *My Cousin Rachel* and – my favourite – *Frenchman's Creek*.

Cannon Place and Cannon Hall are named after the cannon that were placed in the ground by James Melvill, who was the last secretary of the East India Company. The bollards along Cannon Lane are actually real cannon, probably captured from the French or Spanish during various campaigns over the years. It used to be common to use them for this purpose and you can see them dotted around London, usually with a cannonball lodged in the muzzle. When they ran out of cannon they started making replicas in the same style – but you can tell these are original because the sizes are all different.

Points galore!

Now walk left along Cannon Place straight past the church, across the paved area with the bench and straight on down Hampstead Square. Then turn right and walk up Heath Street.

By hook or by crook we have found ourselves at **WHITESTONE POND** **7**. It might be that you decided to blend **Walk 5** into this one here. Don't worry, it's one of the highest points in London, so at least you'll be going downhill from here.

Whitestone Pond used to be a dew pond, used mostly for horses to cool off, and was named after the white milestone, which is still there. You have to look in the bushes by the side of the road, but it's pleasing that it survives. If you turn left before the pond (onto West Heath Road) and then immediately left, as if to go to Hampstead Grove, you should see the milestone in the bushes on your right. It tells you that it's four miles to St Giles (which nowadays means the Centre Point Tower at the end of Oxford Street).

In later years the pond was enlarged and I remember my dad taking me there as a boy to sail our toy yacht. Some people had these new-fangled boats with engines, but I liked how ours would just go wherever the wind blew it.

You should be able to see **JACK STRAW'S CASTLE** **8** from here, just north of the pond near the mini roundabout. It's named after one of Wat Tyler's brethren, Jack Straw, who lived around here in 1381 and helped lead the Peasants' Revolt. In the 18th century it became a pub, which was popular with the likes of William Thackeray and Charles Dickens (who said that they served 'a red-hot chop for dinner and a glass of good wine'). I must say, after a brisk walk across the Heath it sounds like just the thing! Indeed, in Bram Stoker's *Dracula* Van Helsing dines here with Seward before hailing a cab at the Spaniards Inn.

Sadly, the pub closed in 2002 and ended up being turned into luxury flats. I don't like what they've done with the exterior – it looks rather tacky to me and looked much more charming in its pub days.

Opposite Jack Straw's Castle is the 18th-century **HEATH HOUSE** 9, behind the Hampstead War Memorial.

This building has always been a mystery to me, since I was little. I cannot remember a time when it was in a good state of repair, but it must be one of the most desirable properties in London. Back in 1790 it was the London home of banker and philanthropist Samuel Hoare, who was one of the founding members of the Society for the Abolition of the Slave Trade. However, down the years it has had various owners, been hit by bombs and remained in such a state of disrepair that I have never seen it without scaffolding. Naturally, they wanted to turn it into luxury flats, but permission was denied.

Let's head back down past the milestone and turn right into Hampstead Grove. On your left is what most people ignore as a reservoir; what a lot of people miss is **HAMPSTEAD OBSERVATORY** 10, which has been here since 1910. It was opened by the Hampstead Scientific Society, founded in the 1890s, who wanted to give people the chance to learn about astronomy, since they felt that everything reported in the newspapers or on the radio was invariably wrong. It's open to the public on various evenings (which can change, so it's worth booking ahead on their website).

Now carry on along Hampstead Grove and it becomes Lower Terrace. It's all so meandering around here, making it difficult to choose the most efficient route, but that's all part of the charm. The little streets and passages winding up and down retain the village atmosphere of yore.

Now turn left up Admiral's Walk (grabbing yourself some **points** for the Queen Victoria post box recessed into the wall) and you'll come across **ADMIRAL'S HOUSE** 11, which was built in 1700 and appears in a few Constable paintings. The plaque for George Gilbert Scott, who lived here, is not to be confused with his grandson Giles Gilbert Scott, who designed the red telephone boxes. George designed the Albert Memorial and St Pancras station; Giles designed Battersea Power Station.

I call this the *Mary Poppins* house, because this is the one that inspired the character of Admiral Boom, who fires cannonballs from his roof in the book. In the late 18th century a naval captain lived here and added a quarterdeck, bulwarks and portholes – but the real admiral (Admiral Barton), who did actually fire cannonballs from his roof on the King's birthday, lived nearby and everyone just assumed the cannon fire came from this one. If you don't sing 'Chim Chim Cher-ee' as you walk by, I'll be very surprised. I did!

Continue around the corner to the right and you'll be in Hampstead Grove again, where you'll come across **FENTON HOUSE** 12, which is the oldest house in Hampstead. Dating from 1693, it was remodelled in the 18th century by a Riga merchant called Philip Fenton, but now it's run by the National Trust (don't forget to get your tickets in advance on their website). You can visit the 300-year-old orchard and learn to make cider the old-fashioned way, if you go at the right time of year.

That said, there's a lovely pub around the corner, so I think I'll pop in there for a pint.

Continue down Hampstead Grove and into Holly Hill, and then turn left into Holly Mount.

In front of you is the **Holly Bush**. Actually, they've turned half of it into a restaurant now, what they call a gastropub, which annoys me when I just want to go for a drink, but when I fancy a nice pub lunch I'm less bothered by it! Try to sit in the front room, though; it's nicer and cosier. Whilst you peruse the plaques that the landlord has installed for regulars who drank their last pint here, I shall raise a glass to my old friends Steve Donnelly and James O'Halloran, whom I last saw at this pub many years ago. I must check if there's a plaque for them.

To Steve and James…Cheers.

Once refreshed, head back out and just opposite the entrance of the pub look out for the 'TRADESMEN'S ENTRANCE' sign next to a small door. (Well, it's small if you're 6' 6" tall, like me!) If you then stand on your head you will see that the old doorbell is marked 'SERVANTS'. It's a nice indication of how the servants in some of these grand houses had separate entrances.

It's also worth checking out the view of London from the little dead end in front of the pub.

Now head back past the pub the way you came. Cross over Holly Hill and up the steep path to Mount Vernon. The houses around

PUB

The Holly Bush

here are so beautiful and make one feel as though one is in the English countryside or an Agatha Christie novel.

Above the door of number 6 you'll see what I'm sure must be a fire insurance plaque. In the 18th and 19th centuries, before the modern emergency services, homeowners would have to buy fire insurance, and if the firemen showed up and found you didn't have insurance, they would just let you burn. Different insurance companies had their own fire brigades, which is why the plaques differ. Followers of Joolz Guides will know that I have several obsessions: post boxes, parish boundary markers, cattle troughs and fire insurance plaques! You don't see them that often, so when I spot one it's rather pleasing. I notice that the author of *Kidnapped* and *Treasure Island*, Robert Louis Stevenson, who lived next door, didn't have one – but he didn't need it in the end. Like many people with tuberculosis, he moved to Hampstead to improve his health, but it didn't work; so he moved to Samoa, where he died.

Carry on and then turn left down Holly Walk.

The Flask

Usually, I'm not a fan of modern buildings amongst old ones, but there is a rather cool building on your right. I don't object to this one myself, and wouldn't say 'no' if someone offered it to me!!! Imagine living here. It's right opposite a **WATCH HOUSE** ⑬ – another one of my obsessions.

The Metropolitan Police wasn't established by Robert Peel until 1829. Before that, they just had night watchmen, who were elected but unpaid. We saw the lock-up they used earlier in this walk, but once Hampstead got a proper police force, they moved here.

Now continue down Holly Walk and you will see before you the parish church of **ST JOHN-AT-HAMPSTEAD** ⑭. This parish stretched as far as Primrose Hill – I know this because there's a 'St J' boundary stone on the slope of Primrose Hill (which we shall see in **Walk 8**). To your right, where Frognal Gardens meets Church Row, there used to be a toll gate, which is why the architect of the church placed the entrance on the east side: this meant that most of the congregation could avoid paying the toll, as the majority lived on the Hampstead side.

Several notable celebrities are buried here in the southern part of the cemetery, including the comedian Peter Cook and the artist John Constable, who was most famous for his painting *The Haywain*. Constable lived in Hampstead, on Well Walk, and said:

I love every style and stump and lane in the village: as long as I am able to hold a brush, I shall never cease to paint them.

Personally, I find cemeteries spooky, and even more so this one, because in *Dracula*

this is where Van Helsing comes to drive a stake through Lucy's heart:

Lucy lies in the tomb of her kin, a lordly death-house in a lonely churchyard, away from teeming London; where the air is fresh, and the sun rises over Hampstead Hill, and where wild flowers grow of their own accord.

In the northern part of the cemetery (across the road from the church) you will find **THE ACTUAL GRAVE OF PETER PAN** ⑮ – or the boy he was based on, at least!

J. M. Barrie was inspired to write *Peter Pan* after meeting Sylvia Llewelyn Davies in Kensington Gardens around 1900 and befriending her five boys; Peter, Jack, George, Nico and Michael. It all sounds a bit suspicious these days, but apparently she trusted him, and he used to hang out with them quite a lot, playing games and telling them stories. The Llewelyn Davies boys (who were related to Daphne du Maurier) became the inspiration for the Lost Boys in *Peter Pan*, and are buried here in the family tomb, six coffins deep!

Many of them met untimely ends. One jumped into a river in Oxford and drowned; another two died in the First World War; and Peter was terribly depressed and didn't enjoy being constantly associated with *Peter Pan*, eventually throwing himself under a train at Sloane Square.

Leading up to the main entrance of the church is one of the finest examples of a Georgian street in London: Church Row, built in the early 1700s. If it weren't for the cars, you might think you had travelled back in time to an age when men would parade in their powdered wigs after having taken the waters at the healthy local springs, alongside women in their farthingales and 'hoops of wondrous size'. Some of its famous residents down the years have included Lord Alfred Douglas (Oscar Wilde's boyfriend), H.G. Wells and Peter Cook.

At the end of Church Row, cross over Heath Street and turn right. Look back at the building you passed on the corner, for the lovely old ghost sign for the estate agent and decorator. Why? Just because I like old stuff like that.

Coming up on your left is a nice little antique craft emporium, where there are more cute cafés and second-hand bits and bobs… Stop me if you've heard this one before.

There are of course many places to have a cup of tea in Hampstead. Turn left down Perrin's Court and then turn right onto Hampstead High Street. To your right you'll see another cute iconic coffee house, the **COFFEE CUP** 16, which has been there since the 1960s. It's one of those places that is bigger on the inside than the outside and is still very good value, despite being in Hampstead. They do a

pretty good selection of food, from English fry-ups to soups, pasta and burgers. You can even get fried liver here!

Just further along, though, outside the **King William IV**, is the **CREPE VAN** 17, which has been there certainly since I was young. I have never understood the people who order a savoury pancake with cheese and ham on it. I must have a sweet tooth, but it's chocolate, coconut and lashings of rum for me, every time! It was called a Caribbean Surprise last time I had one, and worth queuing up for. Yum!

We're going to nip down the hill now. Cross over the zebra crossing at the King William IV and turn right down Hampstead High Street. I do like the street furniture around here, for example the Queen Victoria post box, and the telephone box which has been turned into a café. Because they are listed buildings, it has become quite a conundrum, what to do with all these phone boxes that no one uses except drug dealers and people dying for the toilet, judging by the smell! Some are turned into libraries or book lending services, and others are ATM machines, but this one was a café last time I checked.

As you walk down Hampstead High Street, opposite HSBC you will see a steep bank on your right with **STANFIELD HOUSE** 18, which has been cut in half to make way for Prince Arthur Road. It used to be occupied by the painter Clarkson Stanfield, who was a friend of Charles Dickens – but he moved out when they cut it in half, saying that it was too small for him. I don't know what he was talking about, because it still looks pretty big to me! Maybe he had a lot of paintings…

Sorry to drag you even further down this hill, but I couldn't resist the **SNAPPY SNAPS** 19 on the corner of Willoughby Road. In 2010 George Michael was arrested after crashing his Range Rover into it at 3.30 a.m., so it has had a special place in the hearts of all locals ever since. One hilarious joker wasted no time in adding graffiti beneath the broken windows, before the paparazzi arrived. They simply wrote: 'WHAM!'

At Snappy Snaps turn down Willoughby Road.

On your left is a groovy-looking house, number 1a. A bloke down the pub told me that German football legend Jürgen Klinsmann used to live here when he played for Tottenham Hotspur. Well, he certainly lived *somewhere* around here! He'd arrive home in his old VW Beetle while all the other players were driving Ferraris.

Carry on down Willoughby Road to the end and then turn right into Willow Road.

At the junction with Christchurch Hill you will notice another one of my slight obsessions: a **HORSE DRINKING TROUGH 20**, installed by the snappily named Metropolitan Drinking Fountain and Cattle Trough Association, founded in 1859. They installed around 800 all over London, but the only one I've ever seen in actual use today is just behind the King's personal bodyguard at the entrance to the Household Cavalry Museum on Whitehall. I suppose in 100 years the Joolz Guides of the future will look at telephone boxes and post boxes in the same way that we look at these cattle troughs today, as if we're looking at a ZX Spectrum or Sony Walkman.

Continue down the street and on the right is **2 WILLOW ROAD 21**, which was built in 1939 by architect Ernő Goldfinger, who lived here with his family until 1987. It's an excellent example of modernist architecture

WILLOW ROAD

and has been preserved as a museum run by the National Trust – in fact, you can get a discount if you are visiting Fenton House together with 2 Willow Road.

Inside it's like a time capsule taking you back to the 1960s, with an interior that looks like something out of *The Man From U.N.C.L.E.* Goldfinger was also responsible for designing Trellick Tower, that hideous Brutalist eyesore in Westbourne Park. He famously didn't get on with his neighbour Ian Fleming, which is why Fleming named his most famous James Bond villain after him.

Carry on down Willow Road until it becomes South End Road.

Then turn right onto Keats Grove, where you will find **KEATS HOUSE 22** on your left.

John Keats was, of course, one of our famous Romantic poets, and friends with Lord Byron and Percy Shelley. For some reason he was called 'the Cockney poet', maybe because he was born in Moorgate, within the sound of the Bow Bells. He only lived in this house for 17 months before moving to Italy to die. He managed to make quite a name for himself in the short time he was around – he only lived to the age of 25 – and they've now turned his house into a sort of museum. It is claimed that he wrote 'Ode to a Nightingale' under the plum tree in the garden here, which I find more likely than the claim that it was written at the Spaniards Inn, which is what the pub claims. Although he might have done a bit in both!

When his tuberculosis got worse he was advised to move to Italy. He died in Rome, in a house on the Spanish Steps, after being restricted by his doctor to a diet of one anchovy and a piece of bread per day. That is probably enough to kill anyone off, I should think. Anchovies, yuck!

Come along now, the sky's beginning to bruise, night must fall and we shall be forced to camp! We've actually just passed a perfectly good pub, but as this is such a lovely area, may I suggest a slightly circuitous route?

Just carry on up Keats Grove until you get to the church of St John's Downshire Hill,

and very pretty it is, too. I just wanted you to see the lovely houses around here, but time waits for no man.

Turn sharp right and down Downshire Hill.

In deference to my friend Ted, who always decides to go to the nearest pub, we shall invoke 'The Rule of Ted' and decamp to the **Freemasons Arms** on your left. It's more suited to dining than drinking, but it has a lovely large garden and certainly enough room inside to cater for a few drinkers. Apparently, downstairs they have one of London's only olde English full-size skittle alleys (skittles being a precursor to ten-pin bowling), but it tends to get flooded now and then, because it stands on a tributary of the River Fleet.

But what of it? I'll have a pint of bitter. Chin chin!!

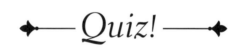

Quiz!

Why was Israel Lewis, resident at Burgh House, fined £5?

Which character in a Walt Disney film was inspired by Admiral's House?

What happens at St John-at-Hampstead churchyard in a famous gothic novel from 1897?

What happened at Snappy Snaps at 3.30 a.m. in 2010?

Who lived at 2 Willow Road and didn't get on with his neighbour, Ian Fleming?

Joolz's Guide to...

TRAVELLING ON PUBLIC TRANSPORT

• Don't just arrive at the ticket gates and be suddenly surprised that you need to scan your card or phone like you weren't expecting it. Don't just stand there blocking the entrance. *Get out of the way!*

• On the escalators, *please stand on the right*! The left-hand lane is for people who are much busier than you. If you have so much as a bag or half an arm encroaching into the left-hand lane, you basically have no human rights and will get ploughed out of the way by someone descending at speed.

• When you get to the platform, don't just stand there blocking the entrance, looking at the map. Move down the platform!

• When jumping on a train just as the doors are closing, use your momentum to carry you further into the train. Don't stop stock-still, looking smug to have caught the train. There will be some poor bugger like me who is cutting it even finer just behind you, and you'll be blocking the way!!

• Rucksacks: on any bus or train, hold your rucksack in front of you or by your feet. Don't jump on and get it stuck in the door like an amateur, and don't swing around causing it to wipe out a fellow passenger!

• On no account talk to anyone or catch their eye!!! If you see anyone talking to a stranger on the tube or bus they are clearly not from London (or they are totally weird).

• If you must talk, no loud comments to your companions please about 'how hot' or 'how packed' it is – or the dreaded 'I couldn't do this every day'. This will only annoy passengers who *do* actually do this every day and cause them to view you as an alien body in their space who is making it more hot and more packed.

• Top tip: whichever line you desire to use at King's Cross St Pancras station, initially *always* follow signs to the Metropolitan line. These take you to the old ticket hall from where all lines are quickly accessible. If you make the mistake of following signs to the Victoria, Piccadilly or Northern lines from some entrances, you will end up walking 10 miles in seven circles of hell.

• Don't manspread! The seats are small enough as it is, so please don't spread your legs overhanging my section when sitting next to me.

• At all costs you must find it hilarious when the announcement comes telling you to MIND THE GAP'. It is customary for anyone who hasn't heard it before to repeat it loudly several times, much to the joy of everyone else.

• Don't leave litter on the train unless it's the free *Evening Standard* or *Metro* newspapers, and don't eat disgusting smelly food!

• It's okay to put your bag on the seat next to you, to try to dissuade everyone from sitting there – except when there are no more seats left. Then you need to remove your bloody bag!

• There is always at least one weirdo on the bus or Tube, and they will almost certainly sit next to you. If you cannot see a weirdo then the chances are it's you!

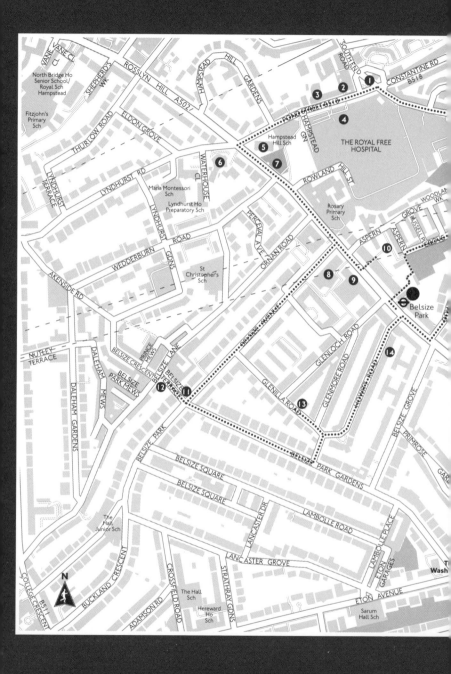

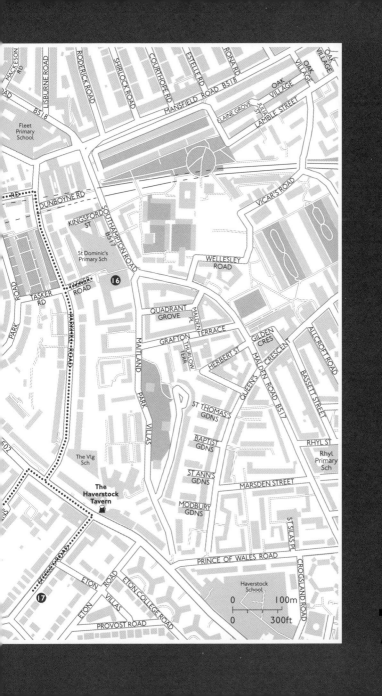

MACKESON RD

LISBURNE ROAD

RODERICK ROAD

SHIRLOCK ROAD

COURTHOPE RD

ESTELLE RD

RONA RD

OAK VILLAGE

B518

MANSFIELD ROAD B518

ELAINE GROVE

OAK VILLAGE

JEFFREYS STREET

LAMBLE STREET

Fleet Primary School

VICAR'S ROAD

DUNBOYNE RD

KINGSFORD ST

SOUTHAMPTON ROAD B518

WELLESLEY ROAD

St Dominic's Primary Sch

TASKER RD

TASKER ROAD

16

PARK ROAD

QUADRANT GROVE

MALDEN PL

GRAFTON TERRACE

GILDEN CRES

THURLOW TERR

HERBERT ST

MAITLAND

MALDEN ROAD B517

BASSETT STREET

ALLCROFT ROAD

QUEEN'S CRESCENT

PARKHILL ROAD

PARK VILLAS

ST THOMAS'S GDNS

BAPTIST GDNS

RHYL ST

Rhyl Primary Sch

The Vlg Sch

ST ANN'S GDNS

MARSDEN STREET

The Haverstock Tavern

MODBURY GDNS

PRINCE OF WALES ROAD

ST SILAS PL

CROGSLAND ROAD

17

ETON ROAD

ETON COLLEGE ROAD

ETON VILLAS

PROVOST ROAD

Haverstock School

0   100m

0   300ft

7

7 A SOULFUL SAUNTER THROUGH BEAUTIFUL BELSIZE PARK

DISTANCE
5.1 km (3.2 miles)

TIME
2 hours

NEAREST STATION
Belsize Park

The walk starts in earnest in South End Green, at the bottom of Pond Street, which you can reach via buses 168, 24 or C11 to the Royal Free Hospital, or by Overground (Hampstead Heath station). If coming by bus or Overground, you can skip the next section in italics. However, I recommend coming from Belsize Park tube station, via the following fun little route, to avoid going back on yourself later.

Turn right out of the tube and right again, immediately towards the tennis club house. Walk around the tennis courts to the end and you will come to Belsize Wood.

There should be a little path through the wood, which you can follow until you reach Lawn Road. (Ignore the big white building at the bottom of the path, we'll come to that later!)

I'm delighted that they kept this wood when they built all these houses, because it's where we used to ride our BMX bikes as kids. A whole bunch of my brother's friends took shovels and spades and created a whole BMX assault course, with all sorts of challenges – and it was good, too! You might still be able to make out some of the steep banks and big dips that they dug...a bit like the overgrown trenches of the First World War.

Turn left on Lawn Road and follow it round to Fleet Road and turn left at the **Stag** *(unless you fancy a pint). Ignore the post box on the corner, which annoys me because it doesn't have the initials of any monarchs on it! No points!!!! (See the* **STREET FURNITURE CHALLENGE***, page 8, for the rules.)*

Fleet Road is named after the underground river (which we saw in **Walk 5***) running beneath it.*

At the end of Fleet Road you'll see a triangle of grass with an old abandoned fountain and we're ready to start!

What ho! Here we are in **SOUTH END GREEN** ❶, a good place to start our walk, or to continue from either **Walk 5** or **Walk 6**, which both finish nearby.

Belsize Park first appears in records in 1317, when it was left by Sir Roger le Brabazon (who had no heir) to Westminster Abbey. The Kings back in those days were Plantagenets, so it's not surprising that the name 'Belsize' comes from the French name for the area, '*bel assis*', which means 'beautifully situated'.

Later the monks of Westminster Abbey gradually started to section off pieces of land, which consequently got sold.

We're starting at the bottom of Pond Street, one of the oldest streets in Hampstead, where there was once a pond connected with the River Fleet, until 1835 when it got filled in because it was all too muddy. By then, some houses had been built on the street and around the pond itself, although it was still very much a rural village with a handful of cottages.

Much of what I remember from my childhood has been torn down, such as the cinema where I first saw *Star Wars*, which stood where Marks & Spencer is now. It was once called the Picture Playhouse and was regarded as one of the finest in London, but by the time I started going there it was called the Hampstead Classic and smelled of fried eggs.

One thing that hasn't been removed yet is the Victorian public lavatory, with its beautiful wrought-iron work. There aren't many of these left in London, but I've always found them less cramped and unpleasant than more modern conveniences. Most of them seem to have been turned into bars or cafés. I mean, who would want to have a coffee in a toilet?

The area where the pond used to be is now occupied by some benches and yet another fountain dedicated to someone who, let's face it, no one has heard of. Miss Crump erected it in 1880 in memory of her cousin, William Warburton Pearce, and her uncle, James Bradley Chamberlain. These days people tend to dedicate park benches to their loved ones, but in Victorian times wealthy families seemed to favour granite drinking fountains. It's a pity they don't work any more, but I like to think that in years to come the Joolz Guides of the 23rd century will look upon my dad's bench with the same sense of wonder that I do these fountains. People from the past who all mattered to someone. Perhaps Miss Crump stepped onto a tram here and headed into town, as this was the terminus for the London Tramways Company, who erected the tramwaymen's shelter, still in use today.

Nearby is another telephone box, which has become one of the smallest cafés in the world, from which you could take a coffee whilst perusing the fun quotations on the ground of various people associated with the area. They're rather good, I think. Robert Louis Stevenson says, for example: 'To travel hopefully is a better thing than to arrive.'

On the opposite corner, where at present stands a Gail's Bakery, there's a plaque on the wall with George Orwell's face poking out.

He used to live and work here in 1934, when it was Book Lovers' Corner, and he describes many local scenes in his novel *Keep the Aspidistra Flying*. The alley next door with a gate on it is known as **TRIFFID ALLEY** ❷, after an incident from John Wyndham's *The Day of the Triffids*. In Chapter 8 the hero is surrounded by man-eating plants in a shop here, but makes good his escape: 'The door, I could see, gave into a narrow alley running the full length of the block.'

Let's walk up Pond Street.

The oldest houses are numbers 17 to 21, which date from the late 18th century and probably housed doctors, because Belsize Park was known as 'the Harley Street of Hampstead' – quite prophetic, really, given that the Royal Free Hospital didn't open until the 1970s!

Further up the street, at 22–25, is the drill hall, or **ARMOURY** ❸, built around 1900 as headquarters for the Royal Fusiliers, but also used in 1908 by Hampstead's first scout troop. Robert Baden-Powell's call to action came that same year, so this is possibly the oldest scout troop in existence. (It also happens to be where I attended a salsa class with a young lady in my youth and decided to introduce her to my mother, at which point my mum said: 'Hello. Oh… You have a nose that doesn't sit well on a young girl's face.' Charming! I never saw the girl again. Thanks, Mum.)

POND STREET

The ugly carbuncle opposite is the **ROYAL FREE HOSPITAL** ❹. The original Royal Free Hospital was opened in the early 19th century in Hatton Garden by William Marsden, who revolutionised healthcare by offering it for free. When they moved the hospital to newly constructed premises in Pond Street, they brought with them the original iron tympanum, which you can see on the wall. William Marsden also founded several other hospitals, including the Royal Marsden.

Carry on to the top of the street and turn left at **ST STEPHEN'S CHURCH** ❺. It was built in 1869 and must have looked vastly different without all these big buildings around it back then. When they started digging the foundations for the new hospital in the 1970s the church started to suffer from subsidence and had to be abandoned. For my whole childhood it was empty, except for a scary guy with a spiderweb tattooed on his face, who used to live inside with about ten dogs. I always supposed he was just squatting there, but no one was using it, so good for him. Eventually, in the last 10 years or so, they've renovated it and it's now available to hire for events. I don't know what became of old spiderweb man, though. Maybe he's in an abandoned church near you. He was like a Disney character!

The church opposite isn't actually a church. It's a recording studio called **AIR STUDIOS** ❻, founded by the producer of the Beatles, George Martin. They do a lot of recordings of film and TV scores, as well as pop and classical music.

Carry on down Haverstock Hill and immediately on your left you'll see a little shack selling coffee and tea, which looks a bit like some sort of prefab from IKEA. It's like a cabmen's shelter, but it isn't painted green like all the others. Remarkably, it is a listed building, the **WHARRIE SHELTER** ❼, named after Mary Wharrie, daughter of the first mayor of Hampstead, who donated the shelter in the 1920s. When it's open don't forget to look at the mosaic floor – probably the nicest thing about it.

Further down on the other side, on the corner of Belsize Avenue, is the old **TOWN HALL**. ❽. Imagine: the council wanted to knock it down in the 1960s, no doubt to make way for some ugly block of flats! But luckily, locals fought for its survival. Now it's used as a performance space and recording studio, amongst other things. I always find it a pity that if you need to go to your town hall to retrieve some document or other you are sent to a dark, grey, ugly office on the outskirts of town. It must have been so much nicer when you could go to a grand building like this.

A little further along is the **EVERYMAN CINEMA** ❾ and a Budgens supermarket, which both lie in a block which was once a beautiful art deco Odeon Cinema. If you look above Budgens you can still make out the shape of the original building, with its typical 1920s curved edges. I wish they would leave beautiful buildings alone, but I guess if they hadn't changed it, the guy who designed the album covers for Pink Floyd couldn't have moved in upstairs.

Directly opposite there is a path leading down beside what is currently a Costa Coffee. When I was a boy this led to the tennis courts. There were over 20 clay courts here, but they have all been built on now, and replaced with houses that look like toy town. They say that everyone remembers where they were when (a) Kennedy was shot;

(b) the Twin Towers fell; and (c) Live Aid was taking place in 1985. Well, I wasn't born when Kennedy was shot, but in 1985 I was here playing a tennis match while my sister was in the front row at Wembley Stadium, watching Freddie bloomin' Mercury!!!! She then went backstage and stole Tony 'Spandau Ballet' Hadley's ripped jeans! I like to think that this inspired her to become a songwriter and compose many tunes for Joolz Guides!

At the end of the path is a strange round structure, which is the entrance to the old **BOMB SHELTER** ❿ from the Second World War. This is the northern entrance and we'll see its twin further down Haverstock Hill. They were started in 1940; in fact, eight were built in London, and you'll see them in Goodge Street and Clapham, amongst other sites. However, by the time they were finished in 1942 the Blitz was over, so they didn't get used much except in 1944, when there was a bit more bombing. Some of them, like the one in Clapham South, offer tours and still have the steel bunk beds in place – but this one is just used as a storage facility, the bunk beds making useful storage racks!

Now head back the way you came, up Haverstock Hill briefly, and then left down Belsize Avenue (next to the Town Hall).

It's extraordinary to think that fewer than 200 years ago this was a driveway leading up to the grand manor, Belsize House. Belsize House was first built in 1496 and stood in open fields, as can be seen on John Rocque's map of 1746. John Rocque was an 18th-century cartographer, commissioned to draw a map proving that London was bigger than Paris. Apparently size does matter!

1

1

1

4

7

8

Perhaps the most famous resident of Belsize House was Spencer Perceval who, in 1812, became the only British Prime Minister to have been assassinated while in office. The nearby Perceval Avenue is named after him.

After the restoration of King Charles II to the throne in 1660, the dark days of Puritanism were put into the past as theatres and pubs started to open and the mood of the nation improved. There was much debauchery and the area around Belsize House became a pleasure garden known for its deer hunting, shooting, gambling and dancing, on a par with the Vauxhall Pleasure Gardens. Samuel Pepys once visited and recorded in his famous diary: 'too good for the house the gardens are, being, indeed, the most noble that ever I saw.' Eventually the other residents nearby got it closed down in 1745. Always seems the way whenever there's something fun happening. Some things never change.

Walk down Belsize Avenue until you reach Belsize Terrace and turn right, but take note of the **MULBERRY TREE** ⓫ on the corner. It looks rather old – and that's because it is! Belsize House was demolished in 1853 to make way for all these housing developments, but this mulberry tree demarcated the corner of the grounds of the house. It's all that's left to mark Belsize House, so I hope it remains there for many years, even if it does create quite a mess on your car if you leave it parked underneath. The ground is always stained with mulberries!

Belsize Terrace leads to Belsize Village, which retains its charm partly due to being blocked to traffic. I remember it as a child, when the local boys used to do break dancing and body popping on a linoleum mat with a ghetto blaster in the middle of the square. A very 1980s scene, but so many people will have their own memories, like in the Edwardian photographs I've seen of the same square where children are playing with a hoop and stick. I always find it extraordinary that Harvey Keitel (whom I always imagine being from a different world of Hollywood and stardom) has graced this street in a recent TV commercial for an insurance company, reprising his character as Winston 'the Wolf' Wolfe. 'Traffic warden!' he warns one motorist. I always wondered what Tarantino thought about his character being used to sell insurance.

Over on the wall on the left is a piece of **STREET ART** ⓬, which many people attributed to Banksy for a while. The image is of the elderly June Beechey, a local shopkeeper whom I remember in Primrose Hill, with the caption 'Make Tea Not War'. I often wondered how long her traditional old shop selling household items would last amongst the boutiques and cafés. Anyway, it transpired that the artwork was created by Bambi, who is also quite a sought-after artist, boasting fans such as Robbie Williams, Brad Pitt and Rihanna. She does similarly witty stencil work to Banksy, including a tribute to Amy Winehouse in Camden, and Donald Trump dancing with the caption 'Lie Lie Land'.

The square itself is quaint and beautiful, with many shops (I would recommend a bagel from Roni's if you're feeling peckish). The site of the original Belsize House can be seen at the bottom of Belsize Place where there is currently a bar, although it keeps changing. The current building was a pub called the Belsize Tavern when I was small. It's odd that they closed it, as the area could do with a traditional pub, in my opinion.

Splendid. Let's walk back down past the mulberry tree now and down Belsize Park Gardens, which used to be known as 'Cut-Throat Alley'. Charles Dickens recalled one of the most gruesome murders he'd ever read about taking place down here. It has been home to many celebrities, but the ones I remember from my youth were radio DJ Chris Evans and Yazz from the band Yazz and the Plastic Population, who sang 'The Only Way Is Up'. Last I heard, she had found God and moved to Spain to get more involved with a Baptist church.

My mum always called it Belsize Poo Gardens because for some reason there is always loads of dog poo everywhere. It's quite odd for a posh area like this, but it's definitely something I've noticed when walking here. A lot of the dog-walkers seem to think it's sufficient to put the poo into a poo bag and then just leave it on the pavement. Don't worry, mate. Someone else will pick it up!

Now turn left into Glenilla Road. This was added later than the other developments, and you can see where they had to knock down number 36 to create the opening to the road.

Follow Glenilla Road round to the left and have a quick look at **NUMBER 17** ⓭, which was owned by the son of H.G. Wells. People often argue about whose likeness is painted above the door, but a bloke down the pub told me it was H.G. Wells's girlfriend.

Now turn around, back towards the curve in the street, and go up Howitt Road. **NUMBER 9** ⓮ has a plaque telling us that Ramsay MacDonald, the first Labour prime minister, lived here from 1916 until 1925.

Now turn right down Haverstock Hill and then left into Downside Crescent, past the south entrance of the bomb shelter. Walk to the end and the turn left on Lawn Road.

If you like, you can hum the 1985 song 'Kayleigh' by Marillion.

Do you remember, barefoot on the lawn with shooting stars?

Do you remember, loving on the floor in Belsize Park?

Whilst Belsize Park is a lovely area and many artists have lived here over the years, it is seldom referenced in any songs, so I must credit Marillion for achieving this.

Down Lawn Road you will see the **ISOKON BUILDING** ⓯. You can't miss it – and you'll either love it or hate it. If you ask me, it looks like it belongs in the former Soviet Union. In fact, back in the 1930s a fellow called Jack Pritchard, who ran a furniture business out of Estonia (a country which was later absorbed by the Soviet Union), commissioned Wells Coates to design this eyesore. It became one of the most architecturally important buildings in Britain, achieving Grade I listed status. There were services like shoe cleaning and food sent up by dumb waiter, a bit like a hotel; and after they added a restaurant in 1937 called The Isobar it became quite famous for its parties. It attracted the cream of intellectual life in London, with famous residents including Agatha Christie, who said it looked 'just like a giant liner, which ought to have had a couple of funnels'. Parties would be attended by artists Henry Moore and Barbara Hepworth,

The Washington

and Bauhaus architects Walter Gropius and Marcel Breuer; it also became the centre of a Cambridge-educated Soviet spy ring led by Jürgen Kuczynski (brother of Red Sonya!).

You couldn't make it up. What were MI5 doing? I mean, it couldn't have been more suspicious if they painted the building red and hung a hammer and sickle over the door!

Turn right on Garnett Road and then second right up Parkhill Road.

Tasker Road crosses Parkhill Road, leading (to the left) to **ST DOMINIC'S CHURCH** 🔟. There are some cottages hidden on the left behind the main houses called Mall Studios, which were popular with artists. Arthur Rackham lived here, as did Walter Sickert (who some people think was Jack the Ripper!), as well as Barbara Hepworth and Henry Moore.

I must say, it's all very lovely around here, but we must be getting on.

Return to Parkhill Road and continue on, all the way to Haverstock Hill, and then turn left. I love this view, because you can see St Paul's Cathedral and London stretched out before you. However, it's quite different to the view painted by John Constable from this point around 1832, called *Sir Richard Steele's Cottage, Hampstead*. In the painting you can see the **Haverstock Tavern** on the left, which was mentioned in licensing records as far back as 1721. It would have been a popular and standard stop on the way up the hill for weary travellers, or for those heading into London. Its most famous landlord was poor Joe Davis, a large, boisterous but convivial fellow with a red face, who liked to drink and rub shoulders with nobility. He was often characterised

in prints that can be seen on the walls of the pub.

One day in 1806 Joe Davis had been drinking in the morning (as usual) and people came to the pub (as usual) to find him slumped on the bar (as usual). They thought he was asleep and apparently he remained there all day until closing time – when they discovered that he was actually dead!

On the other side of the road is, wait for it…no, not a boundary marker, but a milestone! I like milestones because people often see boundary stones thinking that they are milestones. I haven't seen that many in London, but this one is definitely a milestone. It tells us that we are four miles from the Post Office, meaning the one which used to be beside Postman's Park (see **Walk 4**).

The milestone is just outside where Sir Richard Steele's house stood, before getting knocked down to make way for Steele's Road. Sir Richard Steele was a poet and writer whose most lasting achievement was the creation of *The Spectator* magazine. Apparently he moved here because he wanted to avoid his creditors in London, thinking that they wouldn't bother chasing him all the way up here. I don't think the ruse worked, however.

Further down Steele's Road is **SUPERNOVA HEIGHTS** 🔢, where Noel Gallagher from Oasis lived – but we're going back up Haverstock Hill and turning left down England's Lane.

England's Lane existed on maps of 1745 as a little country path leading to the farms of Chalcot, or Chaldecot (originally Upper Chaldecot Farm and Lower Chaldecot

Farm), which is where the name of the 'Chalk Farm' area comes from.

There are some lovely late-19th century houses here, which are popular with celebrities. I've only ever been in one of them, when I was little, because my mum had a friend called Nina who lived in a beautiful artist's studio set back down a little gated path off Chalcot Gardens, smoking endless Gitanes. (I think it was eventually sold to Helena Bonham Carter.) They have beautiful skylights and big spaces, ideal for bringing in large canvases.

But enough of all this. There are some pleasant cafés along here, but I'm headed for the **Washington**. It has nothing really to do with George Washington, as far as I can tell, except being named after him. I do like the original 150-year-old fittings, though. It retains its Victorian atmosphere with the cut glass and beautifully decorated mirrors. A perfect place to relax after a long walk.

I'll have a lager.

Cheers.

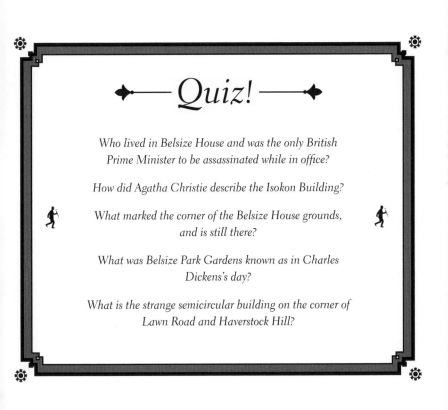

✦ —— *Quiz!* —— ✦

Who lived in Belsize House and was the only British Prime Minister to be assassinated while in office?

How did Agatha Christie describe the Isokon Building?

What marked the corner of the Belsize House grounds, and is still there?

What was Belsize Park Gardens known as in Charles Dickens's day?

What is the strange semicircular building on the corner of Lawn Road and Haverstock Hill?

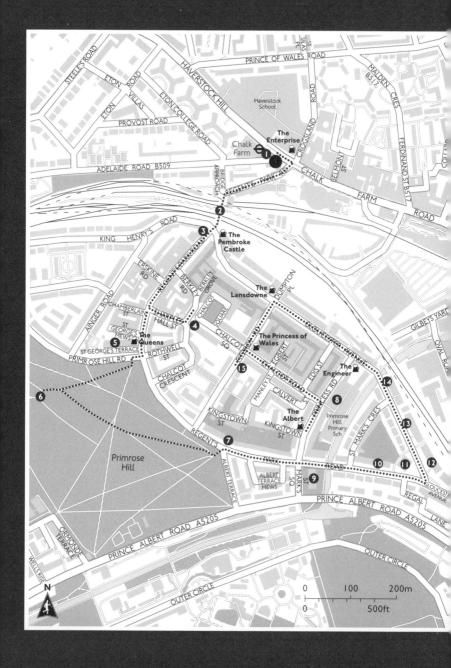

8

8 A PEACEFUL PROMENADE AROUND PRIMROSE HILL

DISTANCE
3.1 km (1.9 miles)

TIME
1 hour 20 minutes

NEAREST STATION
Chalk Farm

What ho!

Let's start here at Chalk Farm Station (the area is named after Chaldecot's, or Chalcot's, farm, as I mentioned in **Walk 7**). If you're waiting for a friend, you can always wait in the **Enterprise** across the road, which is perfectly nice and recently refurbished. (I prefer pubs when they just leave them rough around the edges, but I suppose they know how to make money better than I do!)

You might recognise **CHALK FARM STATION ❶** from the cover of the Madness album *Absolutely*. Madness liked singing about Camden because they were from around these parts. Actually, a few doors up from the station, on Adelaide Road, is where the original Winchester Club was based in the 1980s TV show *Minder*. You see Arthur Daley and Terry McCann walking in there in the still pictures during the credits. R.I.P.

The whole area used to be owned by the Eton Estate (the same one that owns the famous Eton School, which all our politicians seem to attend). That's why when they first started building these streets here in the 19th century they called them things like Eton Rise and Eton Avenue. One of the first buildings was (naturally) the Adelaide Tavern, which was the yellow brick building opposite the station. Now it's flats, of course, but you can still catch a glimpse of it in early episodes of *Minder*!

Just between here and the Enterprise is where the trams arriving from Tottenham Court Road used to terminate and turn around, because they couldn't get up the hill. You can see that there is space for the tram tracks to curve all the way around here. (Look out also for horse troughs and abandoned fountains for extra **STREET FURNITURE CHALLENGE** points!)

But enough of hanging around in this busy traffic; let's head up Regent's Park Road, where there tends to be lots of graffiti (or 'street art', as we now have to call it). It's hard to believe that 150 years ago this used to be a little country lane leading up towards Primrose Hill. When the railway was built, they sliced straight through the lane and had to build a bridge. Regent's Park Road now follows the route of that same path, starting here and going over the bridge and past the park. Until the 1820s the whole southern part of Hampstead was almost completely rural.

PUB

The Pembroke Castle

The **RAILWAY BRIDGE** ❷ was designed by Robert Stephenson – son of George Stephenson, the father of the railways – after he signed a contract in 1833 to build a railway from Camden Town to Birmingham. It was his first iron bridge and came before the famous one in Newcastle and the huge one across the Menai Straits. Meanwhile, after much deliberation, they decided that a snappy, concise name for the railway should be 'The East and West India Docks and Birmingham Junction Railway'. If you are as tall as me you can see over the bridge to the railway lines and the abandoned Primrose Hill Station, which I remember as a boy. It's all being redeveloped for the long-awaited 'white elephant' HS2 high speed railway, which should be finished some time before Halley's comet next comes around. Tall people should also be able to see the Primrose Hill tunnel, which was the first railway tunnel in London and a wonder of the age. Many people flocked to witness its construction in the 1840s. It wouldn't have had all these houses around it, so they could have just sat on the banks with the lush green hill in the background.

If you're already thirsty you could pop into the **Pembroke Castle** for a quickie. The nearby houses in Gloucester Avenue were built for the railway workers and because they came from all over the UK there used to be a lot of fights when they went to the pub. To solve this problem, four pubs were built in order to segregate them: the Dublin Castle for the Irish, the Edinboro Castle (yes, that's how it's spelt) for the Scots, the Windsor Castle for the English, and the Pembroke Castle for the Welsh. If you don't believe me track down the bloke outside Sainsbury's who told me that fact. I like it and I'm sticking with it.

Opposite the Pembroke is another contender for the snappiest name competition. These days it's luxury flats, with David Birkett estate agents on the ground floor, but in 1865 this was the imaginatively titled…*deep breath*… **BOYS' HOME FOR THE TRAINING AND MAINTENANCE, BY THEIR OWN LABOUR, OF DESTITUTE BOYS NOT CONVICTED OF CRIME** ❸…*and relax.* (Lucky they didn't have to write their address on an embarkation card or anything.)

I find these sorts of places always evoke Charles Dickens, who often wrote about poverty and workhouses. Indeed, he would have known this boys' home as he lived and went to school in Camden. Boys here were trained in things like playing band instruments (useful for the army), sewing and carpentry, until it closed in 1920.

Continuing along Regent's Park Road you'll come to a pleasant parade of shops, boutiques, cafés, more cafés, and some more boutiques. Oh, and some cafés…in case I missed that out. Actually, I remember them having normal things when I was a boy, like a fish and chip shop and a launderette, but towards the new millennium more and more media types started moving in and it became ever so trendy and quaint. Jude Law and Sadie Frost lived here, among many other famous people, and their gang started to be known as 'The Primrose Hill Set', which included the likes of Kate Moss, Jonny Lee Miller and Sienna Miller. There's a bookshop, too, which insists on displaying copies of books written by famous local residents in the window. However, back in the 1980s it was a pretty ordinary place to live.

One place that is consistently good is the Greek restaurant Lemonia. When I were a lad, this was the Chalk Farm Tavern, which had been there as far back as 1678, when it was the only building in the vicinity. When Sir Edmund Berry Godfrey (a missing magistrate) was found murdered in a ditch on Primrose Hill, his neck broken and a sword through his body, he was brought here 'to a very modest tavern'. He had been accused of a Catholic plot to overthrow King Charles II.

If you want to stop in one of the numerous cafés, you can. I like Greenberry because it's slightly bigger and has more room for my long legs. It also does good food and amazing carrot cake. It is either named after the erstwhile name for Primrose Hill, 'Greenberry Hill', or the

alleged murderers who were hanged for killing Edmund Berry Godfrey: Robert Green, Henry Berry and Lawrence Hill. They were probably innocent, but it was considerate of them to have the words 'Green', 'Berry' and 'Hill' in their names. Was the hill named after them, or was it just a coincidence?

Just nip to the left down Sharples Hall Street and you'll find yourself in Chalcot Square, with its colourful houses surrounding a little garden full of parents and their kids. Just before you reach the square you'll see a door to the right, which is **NUMBER 1** 4. Above it is the balcony where Hugh Grant comes out in the film *Paddington II*. Just beneath this balcony is where the green newspaper kiosk was in the *Paddington* films. In fact, the Browns, at whose house Paddington Bear stays, is in Chalcot Crescent, a very pretty street to the right, which also has lots of colourful houses and young people constantly taking photos for their Instagram profiles.

Now follow the road back round to Regent's Park Road and you might fancy stopping for a cheeky pint at the **Queens**, where they also have a nice restaurant upstairs and if you're lucky you can get the seat on the balcony overlooking the park.

Just next to the pub is St George's Terrace, where Lord Byron's widow lived and died (in 1855) at **NUMBER 10** 5. Her daughter, Ada Lovelace, Lord Byron's only legitimate daughter, is credited with being the first ever computer programmer, after working on Charles Babbage's mechanical computer.

Now, if you're visiting in the summertime, **PRIMROSE HILL** 6 will be awash with sunbathers, fitness fanatics, kite-flyers and dog-walkers. It's a lovely place to take your

PUB

The Queens

picnic, commanding spectacular views of London stretching out before you. (Unless some inconsiderate moron starts blaring out loud music from their loudspeaker. I mean, who died and made them the bloody DJ?!)

This is where, in the Madness song 'Driving in My Car', he buys his car.

> *I bought it in Primrose Hill*
> *From a bloke from Brazil.*

Back in the 1830s Primrose Hill almost got turned into one of the great cemeteries of London, along with Highgate and Abney Park, but there was so much opposition to the plan that Eton (who owned the estate) exchanged it for ground near Eton School, and subsequently the government secured it as a park. Like nearby Regent's Park and many other parks in London, it was originally owned by the Crown and used for recreational activity such as hunting. That's why these are called 'Royal Parks', and on the lampposts you will see the initials of King William IV – WR IV – who was on the throne for most of the 1830s.

This is another one of the protected views of St Paul's Cathedral which I mentioned in **Walk 5**. I think you get a better view from here than from Parliament Hill or Kenwood. What you might not get a great view of, however (at least if it's snowing), are the two boundary markers sticking out of the ground in the middle of the hill. As children we

would sledge down this hill and no matter where I started, I always ended up colliding with these obstacles, usually injuring my testicles! If you look around the parks you notice these all over the place, but they are not milestones. They denote the boundaries of the old parishes – in this case, Hampstead (St John) and St Pancras.

Whenever I stand on the hill and look towards the zoo and the canal, I always think of H.G. Wells's *War of the Worlds*:

> *Wondering still more at all that I had*
> *seen, I pushed on towards Primrose Hill.*
> *Far away, through a gap in the trees, I*
> *saw a second Martian, as motionless as*
> *the first, standing in the park towards*
> *the Zoological Gardens, and silent.*
> *A little beyond the ruins… I came*
> *upon the red weed again, and found*
> *the Regent's Canal, a spongy mass of*
> *dark-red vegetation.*

If you are here during the autumn equinox at 1 p.m. (around 22–24 September), when the day and night are of equal length, you should see a procession of Druids celebrating. This tradition dates back to 1792, when a group of Welshmen, led by Iolo Morganwg (who claimed to be the last living Druid) gathered here to perform the Gorsedd of the Bards. They made a circle with stones Iolo had in his pockets and recited poems in Welsh and English, declaring themselves to be the new keepers of the Druid tradition.

The Druid Order claim that their 'chosen chief' from 1799 was William Blake, although there isn't any evidence for this. A good friend of his, William Owen, was present at this original ceremony and it's likely he got William Blake to attend. Blake's local pub in Soho was the Old King's Arms on Poland Street, where he

lived, and they have a plaque stating that the Ancient Order of Druids was revived there on 28 November 1781. This probably explains why Blake's words are carved into the stone surrounding the summit:

> *I have conversed with the spiritual sun. I saw him on Primrose Hill.*

Now head down to the bottom of the hill (in the direction of St Paul's, slightly to your left). Just outside the gate, at the junction of Albert Terrace and Regent's Park Road, you will see another one of these fountains left in memory of someone you won't have heard of. In this case, Joseph Payne Esquire, a deputy judge who was apparently a zealous, teetotal abstainer. I do like how these memorials are dotted around the place, especially if they amuse me in some way. An abstemious judge? Never heard that one before!

Just opposite is **NUMBER 60** ⓻, where Stanley Johnson, father of former Prime Minister Boris Johnson, used to live. It was known as the 'Rocking Horse House' because for years there was an ancient-looking wooden rocking horse in the window. The house recently sold for over £11 million.

Continue along Regent's Park Road, past the church and over the humpback bridge. From the bridge you get a beautiful view of the canal, and also **PRIMROSE HILL PRIMARY SCHOOL** ⓼, a typically Victorian red-brick building, which Boris Johnson attended. I rather like these forbidding buildings, but I don't know if I'd have liked it on my first day at school. Intimidating, I would have thought!

Poor Boris Johnson. He reminds me of the character Victorian Dad from *Viz* magazine.

Wooden rocking horses, Victorian red-brick primary school, followed by years at Eton wearing top hat and tails. Goodness.

In the other direction you'll see **ST MARK'S CHURCH** ⓽, behind which the canal bends to the right. This is where Charles Dickens witnessed the sad sight of a dead woman, which he describes in *The Uncommercial Traveller*:

> *…when I came to the right-hand Canal Bridge, near the cross-path to Chalk Farm, the Hansom was stationary, the horse was smoking hot, the long pole was idle on the ground, and the driver and the park-keeper were looking over the bridge parapet. Looking over too, I saw, lying on the towing-path with her face turned up towards us, a woman, dead a day or two, and under thirty, as I guessed, poorly dressed in black.*

> *A barge came up, breaking the floating ice and the silence, and a woman steered it. The man with the horse that towed it, cared so little for the body, that the stumbling hoofs had been among the hair, and the tow-rope had caught and turned the head, before our cry of horror took him to the bridle. At which sound the steering woman looked up at us on the bridge, with contempt unutterable, and then looking down at the body with a similar expression.*

On a less depressing note, imagine living in one of those houses on St Mark's Crescent, just coming up, with a garden backing onto the canal. I'd fancy having a cold Pimm's and then hopping into my boat for a jaunt along the canal to Little Venice. One day, perhaps…

Further along at **10 REGENT'S PARK ROAD** ⑩ is a modern-looking house that doesn't quite fit in with the rest of the street. This is because it was hit by a bomb during the war, and in their infinite wisdom they decided to build something totally different. If you've done **Walk 6** you will have seen Ernő Goldfinger's house in Hampstead. This was also designed by Goldfinger, which is why it looks very similar.

A bit further along you'll see a big building on the corner called **CECIL SHARP HOUSE** ⑪, which accommodates all English folk arts. Cecil Sharp founded the English Folk Dance Society in 1911 and went all around the world trying to discover classic old folk songs, including favourites such as 'A Frog He Would A-Wooing Go' and 'There Was a Frog Lived in a Well', and many others that we used to listen to during country dancing at school. The songs didn't have to feature a frog, but it seemed to help. Inside you can learn English country dancing and Morris dancing, and they put on afternoon tea dances, too. The building also houses the Vaughan Williams Memorial Library, containing the largest collection of folk resources in the UK.

Go to the other side of Cecil Sharp House (you can either walk round the front or cut through the back) and then turn left.

The ugly apartment blocks opposite comprise **DARWIN COURT** ⑫, which used to be a lovely line of Victorian villas before the council knocked them down in the early 1970s. The locals were so outraged that it led to Primrose Hill being made into a conservation area. I would actually describe anything beyond Cecil Sharp House as being Camden Town, but some people who live towards this end of Regent's

Park Road think it more prestigious to say they live in Primrose Hill. This is known as 'Postcode Snobbery'.

Anyway, we're not going to Camden right now. We're heading up Gloucester Avenue to find a pub. Whilst doing so, have a quick look at the base of the **STREETLAMPS** ⑬, which feature St Pancras trampling a Roman centurion underfoot on the access hatch. The Christian St Pancras was only 14 when he was beheaded by the emperor Diocletian for refusing to perform a sacrifice to Roman gods. The ancient parish of St Pancras has mostly been absorbed into the London Borough of Camden now, but you still see it featuring on the parish boundary markers, like those we saw on the hill. And if you spot any old street signs which still say 'Borough of St Pancras' on them, you know they are from before 1965 when the borough was abolished.

Carrying on towards the little canal bridge you'll see an **ELECTRICITY SUBSTATION** ⑭ on the right, which was built after they electrified the railway tracks in 1910, once again knocking down the nice houses that used to be there.

On the other side of the road is the **Engineer**, which seems to reserve more space for dining than drinking these days. In the heady days when we used to play football with Woody Harrelson in Regent's Park, he took us here for a goodbye meal. I only mention it to show off, frankly.

In the noughties I used to play football every Sunday with a group of friends in Regent's Park. One summer's day an American fellow arrived, asking if he could join in. Then for the next 45 minutes I kept teasing him, saying, 'Hey, Woody, pass the ball… Come on,

PUB

The Engineer

Woodster... Woody Woodward...' and so on.

At half time he said to me, 'Why do you keep saying "Woody" in that stupid way?'

I replied, 'Well, you look just like that actor on the *White Men Can't Jump* posters, called Woody Harrelson or something.'

And he said, 'I *am* Woody Harrelson!!!'

Unfortunately, I hadn't seen many of his films back then – but he ended up playing with us every week while he was performing in a play in the West End.

I bumped into him in the pub more recently and we had a drink. Having watched some of my early Joolz Guides he said, 'Joolz, you're a funny guy. Why don't you be more funny in your videos?'

I figured he's someone whose advice I should take, so hopefully I've managed!!!

The Engineer originally catered to thirsty engine drivers and railway workers and there's a secret tunnel that went under the road so that horses could get from the railway or canal to the beer store. These days the entrance on the canal is sealed, and mostly used by drunks who urinate against the door. Delightful.

By the way, a walk along Regent's Canal is

another lovely thing to do, but that is for another day.

One could stop at any of these pubs, really, and they can be included in a decent pub crawl. Take, for example, the **Lansdowne**, on the corner of my favourite named street in the area, Dumpton Place. It is named after the Marquess of Landsdowne, William Petty, who was the Prime Minister of Great Britain and responsible for having negotiated the peace terms with America that ended the War of Independence. What he has to do with this pub is less clear, but they had to name it after someone, and he seems as good as any.

It doesn't look like one of those old traditional pubs with carpets and Victorian fittings, but it has nice eclectic wooden tables and a wooden floor, and it serves beer and food. I've often seen famous people drinking here – and they do good pizzas! My favourite thing about it, though, is the old Charrington's sign that they've retained on the outside. Charrington's no longer operate but they were once one of the biggest breweries in Britain.

Now turn left up Fitzroy Road.

Keep an eye out for the Victorian coal hole covers on the pavement (the round iron discs). All the houses around here had them. They were used, right up until the 1960s, to prevent the coal man having to come into your house and make a mess. Instead, he could just pour the coal down the chute into your coal cellar. Some of them are pretty ornate and could have been used as a status symbol. If yours was more interesting than someone else's, or made by a more reputable foundry, it meant you had more money than your neighbour! Some are just blank, but the ones with writing on them usually denote the foundry where it was cast, or the name of the person who cast it.

Some of them have the old postal codes on them: just 'NW'. The newer numerical subdivisions were introduced in 1917, so most street signs have 'NW1' on them, meaning 'North-West 1', but if you see a sign or a coal hole cover with just 'NW' on it you know it is pre-1917. How about that for being nerdy!?? Now you've noticed them, you'll keep seeing them everywhere.

If you fancy a pint here, feel free to stop at the **Princess of Wales**, which gets a lot of sun in the afternoon and evening if you're sitting outside. Or you can try a bacon and egg sandwich from Sam's Café opposite. (They do other things, but that's my favourite.)

A few doors after Sam's Café, at **NUMBER 23** 🔢, is the house where poet Sylvia Plath committed suicide in 1963, after struggling with depression for years. By coincidence, it is the same house where another poet, W.B. Yeats, lived – as you can see from his plaque. Sylvia Plath doesn't have a plaque on this house, but she does have one around the corner in Chalcot Square, where she lived with her husband, the poet Ted Hughes.

Now go back to the corner with the Princess of Wales on it and turn right up Chalcot Road to the end, and turn right on Princess Road near Primrose Hill Primary School. There's a nice Italian restaurant here called La Collina, which has a good chef by the way; but I fancy a pint in a pub-looking pub. They recently reopened the **Albert** after years of closure, and I'm glad because I like pubs like this.

I'll have a pint of their guest ale. Down the hatch!

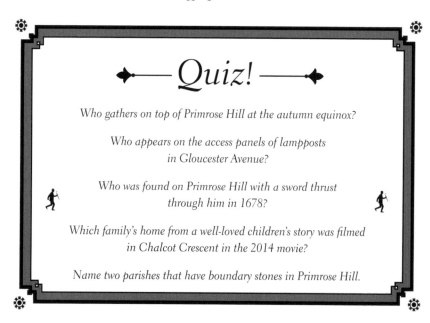

Who gathers on top of Primrose Hill at the autumn equinox?

Who appears on the access panels of lampposts in Gloucester Avenue?

Who was found on Primrose Hill with a sword thrust through him in 1678?

Which family's home from a well-loved children's story was filmed in Chalcot Crescent in the 2014 movie?

Name two parishes that have boundary stones in Primrose Hill.

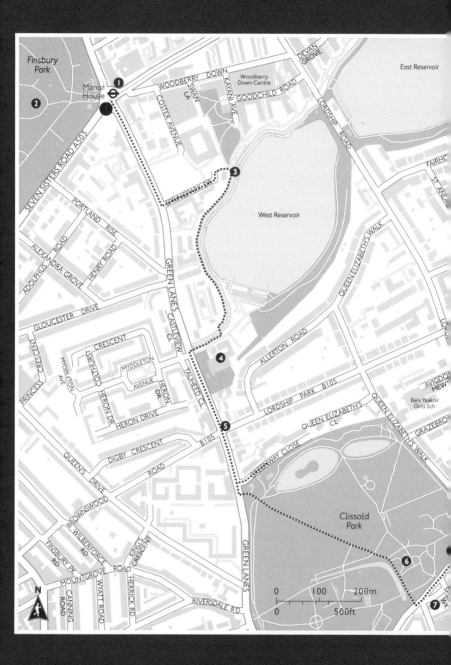

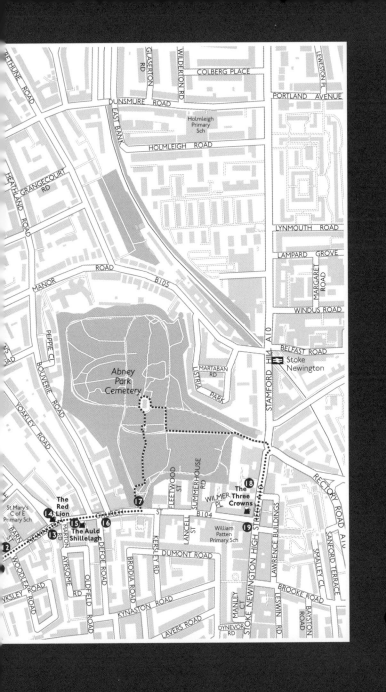

BETHUNE ROAD

GLASERTON RD

WILDERTON RD

COLBERG PLACE

LEWESTON PL

PORTLAND AVENUE

DUNSMURE ROAD

EAST BANK

Holmleigh Primary Sch

HOLMLEIGH ROAD

HEATHLAND ROAD

GRANGECOURT RD

LYNMOUTH ROAD

LAMPARD GROVE

MARGARET ROAD

MANOR ROAD

B105

WINDUS ROAD

PEPPIE CT

BOUVERIE ROAD

JAD

BELFAST ROAD

Stoke Newington

YOAKLEY ROAD

Abney Park Cemetery

MARTABAN RD

LISTRIA

STAMFORD HILL A10

PARK

FLEETWOOD ST

SUMMERHOUSE RD

WILMER PL

The Three Crowns ⑱

RECTORY ROAD A10

St Mary's C of E Primary Sch

The Red Lion

⑭ ⑮

⑬

CHURCH

The Auld Shillelagh

MARTON RD

⑯

⑰

ST

LANCELL ST

B104

William Patten Primary Sch

⑲

LAWRENCE BUILDINGS

STOKE NEWINGTON HIGH STREET A10

SANFORD TERRACE

BERM

⑫

WOODLEA ROAD

AYRSOME RD

DEFOE ROAD

OLDFIELD ROAD

BRODIA ROAD

KERSLEY RD

DUMONT ROAD

SMALLEY CL

VKSLEY ROAD

KYNASTON ROAD

LAVERS ROAD

MANLEY CT

DYNEVOR RD

BROOKE ROAD

LESWIN RD

BAYSTON ROAD

9

9 A TERRIFIC TODDLE THROUGH STOKE NEWINGTON

DISTANCE
3.4 km (2.1 miles)

TIME
1 hour 30 minutes

NEAREST STATION
Manor House

What ho! Marvellous.

You're probably wondering why we are starting our walk here, but 200 years ago this used to be a nice country lane on the edge of the woods. In fact, the original Anglo-Saxon name for Stoke Newington meant 'new town on the edge of the woods', while the **WOODBERRY DOWN ESTATE** ❶, which you can see down Seven Sisters Road, was named after the beautiful Berry Down meadow, in which deer and wild boars roamed freely. Fortunately there is still some green space here, in the form of **FINSBURY PARK** ❷.

Across Green Lanes from the park you can see a group of shops on the north-east corner, within a red brick building which has a sort of 'Dutch gable' effect. This used to be the Manor House Tavern, which had a dusty upstairs room where many famous

performers played gigs over the years. In the 1960s the Rolling Stones held weekly gigs here – Eric Clapton, Cream, John Lee Hooker and Jimi Hendrix all played here – but, most importantly, my sister Lil' Lost Lou played there, too (though not in the 1960s!).

In 1830 there was a chap called Thomas Widdows (apparently a 'lascivious fellow') who lived in a cottage here. When they started developing the area and building Seven Sisters Road, he thought it a good opportunity to make some money by turning his cottage into a pub. Because of its convenient location on the way to Cambridge, he did rather well out of it – Queen Victoria herself even stopped here to change horses. Thomas Widdows had a workshop in Stoke Newington Church Street next to a school called the Manor House School, so he decided to name the pub after it.

In fact, I'm sick of standing at this busy crossroads, especially as the pub isn't even a pub any more! Let's get out of here.

Walk south down Green Lanes and just after the block of flats called Willowbrook House turn left into Springpark Drive. (It probably doesn't have a road sign. Helpful, I know.)

Follow it down and round the corner at the end, and the path to the left of Woodberry Down Children's Centre leads you to a little river and a reservoir.

It's amazing to think that this river is man-made and has been here since 1613! Back at the start of the 17th century a fellow called Edmund Colthurst asked permission from King James I to dig the **NEW RIVER** ❸, to help provide fresh water for the growing population of London. The work was completed by Hugh Myddelton, who designed it to bring clean water from the chalk streams in Hertfordshire all the way down to Clerkenwell and Sadler's Wells. Then in 1833 these huge reservoirs were built using bricks from the old London Bridge, which had just been demolished. The new supply of clean water to London helped reduce the amount of cholera in the capital, but in 1946 the decision was made to shorten the river and end it here. The West Reservoir got turned into leisure facilities where you can now go boating and swimming, although you have to prove that you can swim. (I don't think they make you dive down to the bottom to retrieve a rubber brick, though, like at my school.)

Follow the New River along to the right and then over the little wooden footbridge and you'll see a castle. Except it isn't a castle! These days it's the **CASTLE CLIMBING CENTRE** ❹, where you can do indoor rock climbing. It's very popular and has a nice café and has lots of young healthy people hanging around, as well as some effortlessly cool older people, too.

Back in the 1850s William Chadwell Mylne, chief engineer of The New River Company, was asked to build a pumping station – but the locals didn't want a big ugly block ruining the countryside, so he disguised it as a castle. (God knows what the locals would think if they saw the area now!) Since he was from a Scottish background (his dad, Robert, designed Blackfriars Bridge) people say he based the design on Stirling Castle, with all the turrets and chimneys housing flywheels, chimneys and flues. You can still see his initials on the side of the castle in gold lettering… What a show-off.

Now head out onto Green Lanes past the little bicycle repair hut (which is very cute). It always makes me think of Bicycle Repair Man from *Monty Python's Flying Circus*.

Turn left and keep going south down Green Lanes.

On the corner of Lordship Park is a lovely **LION KEEPING GUARD** ❺. It's rather sad because he used to be part of a couple of sentries on duty here, along with their twins at the other end of the street. His companion was more of a griffin or dragon thingy.

Back in the 1860s there were sixteen four-storey, single-occupancy houses along Lordship Park and some of them, like that at number 4 near the bus stop, still have separate doorbells for the servants and visitors on the outside walls. The lions and griffins reflected the grandeur of the houses in this street.

Continue along down Green Lanes and then turn left into Greenway Close, just before the park.

On the left are some beautiful Art Deco apartments that look like they should be home to Hercule Poirot. I could just imagine having a cup of tea in Aunt Bianca's finest bone china, with a digestive biscuit, on one of those balconies, but I digress… Just past them on the right is what looks like a lamppost without a lamp at the top. **Points, yay!!!!** Viewers of Joolz Guides will know that I have many obsessions: cattle troughs, fire insurance plaques, post boxes and many others, but this is a stink pipe!!! (See the **STREET FURNITURE CHALLENGE**, page 12.)

Running just beneath your feet is what used to be the Hackney Brook, which is now one of London's underground rivers. Like the River Fleet, the Hackney Brook got culverted and became part of the Victorian sewers. Because of all the gases and fumes they had a tendency to explode, causing what can only be described as a rather smelly poosplosion. So to ventilate the sewers they installed these stink pipes, which took all the nasty pong up above people's heads. Usually they are much taller than this one, and I think this has probably been hacked in half.

Now skip joyfully back to the end of the road and head into Clissold Park, where they have a menagerie with birds, goats, deer and two large lakes full of swans, ducks and terrapins!

When they were building the nearby **CLISSOLD HOUSE 6** in 1790, the ponds which you first come to, on your left, were the clay pits they dug for the bricks.

Head across the field towards the church spire

CLISSOLD PARK

and soon you'll see Clissold House, which was built for a local Quaker called Jonathan Hoare who, along with his brother Samuel and William Wilberforce, fought for the abolition of slavery. We are now entering the heart of Stoke Newington, which was famous for its abolitionists, Quakers, non-conformists, writers, trailblazers and anarchists. It is said that an assassination attempt was made on the life of King Charles II in 1675 when a shot was fired from one of the houses here.

By the way, opposite the house is a river that is usually covered in green algae. This is the continuation of the New River, which we saw earlier in the walk and used to stretch down to Islington. This section has been retained as a sort of long pond, but doesn't really flow any more.

Just before exiting the park, past Clissold House towards Stoke Newington Church Street, take a look at the rather excellent boundary stone with '1790' on it. I guess the '1790' refers to the year the big house was built. This stone lies on the boundary of the old parishes of Stoke Newington and South Hornsey, which I know because there are some slightly later Victorian metal ones hidden just behind the railing on your right, near the bus stop as you turn out of the park into Stoke Newington Church Street.

Facing you as you leave the park is a beautiful terrace of houses on Spensley Walk called

PARK CRESCENT **7**, which must be one of the most desirable addresses in the area. Back in the 1980s these were all Housing Association accommodation, but through the 'Right to Buy' scheme some of the people living here snapped up the opportunity to buy their flats for a good price and have remained there ever since. It's a tremendous location.

On Stoke Newington Church Street turn left and you'll see (new) **ST MARY'S CHURCH** **8**. There are actually two churches here, the old one being opposite, on the left side of the road, but it's obscured by the trees. The new church replaced the old one in 1854 and was designed by George Gilbert Scott, who also did the Albert Memorial and St Pancras Station. They were quite a family of architects – it was originally built without a steeple, so later his son came along and put a spire on it, before his grandson, Giles Gilbert Scott, designed the red telephone box and the Pink Floyd album cover (well, Battersea Power Station, actually, not the album cover…) and the Tate Modern.

Cross the road and head into the churchyard of (old) **ST MARY'S CHURCH** **9**, if you're not scared of having nightmares. It's quite unusual to have two St Mary's churches right opposite each other, but this one was the old parish church and is now used as an arts venue. It's the oldest church in the country that was actually built as an Anglican church, and the only Elizabethan church left in London. Personally, I find all the graves really spooky, especially the ones which are half open. It looks like someone has tried to crawl out of them during the night! One of the graves here is that of James Stephen, a lawyer who drafted the Slave Trade Act in 1807. Along with his brother-in-law William Wilberforce and his friends Samuel and

Jonathan Hoare, he set up the Society for Effecting the Abolition of the Slave Trade.

London is full of buildings and street furniture with initials and coats of arms all over the place, and I find it fun to discover what they actually mean. After all, the people in the graves around you, and the people who were commemorated in this church, were just people living ordinary lives, like you or me. They had good days and bad days, fell in love, got irritated because their shoes were the wrong size, pulled stupid faces in the mirror, and did all sorts of normal things, just like us. So when I see a coat of arms above the door of the church with the initials 'W.P.', I'm intrigued. If you've got a moment, read on.

Stoke Newington is recorded in the Domesday Book of 1086 as being located in the Ossulstone hundred (a 'hundred' was an old subdivision of a shire). In **Walk 10** you can read about the 'Brixi-stone', which was a big stone where people met to discuss important affairs. The 'Ossul-stone' (Oswald's or Oswulf's stone) was another one further north, situated near the Tyburn Tree (today's Marble Arch).

Funnily enough, they actually discovered the Ossulstone in the 19th century. It was left leaning against a wall in Marble Arch, but after an article was published about it, someone simply came along and stole it!

Anyway, I digress. The manor of Stoke Newington had been a gift from King Æthelstan to the monks of St Paul's Cathedral in the 10th century and was later sold to William Patten, the lord of the manor, in the 17th century. Hence William Patten's initials and coat of arms being above one door and his family motto *Ab alto* ('from on high') appearing above the other.

As you walk up Stoke Newington Church Street you'll see an array of pleasant pubs, cafés and shops, all of which contribute to my feeling that I wouldn't mind living here at all! Coming up on the right is the **Rose and Crown**, where I would suggest taking libation if you fancy. Like many places along here, this pub is very pleasant and has groovy people in it.

Opposite, you will see **STOKE NEWINGTON TOWN HALL** 🔟, another Art Deco building from the 1930s. If you look carefully you can still make out some of the camouflage paint used in the Second World War to disguise it from the air. I'm sure they did a better job of it at the time, but these days it's very faint.

More of a black smudge!

By the mid- to late-19th century Stoke Newington was no longer a separate village. Many residents were moving in, including Jews fleeing from Poland, Germany and Russia.

As you walk around you will see the remnants of many beautiful old houses, and some listed buildings that are still intact. **173 STOKE NEWINGTON CHURCH STREET** 🔟 is a lovely 18th-century house typical of the area; you have to look out for these because they are dotted all around, sometimes disguised as shops. This one is on the site of a medieval mansion that existed here previously – and there's even a small fragment that still survives on the ground.

One building that didn't survive was the Manor House School. Remember I was saying how Thomas Widdows opened a pub and named it after this school? Well, it stood at **NUMBER 176** 🔢 and was attended by Edgar Allan Poe between 1817 and 1820, which is why there's a bust of him above the current door. He wrote classic scary stories, such as 'The Murders in the Rue Morgue' and 'The Pit and the Pendulum' – and it's perfectly possibly that he was inspired by all these creepy cemeteries around here. Some writers attribute his eccentric ways to the influences of 'nonconformist Newington', but I prefer to imagine him stumbling over some of those open graves in the churchyard and coming up with 'The Masque of the Red Death'!

Carrying on a bit further, on the side of **NUMBER 129** 🔢 there's some graffiti by the famous street artist Banksy, which you might recognise from the cover of a Blur single called 'Crazy Beat'. Actually it looks slightly different on the single. It's supposed to be the British royal family on their balcony, but only a small part of it survives. The stupid thing is that one day the lady who owned the property came out of her house to find the council had shown up and were painting over it. She went absolutely berserk, saying that she was fully aware that it was there and she wanted it to stay. So the workmen had to pack up their paintbrushes and disappear with their tails between their legs, but not before having ruined half of the artwork. That's why it's mostly covered in black paint.

The fools.

Some people try to sell authentic Banksy street art, but I must say that baffles me. The whole point of his art is that it's witty and positioned in particular places where it works. If you smash the wall down and put it in some rich person's bedroom it somehow loses its poignancy... for me, anyway.

Keep going and you'll see more pubs, one of which is the **Red Lion**, where Eric 'The Crafty Cockney' Bristow used to practise darts. All the darts players seem to have nicknames, and some are better than others. We've had Phil 'The Power' Taylor, Andy 'The Viking' Fordham and Steve 'The Bronzed Adonis' Beaton – but possibly the most rubbish name has to be Mervyn 'The King' King. Come on!

There used to be 40 pubs in Stoke Newington back in 1910, but now it's more like 20. (Imagine the pub crawls you could have done!) The landlord in the Red Lion kindly said I could film inside, which you'd think most pubs would welcome, given the free advertising – but actually, many pubs tell me to stop filming. Unfortunately, when I returned to film they were closed due to Covid-19, but I appreciated the gesture and recommend the pub! It's certainly worth popping in for a rest and a pint, before turning down Lordship Road just after the pub.

On the left you'll see a building with little bars on the windows like a prison cell. This used to be the **PARISH LOCK-UP** **14**, where they would keep the stocks and

the whipping post. It's hard to make out the year above the door, but it looks like 1831, which was just around the time the Metropolitan Police Force was coming into existence. Before the police there were night watchmen and justices of the peace, who could make arrests and keep an eye on things. These lock-ups could be used as temporary holding cells for ne'er-do-wells and drunken miscreants! These days it looks like it's somebody's house. No doubt they sit in what was once essentially a prison cell watching television with a glass of Musigny Grand Cru!

Now head back to Church Street and you'll see the **Auld Shillelagh**, which claims to be the best Irish pub outside Ireland. A shillelagh is like a walking-stick made out of knotted wood, with a large knob on the end and often used as a weapon, in case you're wondering.

Don't forget to look up at the walls of the buildings around here. Stoke Newington has many **GHOST SIGNS** **15**, which are old advertisements for businesses which once traded in these premises. There are some nicely preserved ones here for the *Westminster Gazette* and a fountain pen company.

Next, on your left, you'll see Yoakley Road, which is where British national treasure Barbara Windsor was brought up. Anyone my age would remember her helping us through our adolescence in the *Carry On* films – in particular, when her bikini top flew off in *Carry On Camping*! Crikey!

Yoakley Road was originally called Park Road, but was renamed after Michael Yoakley, a wealthy merchant seaman, became so appalled at how his widowed mother was

PUB

The Auld Shillelagh

treated while he was at sea that he built the houses at the Church Street end for the sole use of mothers like his.

Further along Church Street, on the corner of Defoe Road, is a **BLUE PLAQUE 16** informing you that Daniel Defoe (who wrote *Robinson Crusoe*) once lived on this site. Defoe was another one of the many nonconformists, or 'dissenters', who lived in Stoke Newington. These were Protestant Christians who separated from the Church of England in the 17th and 18th centuries in order to practice Christianity in a different way, and included Quakers, Levellers and the pleasingly named Muggletonians.

When Queen Anne came to the throne she started to target many of these groups; when Defoe wrote a satirical pamphlet called *The Shortest Way with the Dissenters*, in which he criticised Sir Thomas Abney (his neighbour and Lord Mayor of London), he was arrested. For a while he had been hiding out in the alleys behind Fleet Street (where many publishers operated) and 'wanted' posters appeared in the area with his name on them. Ultimately he was put in the pillory in three locations along Fleet Street, but instead of the public coming to throw rotten apples

at him, they simply came and cheered and threw flowers, as he was so popular.

A little further along you will come to some iron railings, which now constitute the entrance to **ABNEY PARK CEMETERY 17**. These were once the gates to Abney House where the aforementioned Sir Thomas Abney, whom Defoe wrote about, resided.

In the 19th century London's overcrowded churchyard cemeteries were becoming a real concern, with decaying corpses overflowing and causing disease, so in 1832 Parliament passed an act encouraging private, larger, purpose-built cemeteries. Seven major ones popped up and became known as the 'Magnificent Seven', one of which was Abney Park. Since it was built on unconsecrated ground, it became very popular with many of the dissenters in the area.

Amongst the people buried here are William Booth, creator of the Salvation Army; the Reverend Joseph Jackson Fuller, one of the earliest slaves to be freed in Jamaica under the Apprenticeship Act; Ethel Haslam, the suffragette who spent two months in prison for the cause; and over 200,000 other people. So good luck trying to find any of the graves. It took me ages to find that of George Leybourne, even though I had the coordinates on my phone.

If you are interested in the Victorian music hall you might wish to find his grave and sing 'The Daring Young Man on the Flying Trapeze', because he wrote the words! He was quite a character and one of the first major stars of the music hall. Way before David Bowie created his on-stage persona of Ziggy Stardust, George Leybourne invented the character Champagne Charlie, a dandy who dressed snappily and sang songs about

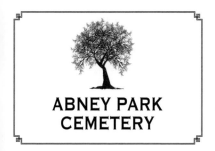

ABNEY PARK CEMETERY

his amazing life and the antics he got up to. I dare say he was fed up with people singing his famous songs 'Champagne Charlie' and 'The Daring Young Man on the Flying Trapeze' to him, so maybe it's best not to sing it by his grave. He was incredibly successful and rather lived the high life of his on-stage persona, drinking heavily and overdoing it, eventually dying aged just 42.

Now, he's pretty tucked away. On one of the paths in the northern part of the cemetery, look for Catherine Smith's grave (which has an angel on it)… He's behind her!

(This feels a bit like describing the location of Arch Stanton's grave in *The Good, the Bad and the Ugly*!)

If you find him you get awarded a whopping **20 points**, because it's a bit creepy and full of nettles and spiders. Don't forget to tag Joolz Guides when you post it on Instagram!

Abney Park Cemetery is huge and you can wander around for hours in the peaceful tranquillity, if you don't find it too creepy. Personally, I've had enough of all these graves, so I'm heading out of the other exit onto Stoke Newington High Street, which was the old road to Cambridge, and turning right.

If you look carefully at the houses in Stoke Newington you will see that many of them are very old. Sometimes they've had bits added or removed, but a lot of them were once very large properties.

187 STOKE NEWINGTON HIGH STREET
18 was built in 1712 and occupied by a wealthy Quaker called John Wilmer. When he died in 1764 he was buried in the garden (which is now a car park) in what was known as a 'safety coffin', with a bell on the tombstone attached to his wrist. This was quite popular in the 18th and 19th centuries, as many people were terrified of being buried alive – a fear known as taphophobia. If they woke up they could ring the bell furiously! In fact, Edgar Allan Poe, who lived nearby, wrote about this in 'The Fall of the House of Usher' and 'The Premature Burial', no doubt contributing to people's fears.

Some people say that this is the origin of the expression 'a dead ringer', meaning someone who looks just like someone else (although I think this could be bollocks). Usually these things are told to me by a bloke down the pub, but since I didn't hear this particular story from this particular bloke I cannot confirm its veracity!

Speaking of the pub, let's continue along the High Street, towards Stoke Newington Church Street again.

Just as you turn right into Stoke Newington Church Street, look up to your left and you'll see a **STREET SIGN 19** simply reading 'Borough of Stoke Newington – High Street', which is a lovely old sign from 1905. Later Stoke Newington became incorporated into the London Borough of Hackney, so it's pleasing when you see these old signs. Much nicer, I think.

In fact, whilst we're talking about street signs, when Church Street was renamed Stoke Newington Church Street in 1937 it became the longest street name in London. It was so long, in fact, that when they cast the old street sign they had to do it in two pieces. See if you can spot it!

Imagine if Arnold Schwarzenegger lived there. The nightmare he'd have when filling out forms with all those letters!

On the corner is the **Three Crowns**, which has been rebuilt over the years but was mentioned as far back as 1683, when it was called the Flower of Luce. The Three Crowns name possibly refers to King James I who, on his way to claim the English throne in 1603, spotted London in the distance from Stamford Hill.

But what of it? They serve beer and food, and I've drunk here before, so it seems as good a place as any to finish this walk.

I'll have what you're having.

Cheers!

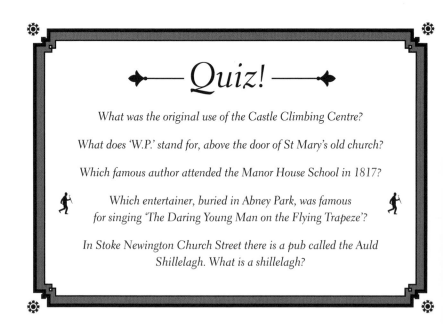

Quiz!

What was the original use of the Castle Climbing Centre?

What does 'W.P.' stand for, above the door of St Mary's old church?

Which famous author attended the Manor House School in 1817?

Which entertainer, buried in Abney Park, was famous for singing 'The Daring Young Man on the Flying Trapeze'?

In Stoke Newington Church Street there is a pub called the Auld Shillelagh. What is a shillelagh?

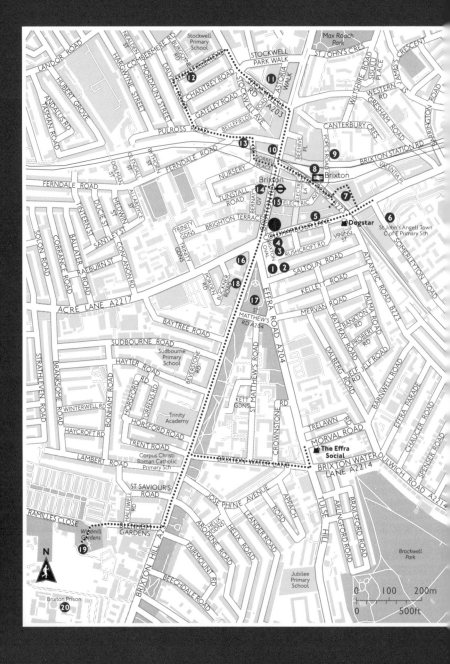

10

10 A JOLLY MARVELLOUS STROLL THROUGH BRIXTON

DISTANCE
4.7 km (2.9 miles)

TIME
2 hours

NEAREST STATION
Brixton

Well, butter my parsnips if I ain't south of the river!!!!

Yes, it does happen occasionally, and for good reason. 'South' isn't a dirty word! I mean, just because your taxi driver might not want to go to south London after a certain time of night, that's just because they probably live north.

One of the most interesting, colourful and culturally diverse areas of London is Brixton, where you can see all walks of life. Over the years it has changed hugely, but many of the old buildings still remain from Victorian times, when it really started to develop.

The name 'Brixton' comes from 'Brixiges-stan', which means 'Beorhtsige's stone'. Beorhtsige was a Saxon lord and is mentioned as far back as 1062. Remember how in **Walk 9** I was describing the 'Ossul-

stone', where the parishes in north London used to meet? Well, the parishes of the local hundred around Brixton used to meet at the 'Brixi-stone', at the top of Brixton Hill.

Some of the main roads around here were originally Roman roads leading to places like Croydon and Brighton. The opening of Vauxhall Bridge in 1816 led to greater access, and the building of more middle-class houses.

By the 1870s the railways were linking Brixton with London, and by 1900 a lot of the larger houses along the main roads started to be converted into flats, which became popular with actors and other degenerates! Charlie Chaplin famously lived in Brixton with his brother when treading the boards of the music halls; and in fact, it wasn't uncommon to see a zebra-drawn carriage in the streets here! Gustav Grais, a

COLDHARBOUR LANE

music hall artiste, ran a nearby circus with baboons and zebras and used to take them out locally for exercise.

Let's start where Coldharbour Lane meets Brixton Road.

The large open space is **WINDRUSH SQUARE** ❶, named after the *Empire Windrush* boat that brought hundreds of people over from Jamaica after Britain had requested help from its empire to rebuild Britain after the Second World War. Of course, no proper accommodation had been arranged for many of the passengers, so they were housed in the Clapham South Deep Shelter. Gradually they settled in the surrounding area and Brixton became one of the biggest centres of African and Caribbean culture in Britain. In the corner of the square you'll find the **BLACK CULTURAL ARCHIVES** ❷, opened in 1981, where there's a nice café serving Afro-Caribbean food and you can access the only repository of Black history in the UK.

Next door you'll see the **BRIXTON LIBRARY** ❸, built in 1891–3 by Henry Tate, who introduced sugar cubes to the UK. You've probably seen bags of sugar in the supermarket bearing the name Tate & Lyle. Before sugar cubes, Victorians would use a pair of sugar nips to cut sugar from a big block called a sugarloaf. It seems ironic that there should be a statue of him in Windrush

Square, given his connection with sugar plantations; although he was only 14 when slavery was abolished in 1833.

In 1806 a law was passed stating that no 'erections' were permitted above ground within 150 feet of the London-to-Croydon turnpike (meaning the Brixton Road), which explains why the library was built further back from the road. (What sort of erections people had below ground is none of my business, frankly!) I like this building because it has gargoyles on it, which people often mistake for grotesques. Gargoyles are the ones with water coming out of their mouths (or drainpipes, in this case). The word 'gargoyle' comes from the French *gargouille*, meaning 'throat', which is where we also get the word 'gargle' from. The scary-looking statues with ugly, contorted faces (which don't siphon water) are known as grotesques.

The next building is the **RITZY CINEMA** ❹, which opened as the Electric Pavilion in 1911 and was one of the UK's first purpose-built movie theatres, with a built-in organ for musical accompaniments to the silent films. Just outside it is a big stone that many people just walk past, but I like these remnants of old buildings. It's the foundation stone of a theatre built by the famous theatre architect Frank Matcham (who also designed the Hippodrome in Leicester Square). Most of the theatre was destroyed by the Luftwaffe, but they didn't get the foundation stone! In the 1980s the Ritzy grew such a reputation for showing left-wing films that the owner took out an ad in the newspaper stating that they didn't *only* show 'left-wing or gay' films!

Let's head down Coldharbour Lane now. Just to the right of the entrance of Market Row at **NUMBER 406** ❺ is where the famous Blacker Dread Muzik Store used to be. Blacker Dread used to bring over artists from Jamaica, put on shows and produce their music, and in the process he became a pillar of the community. Young people would come and hang out in his shop here, while he gave them advice on how to stay out of gangs. He also started the Brixton Splash festival, which grew from a small sound system outside his shop here into a massive annual street carnival.

After financial irregularities in 2013 the shop had to close and Blacker Dread spent some time at Her Majesty's Pleasure. To announce to his customers that he was closing the shop, he simply stuck a piece of paper to the window with the message: 'Oops!'

CLUB
Dogstar

Carrying on down Coldharbour Lane you'll walk past some interesting street art and graffiti, and on your right you'll see **Dogstar**. These days it has become more gentrified, but I'm told that it wasn't the sort of place I could have gone to in the 1980s with my bowler hat and umbrella. Back then it was called the Atlantic, and you can still see the sign on the roof. There have been a few confrontations between the local community and the police down the years, and if they had seen me in there they probably would have thought I was a police officer. A combination of high unemployment, poor housing and the stop-and-searches of 943 Black people in five days

contributed to the Brixton uprisings of 1981, with two days of demonstrations and dozens of arrests.

Carry straight on and under the bridge until you get to a big 1970s dystopian apartment block on your right, which looks like it should be in the film *Brazil*. This is **SOUTHWYCK HOUSE 6**, also known as the Barrier Block.

Many people mistake it for Brixton Prison and it is often joked that the architect Magda Borowiecka killed herself when they built it the wrong way round, but this isn't true.

The plan was to build a raised six-lane motorway cutting straight through Brixton, which is why the windows facing the street are so small – presumably they didn't think people would want a view of the motorway. But when the plans got scrapped, the council (which included future Prime Minister John Major) decided to carry on with the building of this Brutalist housing development.

The famous artist Damien Hirst lived in here at one point before, unsurprisingly, moving to the rather palatial houses around the edge of Regent's Park.

Now walk back the way you came and you should see the entrance to **BRIXTON VILLAGE 7** on your right. These terrific markets are Grade II-listed, but not for their beauty, which is unusual. They are listed for their cultural relevance, because of the diversity retained in the shops and products. It's lovely seeing all the traditional shops, a great many of which are of Afro-Caribbean heritage.

You can spend quite some time meandering through the markets here. If you come out of Brixton Village onto Atlantic Road and go left a bit, there's an entrance to Market Row, where there are even more shops. I particularly like Esme's Roots, where you can buy traditional herbal medicines with names like 'dog blood', 'Irish moss', 'periwinkle' and 'Jack in the bush'. They sound like magic potions from Harry Potter!

Come back out of Market Row onto Atlantic Road again. Head left and you will come to **BRIXTON RAILWAY STATION** **8**. Brixton has a tube station as well as this above-ground railway station. On the platforms at the station here you can find some sculptures of ordinary people waiting for trains. No doubt many people ignore them without realising that they were sculpted in 1986 by Kevin Atherton, making them the first statues of Black British people in a public place anywhere in the UK.

The whole area is full of markets and street traders and as you come out the other side of Brixton railway station you might consider wandering through **POP BRIXTON** **9**, which is an interesting development made out of shipping containers. More bars, market stalls, food outlets and hip-looking young people making me feel old, so I'm off back towards the main road.

Just next to the railway bridge on Brixton Road is **BON MARCHÉ** **10**, opened in 1877 by James Smith after he won a fortune on a horse at Newmarket races. He decided to put the money towards creating this purpose-built department store, making it the first in the UK! Many more successful shops followed (like Morley's, which is still trading) and by the 1920s Brixton was the most fashionable place in south London to do your shopping. Bon Marché closed in 1975.

Walk north up Brixton Road and then turn left on Stockwell Road.

You will see on your right the **BRIXTON ACADEMY** **11**, a concert venue which has one of the biggest stages in Europe. It opened originally in the 1920s as a cinema but down the ages it has played host to many of the world's most famous acts. Most significantly, of course, it's where Wham! recorded the video for 'Wake Me Up Before You Go-Go'!

And speaking of famous musicians, it is time for absolutely the most important stop on this whole walk.

Carry on up Stockwell Road and turn left on Stansfield Road.

Stop outside **40 STANSFIELD ROAD** **12** and look in wonder. Stare in awe. Bow your head, lowly dog, for this is where David Bowie was born!!! We're not worthy! We're not worthy!!!

After worshipping for a few minutes, go to the end of the road and turn left into Dalyell Road. Then at the end of Dalyell Road, turn left into Pulross Road and follow it round past some garages and nice little shops until it becomes Ferndale Road.

You might want to pop into London's only **CHOCOLATE MUSEUM** **13** at 187 Ferndale Road, where you can do tastings and workshops, though it's only open on Sundays.

After the museum turn right into Nursery Road and then left into Dorrell Place, at the bridge. This will bring you back out on Brixton Road. Turn right and look at some of the lovely old Sanders Clockmakers shop signs under the bridge.

A bit further along turn right (opposite the tube station) where you will find the famous **DAVID BOWIE MURAL** , which has now turned into a shrine. Fans naturally gravitated to it on 10 January 2016, the day that Bowie died. It was to prove a disastrous year in which we also lost Prince, George Michael, Muhammed Ali, Gene Wilder and Alan Rickman, to name just a few!

A bloke down the pub once told me that Major Tom from the song 'Space Oddity' was actually inspired by Tom Major, father of former British Prime Minister John Major. It sounds like a fun story that could be true, but I cannot be certain. John Major was from Brixton and his father Tom Major was a music hall entertainer. It is suggested that David Bowie once saw a poster advertising Tom Major's latest show and switched the name around to get Major Tom. Hmmm…

From here you should be able to see **ELECTRIC AVENUE** , just over to the right of the tube station. This used to have beautiful iron canopies, which were damaged by Nazi bombing; after which the only vandals worse than the Luftwaffe, the local council, removed what remained. In 1888 it became the first market street to be fully lit by electricity, giving rise to its name and, of course, the famous song by Eddie Grant… 'We gonna rock down to Electric Avenue…' And as you take it higher, I'm going to continue along Brixton Road and then up Brixton Hill, past the **TOWN HALL** .

I suppose most people ignore the sculptures around the clock, but I like these little details, which represent science, art, literature and justice.

As you continue up the hill you'll see **ST MATTHEW'S CHURCH** , which

is one of the 'Waterloo Churches'. After the Duke of Wellington's victory over Napoleon at Waterloo in 1815, a wave of positive sentiment swept the nation and it was felt that all these new expanding neighbourhoods required more churches to cater for the growing population. The Church Building Acts of 1818 and 1824 led to the construction of many new churches, including this one. I wonder what they would have thought had they known that in the 21st century it would be used as the venue for Torture Garden, a fetish nightclub where patrons dress up in leather bondage gear and walk naked people around on dog leads! I've never been, honest!!!!

Opposite the church is the **ELECTRIC** , or what some might remember as the Fridge, Brixton's iconic music venue and nightclub. Over the years the Fridge played host to bands like the Smiths, the Clash, Marc Almond, the Pet Shop Boys and Grace Jones.

The road behind St Matthew's Church (which we won't go down yet) is Effra Road, named after the River Effra, another one of the underground rivers upon which London is built.

Actually there used to be a farm here called Heathrow (nowhere near the airport) and this 'Heathrow' got corrupted to become 'Effra'.

The Effra now forms part of the sewage system, but before the 1850s it was a proper river, which rose in Crystal Palace and meandered down here, past Brixton Water Lane, which we pass as we continue up Brixton Hill, before it joined the Thames near Vauxhall.

On one occasion back in Victorian times, there was much commotion when a coffin was seen floating down the Effra. When they checked the name on it they saw that it had come from West Norwood Cemetery. However, the grave belonging to the gentleman in question hadn't been disturbed, so the staff were completely mystified. It turned out that the ground beneath his tomb had subsided, taking his coffin into the river below.

Even Queen Elizabeth I used the river when on a booty call to Sir Walter Raleigh. His house was on Brixton Hill, at the end of Blenheim Gardens, where we are heading now.

Something I like about Brixton is that it has a good selection of post boxes. As you know, I am obsessed with the cyphers on these iconic pillar boxes (see the **STREET FURNITURE CHALLENGE**, page 8) and as you wander around Brixton you will see ones with King Edward VII, Queen Victoria, George V and George VI. But for **10 points** look out for the one on Brixton Hill with the cypher of King Edward VIII on it! He wasn't on the throne for very long, because he's the one who abdicated, so there aren't many of these knocking around.

Points, yay!!!! They always seem to be in need of a lick of paint.

Onwards into Blenheim Gardens and past a beautiful old post office with a lovely post box outside (but not Edward VIII, so you only get **2 points** for this one) and continue to the end, where there is a large housing estate. Fans of Alfred Hitchcock might be interested to know that this is where the Ambrose Chapel stood in the 1956 version of *The Man Who Knew Too Much*, where James Stewart comes to find his boy. Americans are probably used to it, but for me to know that Hollywood legend James

Stewart actually walked these streets in Brixton is quite extraordinary.

Over to your left is **BRIXTON WINDMILL** **19**, which was built in 1816. The first owners, the Ashby family, used it to provide flour for the community back in the days when it stood in an open field. With the development of the area, the houses prevented the wind from reaching the sails, so an engine had to be installed. This enabled production to continue until 1934, providing flour to hotels and local businesses. Demolition was proposed after the Second World War, but in the decades since there have been various restoration projects and you can still buy flour from the mill today.

Just behind the windmill is **BRIXTON PRISON 20**, or 'House of Correction', opened in 1820. This was the first prison to introduce the rather barbaric treadmill – which was also used for making flour, so Brixton must not have been short of bread in those days!

But enough of all this. Methinks 'tis time for libation.

Walk back down Brixton Hill and turn right into Brixton Water Lane, where the river used to flow. When you reach the corner of Effra Road, turn left.

Over to your right is the **Effra Social**. This was the Conservative Social Club for over 100 years, but these days it's lost the 'Conservative' while still retaining the look and feel of a working man's club on the inside. Makes a nice change from the usual traditional pub, I think.

I'll have a pint of one of their local beers from Brixton… When in Rome… Tally ho!

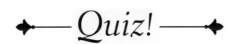

Which animal (other than a horse) could regularly be seen pulling a carriage containing music hall artiste Gustav Grais?

How did Blacker Dread announce to his customers that his record shop was closing down?

Who was born at 40 Stansfield Road?

Whom did Queen Elizabeth I visit by sailing up the River Effra?

Which American actor from the golden age of cinema visited Brixton while acting in a Hitchcock film?

11 A SKULDUGGEROUS SWING THROUGH SURREY QUAYS AND DEPTFORD

DISTANCE
8.2 km (5.1 miles)

TIME
3 hours 20 minutes

NEAREST STATION
Surrey Quays

Ahoy there, matey! Prepare ye for nautical tales of adventure, pirates and other typical weird Joolz Guides stuff on one of my favourite walks. We're starting at Surrey Quays Station, but you might just want to meet your friends at the nearby **Surrey Docks** pub.

Come out of the station taking the right-hand exit, to Lower Road, and turn right. Then turn left into Redriff Road.

Soon you'll come across a marvellous piece of Victorian engineering: the **GREENLAND DOCK BASCULE BRIDGE** ❶, which is painted red. I think it's great for a selfie.

These days it doesn't work, but it must have been amazing to see it in operation. Water would be pumped into the large container on top of the bridge and the weight would make the mechanism open it up, allowing

ships to pass beneath to Canada Dock, which has now been filled in, like so many of the docks that once dominated this area. That said, the ones which remain are still pretty big!

At the end of the bridge take the little stairs leading down to the dock.

This dock has been here since 1696, but it was sold in the 1790s and renamed Greenland Dock after all the whaling ships that came from Greenland; they boiled the whale blubber here to extract whale oil. (You *must* watch that BBC drama called *The North Water* if you're into this sort of thing. Superb!)

Keeping to the left-hand side of the dock, follow it round and pass by the statue of **JAMES WALKER** ❷, the engineer who worked on this dock.

PUB

The Moby Dick

What you really notice is just how extremely tranquil and peaceful it is along here. I'd love to live here. It's quite a contrast to how it must have been in the 19th century, with ships coming and going and all the smells of boiling blubber!

It's a bit early for a drink, but you might fancy a pint at the **Moby Dick**.

If not, just carry on along the dock and over the little footbridge. Go past the boats that people live on and turn right where you see another bridge like the one you just passed. I think you should walk over it for fun.

These are more remarkable pieces of Victorian engineering. At the other end of the bridge you can see all the machinery that opened up the bridge, using high-pressure water from the pumphouse nearby, so ships could pass by.

There are also lock gates separating the dock from the Thames, which they could close depending on the levels of the river. Right at the end, overlooking the Thames, there's a little building called the **TIDE GAUGE HOUSE ③**, where the person operating the lock could check the exact state of the tide and could close the gates to prevent flooding.

Follow the Thames round to the right and you'll go over another cute little bridge at the **SOUTH DOCK ④**. During the Second World War this dock was drained and used to build parts of the famous Mulberry floating harbours which the Allies used during the D-Day landings. Had it not been for these, Britain almost certainly would have lost the war. They were works of absolute genius, fitting together like Lego, and helped armoured vehicles and tanks to land on the coast of France directly from boats.

Keep going and what's this white stone? Points!!! Yay!

This is a beautiful 1819 parish boundary marker (see the **STREET FURNITURE CHALLENGE**, page 11), except it isn't in its original position. They actually moved it because it was originally on a bridge that got destroyed. The fact that they preserved it gives me great hope that there is some sense in this world!

'St. P. D.' denotes St Paul's Deptford, while 'St. M. R.' is the parish of St Mary Rotherhithe.

In fact, until the end of the 19th century it marked the border between Kent and Surrey. These days you just say 'London'.

In the old days you could have taken a canal barge all the way from here along the Grand Surrey Canal down to Peckham. Fully opened in 1826, it connected Peckham and Camberwell with the Thames, but after they moved the docks down to Tilbury in 1972 they decided to fill it in and turn a lot of it into a beautiful parkland walk. Watch my video about Peckham to see what I mean!

Keep going until you see a bunch of cannon and stop for a moment.

We're now in Deptford. Hooray!

Back in 1513 King Henry VIII established the first royal naval dockyard in Deptford. Many great voyages of discovery departed from here in the 18th century and it continued to be a hub of activity in Victorian times, bringing in goods from across the British Empire.

Up ahead of you the rather splendid old buildings overlooking the river were once part of the storehouse of the **ROYAL VICTUALLING YARD** **5**, and also contained the superintendent's house in the 1770s. Victuals are food or provisions, and when ships came to prepare for their expeditions they would come and stock up on various essential items stored here. Captain Cook and Captain Bligh would both have been familiar with these streets.

We're coming back this way in a minute, but let's just turn right here through the little garden. You will come out on a street called Longshore (keep to the right-hand side of the nice garden square).

As you walk up Longshore you will see that the square is overlooked by some beautiful houses to your right. It's interesting to see the contrast between these 18th-century houses and the huge modern apartment blocks nearby.

Turn right at the end of this row of houses and you will come to a line of even cuter **COTTAGES** **6**, called The Colonnade. These were occupied by naval officers based at the Royal Victualling Yard from the middle of the 18th century right up until the 1960s! One gets a tremendous sense of history here and it's difficult not to hold one's head high and shoulders back, whilst

sweeping through this section with an air of importance. For real effect, ask a friend to open the gates for you as you glide through.

Just outside the gates is a great opportunity to score **Joolz Guides points**! The bollards here are wonderfully heavy cannon (real ones!), the biggest I've seen being used as bollards. Also, in the wall nearby is a Victorian post box. **More points!!!**

There is also another little stone that looks like a marker of some sort, but I'm damned if I can read it. Something like 'Rotherhithe and Deptford Turnpike... something... something... conquer London... big bowl of porridge...'

Is the year 1855? I can't read it, but it's a **TURNPIKE MARKER** **7**, which I haven't seen in London before, though there must be others! This one indicates that the land here belonged to the Bermondsey, Rotherhithe and Deptford turnpike.

After you've taken selfies and tagged #JoolzGuides or @JoolzGuidesOfficial in them, return to the cannon on the river and then turn right towards the old storehouses of the Royal Victualling Yard. This whole stretch is littered with the remnants of bygone days: pulleys, cannon, abandoned gateways and bits of machinery.

You will soon come to a marvellous gate with steps leading to the river, called **DRAKE'S STEPS** **8**.

Another famous voyage associated with Deptford was that of Francis Drake, who departed from here before circumnavigating the globe. On his return Queen Elizabeth I ordered his ship, the *Golden Hind*, be drawn into the creek at Deptford as a permanent reminder of his great achievement. After banqueting on board, she proceeded to knight him on the deck.

Some people claim that where we're standing was the location of the famous incident where Sir Walter Raleigh put his cloak over a puddle for the Queen to step over, but I've also heard that it was in Greenwich Park. Besides, it would surely be called Raleigh's Steps if that were the case!!!

Queen Elizabeth also declared that the sea was free of all nations. That is to say, no one could plant a flag and say, 'We own the Pacific Ocean' – although I don't know who died and put her in charge of such decisions!!

After you've finished fooling around and doing pirate impressions, continue along the river until you come to **PEPYS PARK** ❾. Admittedly, it's not much to look at, but it's worth noting that in the area behind the wall, now occupied by Convoys Wharf, used to stand one of the most splendid houses in the area: Sayes Court, owned by the famous diarist John Evelyn. Some of the streets and parks around here still bear Evelyn's name, even though he doesn't seem that famous to me! We'll talk about him more later, but one person who used to visit him was a diarist who really *was* famous, Samuel Pepys.

Samuel Pepys often writes in his diary about his visits to Deptford, in his capacity as clerk of the Navy Board; but John Evelyn wasn't the only person he visited down here. It amazes me that Pepys includes it in his diary, but during the plague he also used to visit one Mrs Bagwell at her home, to get some 'how's your father'! (That's 'nookie' or 'hanky-panky' in plain English.)

Mrs Bagwell was the wife of a ship's

carpenter who seemed to turn a blind eye to these shenanigans. Pepys writes that 'young Bagwell and his wife waylayd me to desire my favour about getting me a better ship; which I shall pretend to be willing to do for them, but my mind is to know his wife a little better.' Later, after procuring a ship for them, he reveals that he had his way with her, 'though with a great deal of difficulty'.

What a bounder and a cad! It would have served him right if his wife had found his diary, but it must have been pretty well hidden. To think he used to buy her strawberries on his way back home after his secret dalliances.

Now head away from the river through the small children's park (which has drunk lampposts that look like they've been hit by a car) and then through a little green area and housing estate until you emerge at Grove Street.

Turn left and walk along Grove Street until you come to **SAYES COURT PARK** ❿.

Sayes Court Park used to be part of the large estate owned by John Evelyn, who had many important visitors. One of his most famous guests was Tsar Peter the Great, who came here in 1698. It is said that the mulberry tree which stands in this park was planted by the Tsar himself! I cannot confirm or deny, but if

SAYES COURT PARK

the local community say so then that's good enough for me!

Now you have a bit of a walk as you follow Grove Street up and turn left into Evelyn Street, then keep going until you come to Deptford High Street on your right. (Notice the tragic sight of yet another closed-down pub on your left, called the Harp of Erin. Why?!!! Why?!! Such senseless waste!)

Walking up Deptford High Street, look out for the classic pie and mash shop at number 204, called **MANZE'S** 11. You don't see many of these in London any more, whereas once they would have been commonplace. It might not be your thing, but eating at these places is a sort of rite of passage. Go on, guv'nor, you know you want to!!

Just nearby, more points are on offer for spotting the old street signs. For example, Hyde Street. Above the modern sign you can make out the original one... Points!!!!! And just opposite is Albury Street, where you can see some good examples of sea captains' houses. Originally these would have been middle-class accommodation but by 1899 they had been divided up for the poor, to house three families in each house. These days I suspect they have reverted back to being middle-class dwellings. They look jolly nice!

Keep going along the High Street and you'll come to the railway bridge. **DEPTFORD STATION** 12 opened in 1836 as part of London's first railway, running from London Bridge to Greenwich. In fact, one of the UK's most famous businesses started as a result of this railway. W.H. Smith, who had a newspaper shop at London Bridge, decided it made sense to open one at Greenwich, too. After that the business expanded to

many other railway stations. (Although it has always been a mystery to me as to why every time I buy a newspaper, the cashier asks me: 'Would you like a blueberry muffin and an extra-large Dairy Milk with that?' I mean, if I had wanted those items I would have selected them, surely.)

If you continue up Deptford High Street you will come to a street market, which feels like a proper market like the one you see in the TV soap *EastEnders*. It's very multicultural and there's no shortage of fresh fish – perhaps unsurprising, given its history. The whole place has the ambiance of a seaside town and makes me feel like I'm on holiday. Lots of new trendy cafés, too!

I think there are some more interesting things if we nip up to the end of the High Street and back.

When you get to Frankham Street just turn left briefly and in the car park there's a **MURAL** 13 of what Deptford used to look like as a naval hub in 1755. One of the ships featured is the *Royal George*, which ended up sinking when they decided to turn it on its side to carry out some repairs. Water gushed in through the gun portals and it ended up being the worst naval disaster in British waters. They ended up salvaging the cannon and recasting them as the reliefs on Nelson's Column in Trafalgar Square!

Carry on up the High Street and look out for another abandoned pub at number 45, the Red Lion & Wheatsheaf. (Sad face emoji...) There's also an old sign above number 26, for Elizabeth Place. All remnants and ghosts of the past.

At the end of the street, near the huge **ANCHOR** 14 reminding us of the area's

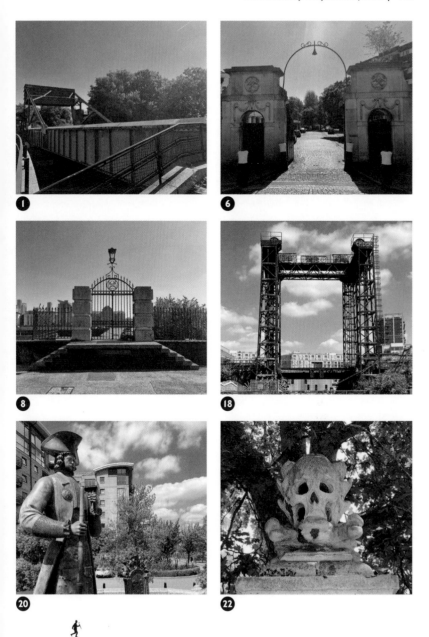

NEW CROSS ROAD

heritage, is New Cross Road. This used to be the Roman road known as Watling Street – the route that the pilgrims took from London Bridge to Canterbury, as described in Chaucer's *Canterbury Tales*. In fact, they would have to 'ford' (cross) the creek at the mouth of the River Ravensbourne, which explains how this area gets its name: the 'Deep Ford' became Deptford.

Now walk back down Deptford High Street and under the railway bridge again.

On the right is **ST PAUL'S CHURCH** **15**, built in the 18th century. As you walk through the churchyard you will notice some of the gravestones piled around the edge, indicating that the area has been opened up for people to enjoy the green space. However, it should be remembered that the bodies are still below the ground. Many 18th-century churches were built with crypts so that the wealthier people could be buried inside, without the danger of being dug up by 'resurrection men' and carted off to be used by medical students for research!

Deptford would have been the last place in London that many sailors saw before dying. This was the case for Captain Cook, who sailed from here on the *Resolution* before being killed by the people of Hawaii. One person who witnessed that incident was Lieutenant Bligh, who later sailed on the *Bounty*, after refitting her here in preparation for his disastrous

voyage to Tahiti. (If you are interested in the mutiny on the *Bounty*, watch my documentary on YouTube called *Take Me To Pitcairn*!!!)

What many people don't realise is that after the famous mutiny, William Bligh returned to Tahiti a second time to fulfil his mission. On his return in 1793 he brought with him a native of Tahiti called Mydiddee.

Poor Mydiddee was terribly shocked by the sight of all the criminals and pirates hanging in gibbets beside the river and in Execution Dock. Quite what he made of the British I don't know, but he must have wished he had stayed in Tahiti, because Deptford proved to be the last place he saw, too. He died when someone tried to inoculate him against smallpox but unfortunately succeeded in actually giving him the disease. He was buried in this churchyard; Bligh paid for a headstone for him, but for some reason it never got put up. Then over 200 years later, Timothy Waters of the Pitcairn Island Study Group organised for a memorial to be placed here, which you can still see.

Considering it was left for so long, it was quite an achievement that from the moment the idea was conceived by Timothy Waters to the erection of the plaque only one month elapsed. I found this particularly amusing because the other way around (from erection to conception) usually takes nine months! Fnarr, fnarr...

Now walk down Crossfield Street (to the right of the entrance to the churchyard), then bear left down Coffey Street, and cross over Deptford Church Street.

Enter the small garden area just before the railway bridge. Walk under any of the railway arches and then turn left to follow the path alongside the arches. Cross over Creekside at the end.

On your right, behind the wall, you will see the **CREEKSIDE DISCOVERY CENTRE** , where you can arrange fun days out wading through the marshes. They will take you on a long, muddy walk up the creek and point out all sorts of fascinating stuff that you won't hear about in Joolz Guides. You will definitely get muddy!

Continuing along towards the big peculiar-looking bridge, you will walk past some more arches which are popular with graffiti artists, if you like that sort of thing.

On the other side of the creek, to your right, you should be able to make out a Victorian industrial-looking building. This is a **PUMPING STATION** , built in 1865 as part of Joseph Bazalgette's huge elaborate sewage network. These days it's run by Thames Water but is still in operation. I call it a poo pump, but I suppose it depends which school you went to!

My favourite piece of Victorian engineering around here is **HA'PENNY HATCH** , the strange bridge that looks a bit like an oil rig. Originally built in 1838, the bridge allowed a section of train track to be raised in the event of a tall ship needing to come under the bridge. It took eight men to turn winches and pull levers to hoist it up, and originally the cost to have it raised was half a penny (a 'ha'penny'). By 1899 inflation had increased the price to an eye-watering whole penny!!

Now head back the way you came, past the graffiti, and turn right along Creekside.

Over to your left is a block of flats; if you're interested, you could divert from our route

and take a quick look at 1 Farrer House, which is where Mark Knopfler used to live when he formed the band Dire Straits in 1977. He was an English teacher at the time and used to hold band practices here in his humble abode. The band Squeeze are also from Deptford.

Keep going past a little park on your left and turn right after the **TRINITY LABAN DANCE FACULTY** . This building won an architectural prize and there are nice views of the creek from here, although they sometimes yell at you if you enter just to take pictures.

Rudolf Laban, after whom it is named, is credited with having created what we know as modern dance. In fact, dance was considered quite important as recreation on long voyages, as our friend Captain Bligh states:

> *Some time for relaxation and mirth is absolutely necessary and I have considered it so much so that after 4 o'clock the evening is laid aside for their amusement and dancing. I had great difficulty before I left England to get a man to play the violin and I preferred at last to take one two-thirds blind than come without one.*

Sorry to go on about the *Bounty*, but I'm obsessed and love the fact that the characters roamed these streets.

On Bligh's infamous voyage on the *Bounty* he ended up taking a fellow from Kilkenny in Ireland, called Michael Byrne, and actually recorded him as being a mutineer in his log book. However, when Byrne was finally brought back to face trial two years later, he was acquitted. Fair enough really, considering he was almost blind. It must have been hard for him to take part in a full-blooded mutiny! In fact, the mutineers who did remain behind in Tahiti, like Byrne, didn't have it easy. The ship sent to apprehend them, the *Pandora*, ended up sinking near Indonesia with some of them drowning. Considering only three of the mutineers actually got hanged in the end, it might have made more sense just to leave them be.

Follow Copperas Street around and then cross over the big main road. Continue ahead into Clarence Road before getting back alongside the creek, and then walk down towards the River Thames.

When I get to the confluence of the two rivers I like to stop and take in the view of the *Cutty Sark* in the distance. That's Greenwich over there, and 250 years ago the whole scene would have been dominated by tall ships filling the river. Meanwhile, activity around the streets we've just walked down would have ranged from dockhands coming and going, women working in laundries, and 'gut girls' cleaning the entrails of slaughtered animals, to impoverished children at play, criminals at work, and prostitutes plying their trade.

After you've finished gazing out and daydreaming, have a look behind you and you'll see a sculpture of **TSAR PETER THE GREAT 20**. As I mentioned earlier, he was the most famous of John Evelyn's house guests at Sayes Court. The Tsar had wanted to study shipbuilding in 1698 in order to upgrade the Russian navy, so decided to spend a while in Deptford. Apparently he was a terrible house guest and had a penchant for being wheeled around the garden in a wheelbarrow, ruining Evelyn's prized yew hedges!

John Evelyn wrote in his diary:

June 9th, 1698. I went to Deptford to view how miserably the Czar of Muscovy had left my house after three months making it his court, having got Sir Christopher Wren his Majesties surveyor and Mr. London his gardener to go down and make an estimate of the repairs, for which they allowed 150 pounds in their report to the Lord of the Treasury.

Always handy if you can call Christopher Wren for a quote, I guess!!! (Perhaps he needed a break from overseeing the building of St Paul's Cathedral.)

I couldn't say for sure if Peter the Great had a pinhead, as suggested by this likeness, but he was 2 metres 3 cm tall (that's 6 feet 8 in in old money).

Now walk up the river and you should see some abandoned landing stages. These were part of **THE WORLD'S LARGEST POWER STATION 21**, opened towards the end of the 19th century. After the East India Company abandoned the area, Sebastian de Ferranti, an engineer from Liverpool, considered it the perfect place for his power station because large amounts of coal could be delivered onto these stages by water.

London already had smaller generators using Thomas Edison's DC system, but Ferranti's system delivered 11,000 volts of AC (the system favoured by Nikola Tesla) to light up London.

Chop, chop! Carry on until you see the Ahoy Centre (a boating club) and turn left up Deptford Green.

At the end of the street you'll see the **CHURCH OF ST NICHOLAS** **22**, which has two large stone skulls on either side of the gate. It was founded in the 12th century, but the tower dates from the 14th century and various parts have been rebuilt over the years. Legend has it that the famous privateer Captain Morgan (yes, he of the rum) based the design of the Jolly Roger pirate flag on these skulls (although it's probably bollocks). They are actually *memento mori* to remind parishioners of the transience of life and to make sure they repent their sins.

Now, have you ever heard someone refer to an 'albatross around their neck'? This means having to bear a burden.

Around the other side of the church, against the west wall, are some chest-style graves. One of them is missing and this is the one that interests me, because it belonged to George Shelvocke, captain of the *Speedwell*, who wrote *A Voyage Round the World by Way of the Great South Sea* in 1726. It was a very successful account of his adventures and included a description of how his crew got scared by an albatross that was following them around Cape Horn. One of his men shot it, thinking it was a bad omen – but later regretted it when they nearly sank, with the rest of the crew accusing him of having brought bad luck upon them. He was then forced to wear the albatross around his neck for the rest of the voyage as punishment. The poet William Wordsworth heard about this story and in turn told it to Samuel Taylor Coleridge, who went on to use it in *The Rime of the Ancient Mariner.*

'*God save thee, ancient Mariner!
From the fiends, that plague thee thus!—
Why look'st thou so?'—With my cross-bow
I shot the ALBATROSS.
Ah! well a-day! what evil looks*

*Had I from old and young!
Instead of the cross, the Albatross
About my neck was hung.*

Over in the corner is a memorial to Christopher Marlowe, the famous playwright who wrote *Doctor Faustus*, among other works. In 1593 he was killed in a fight over in Deptford Strand, where he was staying in a house (near Drake's Steps). At the time there was a warrant out for his arrest and he was buried in an unmarked grave somewhere near this spot.

NEAR THIS SPOT LIE THE MORTAL REMAINS OF

CHRISTOPHER MARLOWE

WHO MET HIS UNTIMELY DEATH
IN DEPTFORD ON MAY 30TH 1593

Cut is the branch that might have grown full straight...
Doctor Faustus

During his life Marlowe was accused of being a spy working against the Protestants, as well as being a rake, a libertine and indulging in women, song, gambling and lavish debts. It was also claimed that he was an atheist, Catholic and a homosexual! (It was later suggested that he might simply have indulged in homosexual acts like many sailors would have at the time. I guess that made a difference in those days.) Don't forget to read *Sodomy and the Pirate Tradition* by B.R. Burg if you're interested in that sort of thing!!

One contemporary of Marlowe's attributed these claims to him:

*That Christ was a bastard and his
mother dishonest.*

That the woman of Samaria and her sister were whores; and that Christ knew them dishonestly.

That St John the Evangelist was bedfellow unto Christ and leaned always in his bosom; that he used him as the sinners of Sodoma.

It sounds like various people had agendas against Marlowe but, whatever the truth, he certainly led an eventful life before it was cut short at the age of just 29.

Outside the church grounds, on McMillan Street, is the **RACHEL MCMILLAN NURSERY SCHOOL** ㉓, named after the person who opened the first nursery school in Britain in 1911.

Walk along McMillan Street and turn right through the gardens. Bear left onto Watergate Street and walk to the bottom until you get to Rowley House.

Points!!! Notice the railings outside this block are actually made from authentic Second World War stretchers. During the war many railings were removed from buildings to be used for weapons, and many stretchers were made for the ARP (Air Raid Precautions) officers. These were easier to clean than the canvas ones and thousands were made. However, after the war some bright spark noticed that they were the perfect shape to turn into railings without having to alter them. So if you spot some stretcher railings award yourself 10 points!!

Behind the big wall opposite is actually one of the oldest houses in Deptford, the **MASTER SHIPWRIGHT'S HOUSE** ㉔, which was part of the original royal naval dockyard, and rebuilt in 1708. Unfortunately it's not open to the public, so it's hard to catch a glimpse of it – but every year in London we have the London Open House event, when many such houses are opened up to the public as a one-off. I shall be keen to get inside this one next time the opportunity presents itself. Alternatively you can hire it for a film shoot (apparently, filming Joolz Guides doesn't count).

At the end of the 19th century the social reformer Charles Booth conducted a survey of London charting all the levels of wealth and poverty. Of Watergate Street he notes:

South along Watergate Street. Cattle Market wall on west side. Men used to be decoyed here and robbed. Faint foetid smell prevails, overpowered in places by disgusting stenches. Rough women; one with head bandaged; others with blank eyes; one old harridan sitting on a doorstep with a dirty clay pipe; shoeless children.

These days it's rather less dilapidated and there is no longer a cattle market behind the big wall, but before someone mistakes me for an old harridan I'm heading to the pub!!

As luck would have it, the **Dog and Bell** is but a few steps away on Prince Street, as it has been for over 300 years. I think it very likely that Lieutenant Bligh and Captain Cook both took a light ale here at some point, and that possibility is good enough for me.

Mine's a pint of grog. Last one to the bar gets a lick o' the cat!!!

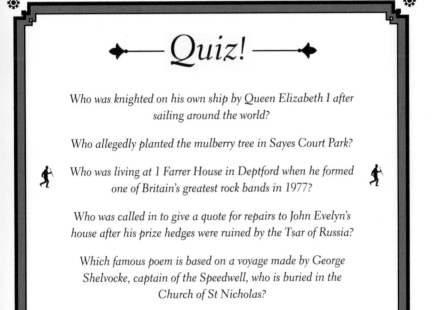

✦ — *Quiz!* — ✦

Who was knighted on his own ship by Queen Elizabeth I after sailing around the world?

Who allegedly planted the mulberry tree in Sayes Court Park?

Who was living at 1 Farrer House in Deptford when he formed one of Britain's greatest rock bands in 1977?

Who was called in to give a quote for repairs to John Evelyn's house after his prize hedges were ruined by the Tsar of Russia?

Which famous poem is based on a voyage made by George Shelvocke, captain of the Speedwell, who is buried in the Church of St Nicholas?

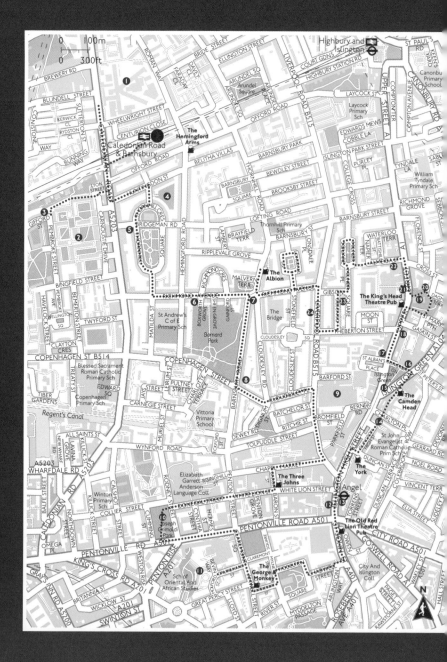

0   100m

0   300Ft

Highbury and
Islington

ST PAUL'S
RD

KEEN'S
YARD

Canonbu
Primary
School

BREWERY RD

BLUNDELL STREET

WHEELWRIGHT STREET

CENTURION CLOSE

The Hemingford
Arms

Caledonian Road
& Barnsbury

Laycock
Primary
Sch

OFFORD ROAD

Arundel
Square

BELITHA VILLAS

EDWARDS MEWS
COBBLE LA

ISLINGTON PARK STREET

PURLEY
PL

TYNDALE
LA

William
Tyndale
Primary
Sch

RICHMOND
GROVE

**The King's Head
Theatre Pub**

**The Camden
Head**

The York

Angel

**The Old Red
Lion Theatre
Pub**

City And
Islington
Coll

**The George &
Monkey**

Sch of
Oriental And
African Studies

12

12 A MOST EXCELLENT PERAMBULATION THROUGH BARNSBURY AND ISLINGTON

DISTANCE
8 km (5 miles)

TIME
3 hours

NEAREST STATION
*Caledonian Road &
Barnsbury*

Marvellous. Top hole. Splendid.

Well, here we are at the Overground station (unless you decided to meet at the **Hemingford Arms** just up Offord Road – a rather marvellous pub with characterful decor!)

This area is called Barnsbury after the Berners family, who acquired a lot of the land here after the Norman Conquest in 1066, and 'bury', derived from the Anglo-Saxon term meaning 'a fortified place'.

Exit the station by following the long path down to Caledonian Road and turn right. Head under the railway bridge (we're coming back in a minute) just to take a quick look at **HER MAJESTY'S PRISON PENTONVILLE** 1, which Michael Gove described as 'the most dramatic example of failure' when he was the Secretary of State for Justice.

Built in the 1840s, Pentonville Prison became a model for prisons throughout Britain and its Empire, originally accommodating people about to be transported to the Colonies. Discipline was very strict and prisoners couldn't talk to each other; their only recreation was walking in silent rows with damp cloths over their faces! Victorian times were harsh, but things have changed somewhat since then. Famous residents have included Oscar Wilde, Dr Crippen, Boy George and George Michael!

Now let's go back down Caledonian Road the way we came, under the bridge and past some new trendy shops and cafés. (It wasn't like this a few years ago. How times have changed!)

Turn right down Lyon Street and walk past the large block of flats, keeping them on your left. Keep going and it becomes Carnoustie

Drive and then Pembroke Street. Stop where Pembroke Street meets Gifford Street.

The council flats you passed (although a lot of them are privately owned now) are the **BEMERTON ESTATE** ❷, which you might recognise from the sci-fi film *Attack the Block*, starring John Boyega and Jodie Whittaker before they were so famous. In keeping with the alien theme, Whittaker went on to play the title role in *Doctor Who* and Boyega starred in *The Force Awakens*!

Look to your right and just behind number **66 GIFFORD STREET** ❸ there used to be a church where Bob Marley filmed the video for 'Is This Love'. In the video you see him walking down Gifford Street with some kids and it turns out one of the young kids in the video is future supermodel Naomi Campbell! Sadly the church burnt down. (Now, of course, it's being turned into flats – although I cannot verify whether they are 'luxury apartments' or just 'flats'.)

In fact, it was here that the famous photo for the cover of his *Legend* album was taken, too. I bet you any money you have that album!!

Now retrace your steps to Caledonian Road and turn right, then left up Huntingdon Street. Take the next right, Crescent Street.

On your left is a small **NATURE RESERVE AND COMMUNITY GARDEN** ❹, which is only open every now and then, but it feels very enchanted and peaceful. It used to belong to the vicarage but then it got bought by the council, who decided to leave it as it is. They even perform plays in there sometimes… and if one of the productions they've put on wasn't *A Midsummer Night's Dream* then I'm a monkey's uncle!

Carry on into Thornhill Square, which is jolly lovely. So lovely, in fact, that they often film TV dramas here, such as the *Poirot* episode 'Murder on Thornhill Crescent'. (Okay, so the episode was actually called 'The Clocks', and it's shown as 'Wilbraham Crescent' on screen, but it was definitely Thornhill Crescent!) There are a great many squares on this walk and they feel a world apart from the busy main thoroughfares nearby. Check out the **WEST LIBRARY** ❺, by the way, one of the most beautiful libraries in London. Just shows what they could do back in the early 20th century.

Exit Thornhill Square along Matilda Street and turn left up Richmond Avenue.

Keep going and around number 54 you'll see some rather splendid **SPHINXES** ❻, which do look a little out of place, I grant you. They commemorate Lord Nelson's defeat of Napoleon at the Battle of the Nile in 1798 (although they were only installed over 40 years later). England had a bit of an obsession with Egyptian architecture back then, which has continued in the years since, and you can find this sort of thing scattered throughout London (e.g. Cleopatra's Needle, Crystal Palace and Mornington Crescent).

Off to the left is Richmond Crescent, where Tony Blair used to live before he became Prime Minister. Hard for some…

Carry on up Richmond Avenue to the cute little garden at the top. Some of the houses around here are jolly spiffing. No wonder Tony Blair and his associates liked the area.

Hmmm… Now we're going to turn right up Barnsbury Road – but before doing so, just take a look at the lovely old **GHOST SIGN** ❼ around the corner on the adjacent

Cloudesley Road, next to the blue shop front. I love these old signs. So much nicer than the ones today. This obviously used to be a chemist.

Okay, so off we go along Barnsbury Road. There's an adventure playground and park on the right, and on the left you'll see the **YOUNG ACTORS THEATRE ISLINGTON** **8**, which does have a lovely weathervane and clock! It is on the former site of the Anna Scher Theatre School, which opened in 1968 and was famously attended by Pauline Quirke, Gary Kemp from Spandau Ballet, and Kathy Burke… 'I am – smoking – a – fag!'

Just while we're standing on this corner, I should mention that a bit further along, on the corner of Dewey Road, is where White Conduit House used to stand. From the 17th century until 1849, this was a leisure resort for people to escape from the city, adjacent to the similarly named White Conduit Fields.

White Conduit Fields stretched to the area just north of here, kind of near where Tony Blair lived, and contained a cricket field that became home to the White Conduit Club (the forerunner of the MCC – the Marylebone Cricket Club). The earliest recorded cricket match here took place in 1718.

After a while they weren't happy with the ground and got one of the bowlers, called Thomas Lord, to find them a new venue. So in 1787 they relocated to what is now known as Lord's Old Ground in Marylebone. Of course, Lord's has since moved to St John's Wood, but it's still called Lord's after Thomas Lord, who played here!!

Now turn left up Copenhagen Street and then continue into Cloudesley Place.

Keep going to the end, where you reach Liverpool Road.

The big building opposite you is the **ROYAL AGRICULTURAL HALL 9**, built in 1862 for the Smithfield Show, where people would display their cattle. A bit like a car show today. 'Oooh, look at this brand-new model of cow… Lovely udders, etc. Yours for ten bales of hay and a pickled egg!'

The hall stood on the cattle-drovers' route down to Smithfield Market; Liverpool Road was originally called the Back Road, where drovers would take their cattle to avoid the High Street. This is why you can still see the raised pavements here, which were installed so that pedestrians wouldn't be splashed by the mud thrown up by the cattle. Ultimately they decided to name the road after Robert Jenkinson, the Earl of Liverpool, who served as Prime Minister between 1812 and 1827.

The first Crufts dog show was held here in 1891. Later, during the Second World War, the building was requisitioned as a sorting office. These days it's part of the Business Design Centre, featuring a modern glass roof that contrasts with the Victorian structure.

Turn right and walk along Liverpool Road, until you reach Chapel Market, where you turn right. This is another good, old-school market which hasn't quite been turned into a commercial excuse to have every stall sell the same thing yet. Many of the shops are succumbing to the great gentrification and spread of chain-store capitalism, but there are a few nice places still, including some street food stalls. Look out for the trainers (sneakers) lobbed over the wire between buildings high up on your right at White Conduit Street. Who throws a shoe??!

PUB

The Three Johns

The building at 89–91 Chapel Market (currently a Sports Direct shop) used to be a pool hall, where I shot pool with Woody Harrelson! (That's right, yeah, I hang out with celebs... See **Walk 8** for my Woody anecdote!)

Hang a left down Baron Street (this is just before you get to the former pool hall) and you'll come to the **Three Johns**, where I suggest you take a beverage – especially if you're plotting a revolution!

You might not know it, but a lot of the meetings that eventually led to the 1917 Russian Revolution took place in London. Lenin spent a lot of time here in exile. In 1903 the second congress of the Russian Socialist Democratic Labour Party took place in London, resulting in a hugely significant vote that shaped Russian history thenceforth! Lenin wrote that a meeting he had in a pub (which researchers have identified as this very one) marked the birth of Bolshevism. These secret meetings were taking place all over London and they didn't always agree on various matters. After the vote that took place here the Bolsheviks (Lenin's side) split with the Mensheviks (headed by Martov) and they decided to do things their separate ways. There was no longer any unity in the party and they chose revolution over reform!

Na zdoróvje!! (Although Russians don't usually say that, apparently.)

Now head right down White Lion Street, which becomes Donegal Street, all the way until you reach **JOSEPH GRIMALDI PARK 10**.

Did you ever hear the famous story about the man who went to the psychiatrist? He said, 'Doctor, I'm so depressed, I don't want to live any more. I just don't know what to do.'

The psychiatrist replied, 'Well, when I was really depressed I went to see Grimaldi the clown at the theatre. He was terrific and it really cheered me up. I recommend you go and see his show.'

To which the man replied, 'But doctor, I am Grimaldi!!'

Joseph Grimaldi performed around the start of the 1800s and was known as the King of Clowns. In fact, the famous clown make-up that we all know (and are probably terrified of) was created by him!

Although Grimaldi was one of the most popular performers of his age, when he died in 1837 he was a depressed alcoholic. He was buried here, and his grave has become a shrine for clowns today. A few metres away from his grave, look for the little stepping stones shaped like coffins. When you jump on them they play a tune and ring bells, although they have suffered a bit of wear and tear.

I love Grimaldi. His mother was only 14 when he was born and when he was a toddler his father used to swing him around on stage from a chain and throw him into the audience, as a popular stunt! He suffered terribly from aching joints in later years and his friends would have to carry him to the pub. Eventually he made a suicide pact with his wife and took poison, but that failed and they ended up with stomach ache. Eventually his wife did die, leaving him sad and alone.

Now, head out of the little park and onto the big, noisy Pentonville Road. Sorry about this, but you'll have to walk up the hill now. (It was worth it for Grimaldi.)

At Claremont Square turn right.

In the film of *Harry Potter and the Order of the Phoenix* the Phoenix HQ is, pleasingly, at 12 Grimmauld Place – 'Grim Old Place' – which was filmed in this square. The family home of Sirius Black appears between two properties here, on the south side of the square (between numbers 18 and 31).

I wonder if it's just coincidence that Grimmauld Place is so near to Grimauldi Park! The 19th-century railings here surround the upper pond of the New River, which I will tell you about later on in the walk.

At the south-west corner of Claremont Square look for Cruikshank Street and walk down it.

At the bottom you will come to a tall building. It's called **BEVIN COURT** ⑪, but I call it the Propellor Building, because from above it looks like a propellor.

Completed in 1954, it's a remarkable piece of architecture designed by the Georgian architect Berthold Romanovich Lubetkin – he also designed the penguin pool in

London Zoo and Highpoint Tower, which you can find in **Walk 5**.

Of course, it didn't look anything like this before the war, and since we've been talking about the Russian Revolution I should tell you that when this was a beautiful terrace of houses in 1902 it was one of Lenin's many residences in London. In fact, it was here that he met Leon Trotsky for the first time. Trotsky showed up in a taxi in the early hours of the morning, with no money and speaking no English. When Lenin's wife answered the door she even had to pick up the cab fare!!!

If you can get access to the building it's worth going up the amazing staircase and looking at the view.

Originally it was to be called Lenin Court and there was a big bust of Lenin outside. But once the Cold War started they felt it was best to remove the bust (which you can still see in the Islington Museum on St John Street) and name it Bevin Court, after Ernest Bevin, who was the (anti-Communist) Foreign Secretary.

Now go back up Cruikshank Street and turn right into Amwell Street.

Turn left onto Inglebert Street at the **George and Monkey**. This used to be Filthy McNasty's, a notorious venue where poets, musicians, philosophers and hell-raisers including Shane MacGowan, Johnny Depp, Pete Doherty and Allen Ginsberg, amongst many others, hung out until it closed in 2013, before relaunching in its current incarnation.

Continue along Inglebert Street, around the very picturesque Myddelton Square and down Chadwell Street until you reach St John's Street. Then turn left.

PUB

The George and Monkey

Sorry to go on about Lenin, but coming up on the right (at the corner of Owen Street) is a hairdressers that used to be a pub called the Crown and Woolpack. It always makes me a little sad to see pubs that have closed down, but you can still see the sign on the ground by the entrance on the left.

Around 1905 Scotland Yard heard that there was going to be a meeting of revolutionaries in this pub and they sent their best man to investigate. The policeman got here early and hid inside a cupboard for hours, waiting for them to arrive.

When they did arrive the meeting went on for ages and the policeman heard every single word. When he could finally escape (after they had all left, several hours later) his sergeant asked him for all the details – but he couldn't report anything at all because the whole meeting was conducted in Russian!!

We are now approaching the Angel Islington!

A little further along on the right is the **Old Red Lion** theatre pub. There are a great many theatres in Islington and many of them

are over pubs like this one. I always find it amusing that they have a picture of a dog on their pub sign, rather than a red lion. It could confuse a stupid person.

Islington was named 'Gisel-dune' by the Saxons in the 10th century. Gisela was the name of the family that owned the land, while 'dune', meaning 'down' or 'hill', indicated that it was the hill near Gisela's land. Later the name became corrupted to become 'Iseldon' and then 'Islington'.

Many people wonder why we talk about the Angel, rather than just Angel. This is because it's actually referring to the Angel pub, which existed here from 1614. It originally belonged to the priory of St John and can be seen as a coaching inn in William Hogarth's The Stage Coach. It would have occupied a large area near the crossroads here, but these days it's the name of a Wetherspoons pub a few doors along Islington High Street.

In the middle of the 18th century there were 56 ale houses along here; by 1870 it had become known as the 'Devil's Mile' on account of its prostitution, crime and drunkenness. Charles Dickens Jr (son of the famous one) described this street as 'amongst the noisiest and least agreeable thoroughfares in London'. In Oliver Twist by Charles Dickens Sr (the famous one) it is described as where 'London began in earnest.'

Now head up Islington High Street towards the tube station. On the other side of the street from the tube there's a little parade of shops which most people probably ignore (unless they want to go into Starbucks). The Starbucks used to be the **ANGEL CINEMA** 🄬, opened in 1913, and you can still see the impressive bell tower demonstrating that they don't make 'em like they used to! Next to this you can also make out the remnants of the old Peacock Inn, dating from 1564. Although it did get rebuilt, some parts still survive from the 19th century. It is mentioned in Nicholas Nickleby and is also where Tom Brown stays before going up to Rugby School in Tom Brown's School Days by Thomas Hughes.

ANGEL UNDERGROUND STATION

13 used to have such a narrow platform, with trains whizzing by either side, that passengers were in danger of falling onto the tracks – so they redeveloped it. Now it has the longest escalator in London and gained internet fame when a Norwegian nutter skied down it and put it on YouTube!

Dotted around, you can see evidence of older buildings all over. For example, across the road on the corner of White Lion Street is an HSBC bank – but you can see that it used to be another one of the numerous pubs, the White Lion. The crest is still visible on the side of the building, with the year 1714 on it.

On the next corner, at the junction of Liverpool Road and Upper Street, above 1 Upper Street, there's an old street sign. Points!!!! You can see how this used to be called Clark's Place before they changed it to Upper Street. On the same corner, under the Liverpool Road sign, you should also be able to see a parish marker which tells you that this was the parish of St Mary Islington. More points!

The splendid Tudor-style building opposite was also once a pub, called the Pied Bull, dating from the 16th century. However, it burned down and was rebuilt in the 1930s and was, pleasingly, designed by an architect

called Sidney Clark – although I don't think that's why the road opposite was called Clark's Place! When I was a teenager it was a pub with a gig venue called The PowerHaus. (Or was that next door? I'm reminiscing…) I saw many a promising band there, most of whom have vanished now. Snuff, Nutmeg, the Senseless Things, Wat Tyler, Mega City Four… Ah, those halcyon days, when I had long hair and we used to tumble around in the 'mosh pit' covered in a weird mixture of dirt, fag-ends, sweat, and a sort of paste formed by alcohol falling onto the non-slip coating on the floor which didn't work.

Now head back to Upper Street, cross to the other side, and turn left.

Just after the **York**, bear to the right (but don't turn down Duncan Street) and you'll come to **CAMDEN PASSAGE** **14**, a charming pedestrianised street. It has an antique market on Saturdays and Wednesdays, but you'll find other little bits and bobs here, too. There are some cute cafés and restaurants and you won't feel like you're in a busy city at all.

After milling around in here (and you can spend a good while nosing around) you will emerge at the other end near the **Camden Head**, where you might wish to stop for a pint. It's a pretty nice pub and I once did a stand-up comedy night upstairs there. I'd rather forget about that, actually, so let's turn left and you'll find Islington Green with a statue of **HUGH MYDDELTON** **15** who, between 1608 and 1613, helped to get the New River built after initial plans stalled. He even got funding from King James I, whose grounds at Theobalds Park were crossed by the route of the New River. It carried fresh drinking water from the River Lea in Hertfordshire all the way to Clerkenwell, or the 'New River Head', where

ISLINGTON GREEN

it filled a huge cistern near today's Sadler's Wells theatre. (Places like Clerkenwell and Sadler's Wells take their names from old wells which used to serve the area.)

The New River got truncated at Stoke Newington in 1946, but you can still see remnants of it in various places, such as the New River Path. Originally it would have been a penal offence to throw rubbish into the river, and doing your laundry in it would 'incur the King's displeasure' – I doubt you'd want to clean anything in it these days! The existing part north of Stoke Newington still serves people today.

As you stand in the middle of the little park area you will see a blue plaque on the other side of Upper Street, indicating that Gracie Fields lived there. She became popular in the 1920s and 1930s singing in her Lancashire accent and performed on many a London stage. One such venue, **COLLINS' MUSIC HALL** 16, was right here where the Waterstones bookshop now stands, incorporating the old music hall frontage. Collins' also played host to another Lancashire singer, George Formby, as well as Norman Wisdom, before it burned down in 1958.

Carrying on along Upper Street, you will find the **SCREEN ON THE GREEN** 17. Opened in 1913, it is one of the oldest cinemas in the UK, although it has subsequently been taken over by the Everyman chain. This, no doubt,

means that they have turned some of their seats into comfortable sofas with blankets where you can have food and drinks with a friend or loved one.

Don't munch crisps loudly or eat smelly food in front of me whilst checking your bright glowing phone – or there'll be trouble in Egypt (as my dad used to say). I'll say 'Shhhhhh!!' (That'll teach 'em, Joolz.)

Okay, rant over.

All along this stretch are various bars, cafés and restaurants; it's a good place to come out and spend a Saturday night if you are not inclined to head into the West End.

On the right you'll come to the estate agent **HOTBLACK DESIATO** 18, after whom Douglas Adams named his rock star character in *The Hitchhiker's Guide to the Galaxy*. Douglas Adams lived in Islington; his phone number was 2–267709, which is why he decided to make Ford and Arthur's chances of being rescued when dying in outer space 'two to the power of two hundred and sixty-seven thousand seven hundred and nine'! As the narrative explains:

> *By a totally staggering coincidence that is also the telephone number of an Islington flat where Arthur once went to a very good party and met a very nice girl whom he totally failed to get off with – she went off with a gatecrasher.*

Coming up on the left, opposite the church, is the **King's Head** theatre pub. There's been a pub here since 1543, when it was called the King's Head Tavern – they say King Henry VIII used to stop here on his way to see one of his mistresses. Many pubs had more Catholic names before Henry VIII, like the Virgin Mary, but in order to please the King and avoid getting their heads chopped off they changed them to names like the King's Head.

This is the oldest theatre pub in London, and the first to exist in London since Shakespeare's time. It's terrific fun to see a performance here. The stage is in the back room, but when I went to see *La Bohème* the singers all came out and performed a whole act in the bar area, much to the surprise of those just there for a normal drink. Many famous actors have passed through its doors, including Steven Berkoff, Richard E. Grant and Joanna Lumley, amongst others. The landlord was also quite a character, refusing for many years to charge people in the new decimalised currency after 1971. For 20 years he continued to charge in pounds, shillings and pence!

The church opposite is the parish church of **ST MARY ISLINGTON** ⑲. Originally this was a 12th-century church, but it had to be rebuilt after the bloomin' Luftwaffe decided to bomb it.

Have a look for the grave of Richard Cloudesley. Many of the streets and buildings around here are named after him. Cloudesley owned much of the land in this area during the 16th century and was a generous benefactor who left so much money for the development of Islington that they were still using it 500 years later to fund various projects.

In 1842 a booklet was published called *The Islington Ghost: A Short Account of the Burial of a Gentleman*, describing what happened after the burial of Richard Cloudesley. He left instructions to be buried in the churchyard but instead (apparently) he was buried in a field nearby, which may have been unconsecrated ground.

Anyway, when an earthquake occurred later, people believed that his corpse was restless in its grave because of some unconfessed sin. It shuddered so much, causing 'tremblements de terre', that in the end an exorcism was performed and he was re-buried in a lead coffin here.

HERE LIES THE BODY OF RICHARD CLOUDESLEY, A GOOD BENEFACTOR TO THIS PARISH, WHO DIED 9 HENRY VIII. ANNO DOMINI, 1517.

There's a charming little path leading down to the right of the church that makes you feel like you are in *Hansel and Gretel*. At the bottom you'll come to the little rector's cottage, the only part which survives from Tudor times.

Wander through the garden to your left and you'll come to the **LITTLE ANGEL PUPPET THEATRE** ⑳, where they hold performances for children like *The Owl and the Pussycat* and *The Pobble Who Has No Toes*, as well as holding puppet-making workshops – they look like a lot of fun!!

Head back to Upper Street. Between number 128 (which has a door number) and the alleyway to Islington Square is **NUMBER 127** ㉑ (which doesn't have a door number). This used to be Granita restaurant, where Gordon Brown and Tony Blair famously had a meeting in which they agreed that Blair would only run for two terms as Prime Minister; in return, he would give Brown sweeping powers over domestic policy. They denied it for years, but everyone knew about it. It was called the 'Granita Pact'.

Carry on up the street whilst perusing some of the nice shops and bars, and then turn left down Almeida Street. This will take you past yet another theatre, the **ALMEIDA** 🔢, and you can then go through a cute little alleyway that – surprisingly – doesn't smell of urine… Well, there's a first!!

Almeida Passage brings you out into Milner Square, which is one of many beautiful squares around here that were built in the early 19th century. The arrival of horse-drawn omnibuses in 1830 led to great expansion and development, which attracted many professionals to the area. These buildings fell into disrepair around the middle of the 19th century, when many slum clearances in central London, making room for the new railway stations, forced poorer people out to the suburbs. This explains why Charles Dickens describes it as a run-down area. Many of the professionals decided to move out and it wasn't until the 1960s that middle-class gentrification set in.

Let's visit one more beautiful square before going to the pub. At the other end of Milner Place is Gibson Square, with another nice garden in the centre for quiet contemplation. Some time ago, the local residents refused to let London Underground install an ugly 15-metre (50-foot) concrete ventilation shaft for the Victoria Line here. So they built this **BRICK AIR VENT** 🔢 instead, which looks like it could be a tomb or a temple. If you listen you can hear trains going past and the air blowing through.

As you wander around the square, try to score some points by spotting all the coal hole covers outside many of the properties. (See the **STREET FURNITURE CHALLENGE**, page 13!)

At the end of Gibson Square turn right into Theberton Street and then right again into Liverpool Road.

You'll walk past some nice houses called **CLOUDESLEY TERRACE** 🔢, built in 1818 and named after Richard Cloudesley, like lots of things around here.

Turn left at Richmond Avenue then have a quick look at Lonsdale Square coming up on your right. It has some remarkable-looking houses with front doors that belong in a church or one of Henry VIII's palaces.

Back in 1818 this square was used as a cattle-pen to hold the herds being taken to Smithfield Market and along Liverpool Road. These houses were actually built in the 1830s, in the Tudor/Elizabethan style.

Return to Richmond Avenue and carry on straight. Then turn right into Thornhill Road. (You'll see that you're back at the ghost sign in Cloudesley Road again.)

We're now back in Barnsbury, I suppose; but depending on your degree of snobbery, residents might choose to describe it as Islington. Both are correct.

At last! I can see the pub from here! Just coming up on the right is the **Albion**. In its time this has been a dairy and (in the 19th century) a tea house, but these days it's a rather beautifully located pub with a splendid interior, which does very fine food.

Last one to the bar buys the drinks. I'll have a pint of their finest ale! Cheers!

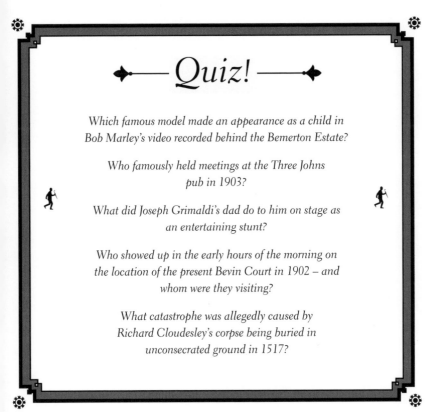

— *Quiz!* —

Which famous model made an appearance as a child in Bob Marley's video recorded behind the Bemerton Estate?

Who famously held meetings at the Three Johns pub in 1903?

What did Joseph Grimaldi's dad do to him on stage as an entertaining stunt?

Who showed up in the early hours of the morning on the location of the present Bevin Court in 1902 – and whom were they visiting?

What catastrophe was allegedly caused by Richard Cloudesley's corpse being buried in unconsecrated ground in 1517?

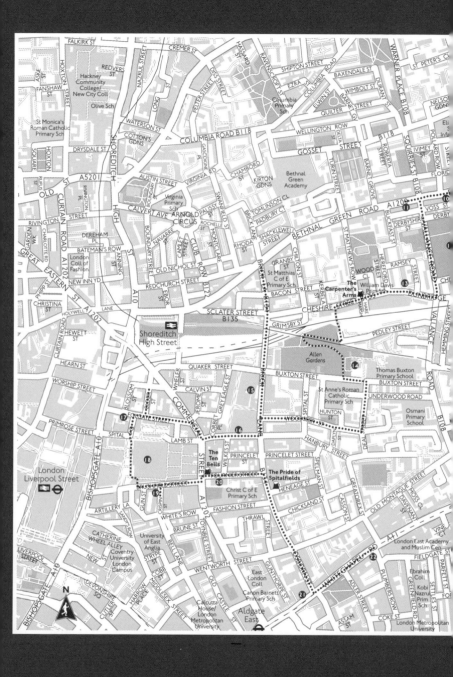

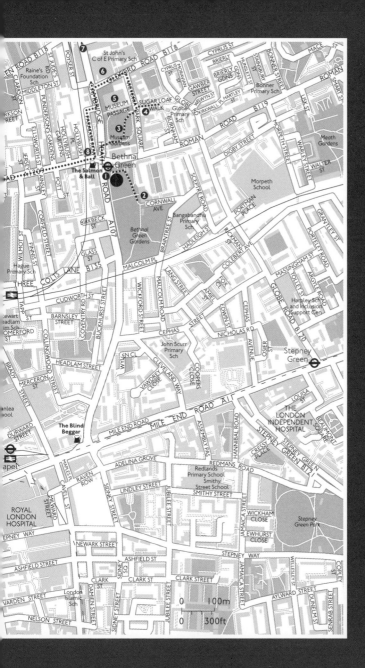

St John's
C of E Primary Sch

Raine's
Foundation
Sch

CYPRUS ST

BRIERLY

BRIERLY
GDNS

BONNER STREET

MACE

ROMAN

SMART ST

MIDDLETON ST

POSSER ST

ST LUKE'S RD

GUILFORD RD B118

CYPRUS ST

MORGAN

GAWBER
STREET

HUNSLETT ST

SELWYN ST

Bonner
Primary Sch

LISK ST

ROAD B118

MCKEAN STREET

Globe
Primary Sch

ROMAN ROAD B119

MORPETH STREET

WARLEY STREET

WALTER
ST

CLARKSON

ELLSWORTH GARDENS

HOLLYBUSH
GARDENS

HOLLYBUSH
PL

GLOBE
STREET

PARK SQUARE

BURNHAM

DIGBY STREET

Meath
Gardens

KIRKSON
STREET

SUGAR LOAF
WALK

Museum
Gardens

Bethnal
Green

Morpeth
School

GRANTLEY ST

JERSEY ST

AINSLEY ST

POTT
ST

The Salmon
& Ball

CORNWALL
AVE

SCEPTRE ROAD

PORTELET ROAD

BIRKBECK ST

Bangabandhu
Primary Sch

RICHMOND

MASSINGHAM ST

GLOBE ROAD B120

ARGYLE ROAD

ST JOACHIM
ST

FINNIS ST

CORFIELD STREET

Bethnal
Green
Gardens

BRAINTREE ST

HADLEIGH ST

COLEBERT AVE

Hartley Sch
and Inclusion
Support Cen

Hague
Primary Sch

GLASS
ST

MALCOLM PL

LANG STREET

DIX

APPLE
STREET

CEPHAS
STREET

TOLLET ST

THREE COLTS LANE B135

TAPP
ST

CUDWORTH ST

WICKFORD STREET

MALCOLM
ROAD

EDWIN ST

NICHOLAS RD

OSIER

Stepney
Green

ewart
eadlam
im Sch
OMERFORD
ST

BARNSLEY
STREET

COVENTRY RD

BUCKHURST STREET

CEPHAS
STREET

John Scurr
Primary
Sch

AVENUE

BRADY
STREET

MERCERON
ST

HEADLAM STREET

WIN CL

CLEVELAND WAY

COOPERS
CLOSE

LOUISA
ST

THE
LONDON
INDEPENDENT
HOSPITAL

BEAUMONT
SQUARE

anlea
ool

COLLINGWOOD STREET

VAWDREY
CLOSE

STEPNEY GREEN

DURWARD
STREET

The Blind
Beggar

MILE END ROAD

MILE END ROAD A11

ASSEMBLY PASS

HANNIBAL ROAD

CRESSY
PLACE

STEPNEY GREEN B121

apel

RAVEN
ROW

MAPLE ST

ADELINA GROVE

LINDLEY STREET

JUBILEE STREET

REDMANS
ROAD

Redlands
Primary School
Smithy
Street School

SMITHY STREET

JAMAICA STREET

WICKHAM
CLOSE

Stepney
Green Park

ROYAL
LONDON
HOSPITAL

EPNEY WAY

NEWARK STREET

SIDNEY
SQ

EWHURST
CLOSE

STEPNEY WAY

WELLESLEY ST

COPLEY
ST

ASHFIELD STREET

CAVELL ST

MILWARD
STREET

CLARK
ST

DAMIEN ST

ASHFIELD ST

CLARK ST

SIDNEY STREET

CLARK STREET

JAMAICA STREET

AYLWARD STREET

DUNELM ST

SENRAB STREET

VARDEN STREET

NELSON STREET

London
Islamic
Sch

JUBILEE STREET

0   100m

0   300ft

13

13 A BLOOMIN' BRILLIANT WALK AROUND BETHNAL GREEN, BRICK LANE AND SPITALFIELDS

DISTANCE
6.9 km (4.3 miles)

TIME
3 hours

NEAREST STATION
Bethnal Green

Tally ho! How's yer father, dog and bone, apples and pears, good to see ya, me ol' China. Enough of that Cockney rhyming slang. Let's get on with it!

Look, if you're planning to visit Brick Lane Market it's probably best to do this walk on a Sunday to see it in all its glory. It really is a good one!

We're starting outside Bethnal Green tube station. Back in the 13th century this area used to be called Blithenhale, which could have meant 'happy corner' or possibly 'the corner near the Blithe', which was an ancient river nearby.

During the Second World War, Bethnal Green tube station saw the biggest loss of civilian life in London in a single night. The Central Line hadn't yet been completed and people were using the station as a bomb shelter. At 8 p.m. on 3 March 1943 the siren sounded, so people headed to the staircase, which was blacked out so that the bombers couldn't see it from the air. Unfortunately, one lady carrying a child fell over in the scramble, causing everyone behind her to fall, too – resulting in 173 people being killed in the crush. Churchill ordered the newspapers to keep quiet about it until after the war, because it would have contradicted his claim that Britain wasn't panicking.

Just inside Bethnal Green Gardens, by the tube entrance in question, there's an award-winning monument in remembrance of this event, called the **STAIRWAY TO HEAVEN ❶**.

Inside the park you'll find **BETHNAL GREEN LIBRARY ❷**, also known as Blind Beggar's House. John Kirby, a wealthy merchant, had originally built Bednal House here in

1570 and almost bankrupted himself in the process. Locals teased him by calling it Kirby Castle; in 1727 it was turned into a lunatic asylum and remained so until the 1920s. Locals still call this Barmy Park today!

Just outside the library entrance you should be able to make out the coat of arms of Bethnal Green, though it's hard to see it well. You get a better idea from the equivalent painting inside the library, depicting 'The Blind Beggar of Bethnal Green' with his dog. Legend has it that Henry de Montfort, a wealthy landowner, lost his sight in the battle of Evesham in 1265. Because he didn't want suitors chasing after his beautiful daughter just for her money, he pretended to be a pauper and was often seen begging with his dog in Bethnal Green. The legend probably sprang from the famous Tudor ballad, but I prefer the version written for Joolz Guides by Lil' Lost Lou!

In reality Henry de Montford died at the battle of Evesham with his father Simon de Montford (who established the first English parliament with elected representatives) but I prefer the story about the beggar.

We'll be coming back this way later, but first let's nip up Cambridge Heath Road northwards. Then turn right into **MUSEUM GARDENS** ❸ on the right and walk through the little park diagonally to the north-east corner. Cross over the road into Sugar Loaf Walk.

Here, until recently, could be found the **VAGINA MUSEUM** ❹ – yes, you heard me right. Roughly half of all human beings have one, yet they remain a mystery to a lot of people, even if they are too embarrassed to admit it! (Naturally I'm an expert, of course.)

These were temporary premises (they are still seeking a permanent location) where you could discover all about anatomy, health, vulva diversity and activism, along with other temporary exhibitions. If the word 'clitoris' makes you feel awkward, perhaps this will help you get over your fears; but I must admit, I probably wouldn't go with my mum again.

Now return to Museum Gardens. On your right is what was until recently the **VICTORIA & ALBERT MUSEUM OF CHILDHOOD** ❺. Here you could find many toys that you would recognise from your own childhood! There's nothing more depressing than finding things from your own lifetime in a museum! However, I've enjoyed some fun nostalgic trips down memory lane here.

The Victoria & Albert Museum was founded in 1852, located first at Marlborough House in Pall Mall and then at Somerset House on the Thames, where it housed exhibits from the Great Exhibition of 1851. It was subsequently moved to South Kensington, where it was temporarily housed in big iron and glass sheds, which became known as the Brompton Boilers because they were so ugly. Prince Albert tried decorating them, but it was no use – so in the 1860s they were moved here to Bethnal Green and covered with bricks and tiles. For three years they contained the Wallace Collection, but eventually that moved to Marylebone (where it is one of my favourite museums), and this became the Museum of Childhood. Further change is now afoot as it transforms into Young V&A ('the UK's premier national museum designed by, and for, young people').

A little further along, on the other side of Old Ford Road, is **YORK HALL** ❻, which opened in 1929 as a leisure facility with swimming pools and a gymnasium. The basement used to house Turkish baths catering to the Polish and Russian Jewish communities who settled here after the pogroms in the 19th century. In the second half of the 20th century it became famous as the home of British boxing, hosting fighters like Lennox Lewis, Joe Calzaghe and David Haye.

Now, at this stage we are going no further up this street – but I know what you're thinking: why didn't we see any actual vaginas in the vagina museum? Well, if you really want to see that sort of thing and you have time, you could continue up Cambridge Heath Road for about 10 minutes and visit the **VIKTOR WYND MUSEUM OF CURIOSITIES, FINE ART & NATURAL HISTORY** **7**. It's just after the canal on the left.

Viktor Wynd is one of the world's true eccentrics and has collected, over the years, some extraordinary exhibits which are on display here. There are ancient Chinese dildos, Amy Winehouse's poo, David Bowie's hair and, yes, the preserved vaginas of Victorian prostitutes in jars. Look, it's a bit out of the way for this walk, but definitely worth a visit if you have time! They even have cocktail classes in their bar – and you can reserve the area to dine on the sarcophagus or, as Wynd puts it, 'have an intimate moment'.

Let's retrace our steps back towards the tube station. On the right you will see Paradise Row, where the famous Daniel 'the Jew' Mendoza lived – he even has a **BLUE PLAQUE** **8**. Daniel Mendoza was the English boxing champion during the 1790s. He perfected the art of scientific boxing and revolutionised self-defence with his book *The Art of Boxing*, and he became the first

English Jew to speak to a king when he met King George III at Windsor Palace.

You now have my full permission to break into a rendition of the Cockney classic 'On Mother Kelly's Doorstep… down Paradise Row'. The song became a favourite in music halls and Mother Kelly was based on a real person who lived here, called Nelly Moss. I can only imagine that the song's composer, George Alex Stevens (who was a close friend of Charlie Chaplin's dad), was in love with her, judging by the lyrics.

On the other side of the road there's a patch of pavement outside the **Salmon and Ball** where a gallows used to be erected for local criminals. This would save local residents from having to travel all the way to Tyburn Gallows for their entertainment! Two such criminals, John Doyle and John Valine, were silk-weavers caught up in riots in 1769, protesting about new imported goods and mechanised looms. 'We don't want your bloody foreign silk over here! And down with these new-fangled machines, too!!! We weave by hand!!' Anyway, it was thought that hanging them here would put an end to some of the violence in the area, which had become popular with silk-weavers.

PUB

The Salmon and Ball

BETHNAL GREEN ROAD

The 'Bloody Code' was a term that referred to the legal system from the late 17th century to the early 19th century. By 1815 there were 215 hangable offences, which included stealing from a rabbit warren, being an unmarried mother concealing a stillborn child, damaging Westminster Bridge, being out at night with a blackened face, and being in the company of gypsies for a month! I assume that 29 days was perfectly acceptable, but I hate to think what would happen if you were a chimney sweep on a late shift, married to a gypsy!

Now make your way up Bethnal Green Road. To me this feels a bit more like an old-fashioned high street, where you might actually see an independent shop or something useful like a launderette.

Nip to the left down Derbyshire Street, where you'll see a big red brick building: **OXFORD HOUSE** **9**. This was London's first 'settlement house', where students from Keble College, Oxford, who stayed in the upstairs rooms, gave lessons to the poor and organised youth clubs and games. These days it's a community centre.

Retrace your steps and continue along Bethnal Green Road. If you feel a bit peckish and want a place full of character, try **E. PELLICCI** **10** at 332 Bethnal Green Road. It's like stepping back in time when you enter, thanks to the original 1940s interior with Grade II-listed status. The

Pellicci family opened this café in 1900 and their descendants, who continue to work here today, are very friendly, funny and welcoming. It feels authentically Italian and chaotic with lots of atmosphere. Infamous gangsters the Krays used to have breakfast here regularly in the 1960s and the lady in the kitchen (who was born upstairs) used to serve them every day. When I was last here the young fellow gave me some of his mama's bread pudding – it was excellent and I recommend it, but I think it might not have been on the menu. Worth asking, though!

Now continue along Bethnal Green Road and briefly cross over at the lights. Stop at number 284, **S. & R. KELLY & SONS** **11**, a traditional pie and mash shop. These were once commonplace in the East End, but now they are a dying breed. Some people love pie and mash, some people hate it, but it's certainly something to experience before they are all consigned to history. Try the jellied eels, an East End delicacy!

Now go back to the traffic lights and turn right down Vallance Road, where the Krays used to live (although their house has been replaced with a block of flats), and then turn right down Dunbridge Street, which becomes Cheshire Street. Along the way you'll pass **WEAVERS FIELDS** **12** on your left, a reminder of all the Huguenot weavers who used to live in this neighbourhood in the 18th century.

Soon you'll come across the Bath House, which is **REPTON BOXING CLUB** **13**, where actor Ray Winstone used to box. He won eighty fights here, but I don't know whether he ever fought the Krays, who also trained here, as did Audley Harrison (who won Olympic gold for Team GB!).

PUB

The Carpenter's Arms

The club was established by Repton School (a well-to-do English private school in Derbyshire) for the benefit of East End boys. Repton School was the one where Roald Dahl went… in case you cared.

A little further along you'll pass the **Carpenter's Arms**, which was the pub that the Krays bought for their mum, Violet, in 1967. They also went to school next door at William Davis primary school.

As you continue to the end of Cheshire Street you will pass some cool second-hand clothes shops, tattooists and other groovy stores staffed by trendy people with beards.

Now, just stop and wait one moment.

If you go this way you will come to Brick Lane, which you will probably want to spend quite a long time exploring. It's cool on any day of the week, but if you want to see the market in all its glory, come on a Sunday when it's buzzing with activity, offering second-hand clothes, a huge variety of food, bars and joviality!

We'll come back to Brick Lane in a moment, but for now we're going to turn left next to 72 Cheshire Street and walk over the graffiti-covered railway bridge.

This whole area was a rather derelict and scary place until a few years ago, when everything became gentrified. There is a lot of 'street art' here and it has often been used in films (*Lock, Stock and Two Smoking Barrels*, for example) because of its rough appearance. Great for Instagram photos!

Follow the long graffiti passage to the right and then to the left under the bridge.

You'll see a big field. Follow the path on your left that bends round to meet Buxton Street.

To your left you'll see **SPITALFIELDS CITY FARM** 14, which is a lovely, peaceful place to take a little rest if you like. They've got a café and lots of nice donkeys, pigs and rabbits to make you feel happy.

Come out of the farm and walk down Deal Street (just to your right as you exit the farm).

When you reach Woodseer Street, check out Albert Cottages (erected 1857) and Victoria Cottages (1864), which are examples of some of London's first social housing. The idea was to have one family upstairs and one downstairs, offering affordable housing for the working classes. All part of the snappily named Metropolitan Association for Improving the Dwellings of the Industrious Classes. There used to be a great deal more of them around the East End until they got bombed in the war. It's interesting to see satellite dishes outside them these days, which makes sense because I expect they are worth rather a lot of money now!

10

15

18

19

20

22

Joolz's Guide to...

COCKNEY RHYMING SLANG

Cockney rhyming slang apparently came about in the 1850s so that criminals wouldn't be understood by the police.

It's easy to pick up. For instance, 'Give me a call on the dog' means 'Give me a call on the phone.' That's because 'dog and bone' means 'phone', but only the first word is required.

Here are a few that are still used today. You can even make them up if you like!

'I'm not well – I've got a touch of the Mileys' (Miley Cyrus = coronavirus)

'I'm creamed' (cream crackered = knackered)

'I'll take a lady' (Lady Godiva = a fiver, i.e. £5)

'Lend me an Ayrton' (Ayrton Senna = a tenner, i.e. £10)

'I've only got a Balinese' (the Balinese Goddess of Plenty = twenty, i.e. £20 – okay, I made that one up!)

'I was all on my Jacks' (Jack Jones = on my own)

'He kicked me up the Aris!' (Aristotle = bottle; bottle and glass = arse)

'A cup of Rosy Lee' (Rosy Lee = tea)

'Let's go for a Ruby' (Ruby Murray = curry)

'He gave me a rubber Gregory!' (Gregory Peck = cheque; rubber Gregory = cheque that bounced)

'I've got an evening planned with the trouble' (trouble and strife = wife)

'See you down the rub-a-dub-dub' (rub-a-dub-dub = pub)

'I didn't like him… He had a dodgy boat' (boat race = face)

'I couldn't give a monkey's' (monkey's pit = shit)

'He's brown bread' (brown bread = dead)

'That's enough of that, me old China' (China plate = mate)

'Get your Barnet cut, mate!' (Barnet Fair = hair)

'Give us a song on the ol' Joanna!' (Joanna = piano)

BRICK LANE E.I.

ব্রিক লেন

Now turn right down Woodseer Street and keep going all the way to the end until you reach Brick Lane.

By the way, the street signs around here are also written in Bangla as there is a large Bangladeshi community here. The area has been home to many different cultures over the years. The Huguenots came from France in the 16th and 17th centuries; then the area was heavily populated by Jews and Irish immigrants during the 19th century; and these days it's more Bangladeshi.

Turn right and you should see a huge chimney with 'TRUMAN' written on it. **TRUMAN'S BREWERY 15** had become one of the largest brewers in London – and indeed the world – by the end of the 19th century, having grown since the 1660s when it was owned by Joseph Truman. As time went by it merged with other brewers and became the Truman, Hanbury, Buxton & Co. Brewery, whose signs you still see above pubs occasionally. Although they stopped brewing in 1989 there was a revival in 2013 and you can once again see Truman's name on beers brewed in the East End, although they aren't brewed on this site. This is now a bunch of offices for cool trendy start-ups and social media people, who hang out in the cool trendy cafés and bars nearby.

Oh, score **points** for spotting the fun coal hole covers! There's one with beer mugs on it that I particularly like.

Now, in my opinion the best part of Brick Lane (certainly on a Sunday) is up this end (the north end towards Cheshire Street) and around the corner in Sclater Street. In the old days they used to say you could come down here and find someone selling your bike that was stolen from you the week before! Hopefully it's not like that any more.

You might want to try one of the bagels from the Beigel Shop at 155 Brick Lane, which are pretty well known and claim to be the oldest in London. Call me unoriginal, but I always have salmon and cream cheese. They're always nice to me in there and they even let me film for Joolz Guides! Look above the doorway near the bagel shop for the old Truman, Hanbury, Buxton & Co. sign that I was talking about.

Anyway, that's all up the north end.

Head back down Brick Lane the way you came, past Woodseer Street, and then turn right into Hanbury Street.

On the right are some shops with glass fronts. Here at **29 HANBURY STREET 16** was the courtyard of the house where Annie Chapman, Jack the Ripper's second victim, was found murdered in 1888. She had previously been seen in the company of a 'swarthy foreigner'. Because a bloody leather apron was found at the scene of the murder, everyone started blaming a local Jewish shoemaker called John Pizer (who wore such an apron for his work). Luckily he had an alibi but the Jews, of whom there were a great many in the East End at the time, continued to be blamed by the increasingly nervous public. Shortly afterwards the residents of the local buildings let out their rooms for sixpence a shot, for people to grab a peek at the gory courtyard.

HANBURY STREET

At the end of Hanbury Street turn right on Commercial Street and then left into Folgate Street.

Keep walking until you get to number 18, which is **DENNIS SEVERS' HOUSE** **17**. Dennis Severs was an extraordinary American who moved to London in the 1960s and used to ride around town in a carriage drawn by horses. Then he bought this house for £18,000 and decided to continue living his remarkable existence. He decided to live as an 18th-century Londoner would have lived, without any of the comforts of today, so the whole place is lit by candles and heated with wood or coal.

After he died the house remained a museum where you can come and experience a journey through time. Each room has been left as if an 18th- or 19th-century occupant has just that minute left, and you've walked in to see their half-eaten Victorian meal on the table, or their spectacles sitting next to the book they're reading. It's really rather wonderful – but don't use your phone in here, or it ruins it!!

Around the corner is Elder Street, with some lovely 18th-century houses, often with vintage cars parked outside! At the junction of Elder Street and Fleur de Lis Street, have a look at the way the cobblestones have been laid out. This must have been done by a proper stonemason taking great care, because it starts with one stone and

then forms a spiral that spreads out in all directions. The street was laid out in 1197 as a part of the Liberty of Norton Folgate, which meant it was outside the laws of the City of London. This is why it attracted many Huguenot silk-weavers fleeing France (the Huguenots were Protestants being persecuted); they weren't allowed to join the livery companies in the City, so they settled here, where rules were less strict.

Return down Elder Street to Folgate Street, before turning right and then left into Spital Square. Straight ahead you'll arrive in an open space where you can buy all sorts of fast food. You should see a staircase going down to a little viewing space.

Spital has nothing to do with spit. In 1197 there used to be a priory here, and they built one of the biggest hospitals in medieval England: the New Hospital of St Mary-without-Bishopsgate. This meant 'without' as opposed to 'within' because it was just outside the City walls, which had various gates to the City of London, this one being Bishopsgate. St Mary Hospital became abbreviated to St Mary 'Spital and eventually the area surrounding it became known as Spitalfields.

When they were doing some digging recently they found part of the medieval priory chapel here, dating from 1320, which you can see at the bottom of these stairs. Now walk over to **SPITALFIELDS MARKET** **18**, which seems to have become more of a place for street food these days, although there are still some second-hand stalls and other retailers clinging on for grim life (as well as the designer stalls trying to sell you a £500 pair of sunglasses). I go there sometimes because it has a pretty good variety of food and a nice buzz of activity as office workers buy their lunch.

This has been a market since the 1600s when King Charles II granted it a licence; but if you're wondering why many of the surrounding streets have names like Gun Street and Artillery Lane, it's because around the 1540s the land was leased to the Fraternity of Artillery of Longbows, Crossbows and Handgonnes ('handgonnes' being hand cannon). This is where the household artillery practised shooting. They ended up becoming the Honourable Artillery Company, whose headquarters we will see in **Walk 18**.

Exit the market on the south side in Brushfield Street and walk towards the big church.

On the right, just briefly walk up Crispin Street and you'll see the very Victorian-looking **NIGHT REFUGE AND CONVENT** , which temporarily housed the destitute. Directly opposite is a group of modern buildings, incorporating the former London Fruit and Wool Exchange (the entrance to which is visible on Brushfield Street). This complex occupies the site of what was one of London's biggest slums in the late 19th century. It was here, in Miller's Court off Dorset Street, that Jack the Ripper committed his final and most gruesome murder, that of Mary Jane Kelly. It was such a horrendous mutilation that the man who discovered it described it as 'the devil's own work'. Incidentally, Mary Jane Kelly is known to have stayed in the aforementioned night refuge when she first arrived in London in 1884.

Looming up ahead is **CHRISTCHURCH SPITALFIELDS** ❷⓪, designed by Nicholas Hawksmoor. In order to rival the ten chapels built by the Huguenots in the area, the Church of England decided to build an Anglican church here with ten bells in it.

PUB
The Ten Bells

That's why the pub over the road is called the **Ten Bells**.

Inside the church there is a large and barely touched dusty organ (no, I'm not talking about myself) dating from 1735 and it is thought that George Frederick Handel played on it. Not many people can boast about having him play on their organ!

If you want to stop for a quick pint you could try the Ten Bells, which they say both Mary Jane Kelly and Annie Chapman used to frequent, and where Jack the Ripper probably eyed them up or made contact with them. Who knows, but it does feature in the film *From Hell*, all about the Ripper murders, starring Johnny Depp.

Beside the Ten Bells walk down Fournier Street, which is another excellent example of the houses occupied by some of the 80,000 Huguenots who once lived in the area. Many of these were silk-weavers and number 14 is where Queen Victoria's coronation gown was woven. As you can see, all the houses here and in neighbouring Wilkes Street and Princelet Street retain their Georgian exteriors (and many ghost signs of old businesses are still visible). As a result, many production companies like to film here (including Joolz Guides!) and that's probably why it's popular with artists like Tracey Emin and Gilbert and George. Look out for the chance to score points, too!! I'm not telling you where, exactly – because you have to have a bit of a challenge – but a couple of the houses in this street have my favourite: fire insurance plaques! (See the **STREET FURNITURE CHALLENGE**, page 8, for more about these.)

At the end of Fournier Street turn right into Brick Lane.

Right, okay, we've nearly finished. If you like, you can skip straight to the pub here, as we are close by. Maybe you already did!

However, there is something quite cool and it's not too far, so probably worth a look!

Walk to the end of Brick Lane, which becomes Osborn Street.

At the end of the road you will come to Jack the Chipper on the corner, where Whitechapel High Street becomes Whitechapel Road.

By the way, they were really nice when I ate at Jack the Chipper; Simon and I had a lovely lunch there after filming a Joolz Guide. Locals don't approve of them using the famous serial killer to promote their business – that said, it doesn't stop the barber, Jack the Clipper!

Cross over Whitechapel Road (the second cheapest property on the English Monopoly board) and look back across the road at the weathervane on the roof of **WHITECHAPEL ART GALLERY ㉑**, which used to be a library. I'm slightly obsessed with weathervanes and

WHITECHAPEL HIGH STREET

this one is rather splendid. It's Erasmus, the 16th-century Dutch philosopher, and he's sitting backwards because he apparently wrote *In Praise of Folly* on his horse on the way back from Italy. I guess the horse's bum was a better writing surface than its neck!

Now walk east up Whitechapel Road until, on your right on the corner of Fieldgate Street, you'll see what used to be **WHITECHAPEL BELL FOUNDRY ㉒**, established in 1570. Sadly, it closed in 2017, by when it had long since become the oldest manufacturing company in Britain. It was here that they cast many church bells, including Big Ben – which developed a crack after they hit it with the wrong type of hammer – and the Liberty Bell in Philadelphia – which also has a crack in it! They also did the 'great bell of Bow' for St Mary-le-Bow in the City – which, as far as I know, didn't have a crack in it! See **Walk 4** for more about the Bow bells.

Anyway, speaking of bells, let's head to the pub before they ring last orders.

Hmm… Well, if you're keen to check out more Krays history, you could head east up Whitechapel Road and finish in the **Blind Beggar**, where Ronnie Kray shot George Cornell, ultimately leading to the brothers' downfall – but that's a little further than I care to walk right now.

Instead let's zip over the road, turn left and then right into Brick Lane again. Of course, if you're feeling peckish you could stop at one of the many curry houses along here. There is certainly no shortage and they will try to lure you in with various deals. I'm not sure why. I think they just enjoy having touts outside trying to get you to go in. I mean, they're usually all pretty full by the evening, anyway!

Me? I'm going to turn right into Heneage Road and grab a pint at the **Pride of Spitalfields**, which David Gray fans might recognise from his 'Sail Away' video. It is

also said that Jack the Ripper was seen by a witness called George Hutchinson drinking here prior to murdering one of his victims – but since we don't know who he was, that could be utter bobbins.

I'll have a pint of Doom Bar. Cheers!

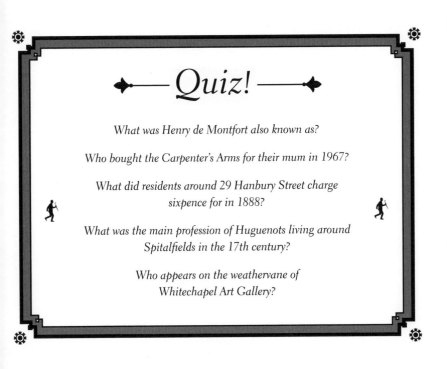

✦ — *Quiz!* — ✦

What was Henry de Montfort also known as?

Who bought the Carpenter's Arms for their mum in 1967?

What did residents around 29 Hanbury Street charge sixpence for in 1888?

What was the main profession of Huguenots living around Spitalfields in the 17th century?

Who appears on the weathervane of Whitechapel Art Gallery?

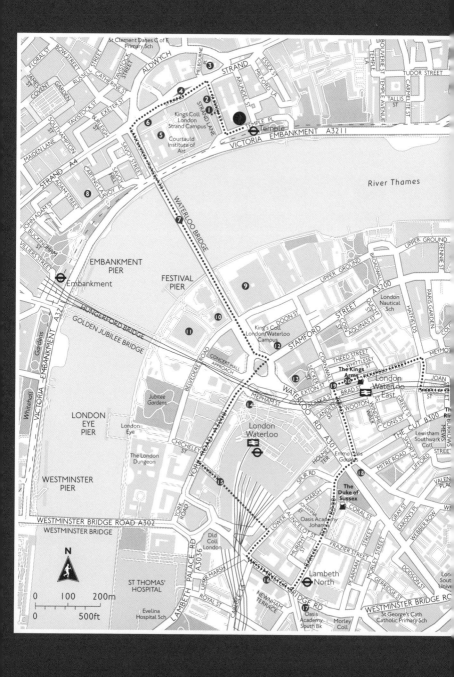

14 A WHIMSICAL WANDER FROM WATERLOO TO BOROUGH

DISTANCE
5.1 km (3.2 miles)

TIME
2 hours 10 minutes

NEAREST STATION
Temple

Pip pip, tally ho!

Here we are at Temple again – where we also started **Walk 3**, but this time we're going the other direction and over the river. From the station go up the steps and turn left.

Yes! Immediate points for spotting the green hut, or cabmen's shelter, to give it the correct name. (See the **STREET FURNITURE CHALLENGE**, page 13, for why these are cool.)

This particular one was originally a bit further up the street, but when a big American company decided to build a hotel here they were completely unaware of its importance. They just thought it was a rubbishy old hut that could be knocked down. Unfortunately, they didn't realise that it is a listed building and their hotel entrance opened right in front of it!

In the end the Cabmen's Shelter Fund agreed to move their green hut a few metres down the road in exchange for a generous donation. Good for them! The building has since been knocked down and redeveloped, so the hut has outlived the hotel, anyway!

To the left there's a nice little space up the stairs with benches, where you can wait for your friends if they are late and take a photo of the river.

Now turn right up Surrey Street.

When you get to the red brick buildings on the left you will see a passageway called Surrey Steps, with a sign above for the **ROMAN BATH** ❶. If the gate is closed you might have to go back to the bottom of the street and turn right and then go up Strand Lane.

The funny thing about the Roman Bath is that it's not Roman, and it originally wasn't even a bath!!

You can see it through the viewing window but it's better to organise a visit by calling the number on the door. Inside you'll find something resembling a Roman ruin, which is actually the remains of a cistern built in 1612 to feed a fountain at Somerset House. Later, in the 1770s, it was turned into a cold plunge pool – and in order to gain attention, the owners advertised it as a Roman bath. The spring actually still flows today, and you can see it's filled with water, but it's more of a trickle really (a bit like me, some nights). Charles Dickens most probably came to this bath as he has David Copperfield take a plunge here in his semi-autobiographical novel; and an MP called William Weddell even died of a seizure here on a hot day in 1792. It doesn't look too inviting to me. I think I'll stick to my usual weekly bath at home, whether I need it or not!

Afterwards, go back through the arch and up Surrey Street to the left.

On your left you will see **STRAND TUBE STATION ❷**, which I remember as 'Aldwych' when I was a boy. (The entrance around the corner still states 'Strand'.)

There used to be a little shuttle service on the Piccadilly Line between here and Holborn, but it seemed to be more trouble than it was worth, so they closed it in 1994. These days you can arrange a tour of the station, which is now often used for film and TV productions – you might have seen it in *Sherlock*, *Darkest Hour*, *V for Vendetta* and *Patriot Games*. During both world wars, many of London's famous artworks and treasures from its galleries and museums were hidden in the tunnels to shelter them from bombing raids. Even the much-prized Elgin Marbles, which Greece have been asking the UK to return for years, were hidden in the tunnels here. I mean, imagine if they had been blown up on our watch!

The tunnels didn't only protect artworks: during the Blitz, hundreds of Londoners flocked here each night to use the station as a bomb shelter.

Now continue to the top of the street.

On the other side of the road, a little to your right, is the **AUSTRALIAN HIGH COMMISSION ❸**. If you're lucky they might have an exhibition going on and you can go and look at the room that was used for the filming of Gringotts Wizarding Bank in the first *Harry Potter* film; or you can cheekily poke your nose in the front door if the security guard lets you. I also recognised it from some of the scenes in the *Wonder Woman* film.

Now turn left and walk past the other entrance of Strand tube station, also passing King's College and **ST MARY LE STRAND ❹**, built in the 1720s.

Just outside where the church now stands, it is said that in the 1630s a Captain John Bailey (who might have sailed with Sir Walter Raleigh) established the first ever taxi rank, getting a bunch of carriages and riders in proper uniforms, and positioning them at this spot because of the huge maypole that existed here at that time. It was twice the height of the current church, and big May Day celebrations were held here every year, so he knew he'd get custom (until grumpy-boots Oliver Cromwell had the maypole taken down – booooooooh!!).

Keep going and you'll pass **SOMERSET HOUSE** ❺ on your left, which was built on the site of the old Tudor palace belonging to the Duke of Somerset. The current Somerset House was built in the 1770s and has lots of things like exhibitions and artistic stuff going on. In the summer they have a big screen in the courtyard to show films and in the winter there's a popular ice rink.

It was in the old Tudor palace here that Oliver Cromwell lay in state after his death; and also, allegedly, where Sir Edmund Berry Godfrey was murdered before his body was dragged to Primrose Hill (see **Walk 8**). Canaletto painted the views of the river from the terrace before the palace went into decline, eventually being demolished in the 1770s, to be replaced by the present building – which has had loads of different uses down the years. At times it has housed the Royal Academy, the Society of Antiquities, the Geographical Society and the Royal Navy. It has also featured in many films, including *Tomorrow Never Dies*, *Sherlock Holmes*, *London Has Fallen* and, most importantly, *Shanghai Knights* starring Jackie Chan and Owen Wilson! Classic.

My favourite institution based here was the Board of Commissioners of Hawkers, Pedlars and Petty Chapmen, established in 1698!

Ooooh… I could do with a curry! And by lucky hap 'tis only a few more yards along the street to the Hotel Strand Continental. On the second floor is the **INDIA CLUB RESTAURANT** ❻ with their 1940s Lounge – it's probably my favourite Indian restaurant in London. Check out the fittings and coat hooks and everything, none of which have changed in years. It's unpretentious and unassuming but very popular amongst those who know about it. My friends Muqu and

WATERLOO BRIDGE

Kishaw (who stole Mr Tweedale's wig – see **Walk 5**) took me here and they know about these things.

There's something about sitting on the old chairs (like the ones we had at school) that just takes you back. The restaurant seems to be constantly under threat of closure, so I hope it's still there when you come. It would be such a pity for them to close.

After your slap-up feed, carry on along the Strand and turn left onto **WATERLOO BRIDGE** ❼.

Dirty old river, must you keep rolling,
Flowing into the night?

Know that song? 'Waterloo Sunset' by the Kinks. Whenever I stand upon Waterloo Bridge I can't help singing it as I look out over one of the best views in London. In one direction you can see the Houses of Parliament, Big Ben and the London Eye, and in the other direction you have St Paul's Cathedral, the Shard and Tate Modern. The reason you can see so much is because of its position on the bend in the river.

Waterloo Bridge started life being called the Strand Bridge, and was much loved for over 100 years, having appeared in paintings by Constable and Monet. With its arches and Doric columns, it was even called the 'noblest bridge in the world' by the Italian sculptor Canova. They changed its name to Waterloo

Bridge when it was officially opened in 1817, to commemorate Britain's victory over the French. Unfortunately it wasn't strong enough for modern 20th-century traffic and had to be rebuilt, a feat they managed to accomplish during the Second World War, to a design by Sir Giles Gilbert Scott (who also did the red telephone boxes). Since there was a shortage of men due to the war, it was left to London's women to complete the bridge. There are some wonderful photos of women hard at work with hammers and welding masks, and ever since then it has been known as 'the Ladies' Bridge'. It must have been quite a kick in the teeth when the man from the council showed up at its opening and said that 'the men who built Waterloo Bridge' were 'fortunate men' because their work would be remembered for generations to come!

In 1978 Waterloo Bridge was the scene of a James Bond-style murder when Georgi Markov, a Bulgarian writer and dissident, was stabbed in the thigh with a poisoned umbrella. The authorities suspected the Bulgarian secret service had engaged the help of the KGB.

Let's head south over the bridge.

Look back at the white building with a clock on it on the north bank. This is **SHELL MEX HOUSE** **8**, with the biggest clock face in London (bigger than Big Ben). It became known as 'Big Benzene'. (You know – because Shell is an oil company… Hilarious.)

Below the clock is a ledge where Winston Churchill used to stand, puffing on his cigar whilst counting the British planes returning from bombing raids during the Second World War. Since this was during the blackouts, the planes would have to follow the line of the river to find their way (and presumably the glow from his cigar!!).

Oh! The horrible big grey concrete block on the left as you proceed south is the **NATIONAL THEATRE** **9**. The theatre company, founded by Laurence Olivier in 1963, was originally based at the Old Vic, but they moved to this purpose-built complex in 1976. Prince Charles described it as 'a clever way of building a nuclear power station in the middle of London without anyone objecting'.

Its matching grey friends on the right are the **HAYWARD GALLERY** **10** and the **ROYAL FESTIVAL HALL** **11**, where you can pop in for a drink, see shows and look at the little models of how the whole of the South Bank was transformed in 1951 for the Festival of Britain. To commemorate the centenary of the Great Exhibition, and to move on from the war, the government decided to put on a huge exhibition celebrating modern Britain and all it had to offer… like vacuum cleaners and toasters. This whole area played host to millions of visitors and it's unrecognisable from how it looks in the pictures.

You might want to nip downstairs and visit the second-hand book market underneath the south side of the bridge, just on the river. This is right next to an area popular with skateboarders who spend all day trying to do tricks. To this day, I still haven't seen any of them perfectly execute a trick without falling off. (Obviously I'm an expert.)

Embedded in the pavement around the South Bank are various plaques to famous people who were associated with the area, one of whom I will mention later!

Anyway, we're back up on the bridge and

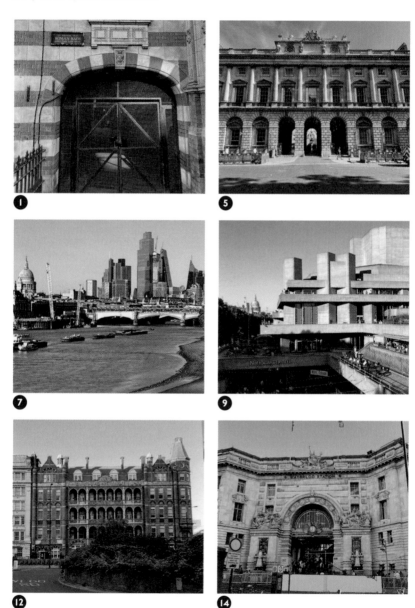

when you reach the end, if you hang around long enough, you might see free-runners jumping around and doing their 'parkour'. This spot is very popular for it and you can see where they've added that grippy material you get on garage roofs. Now these people, by contrast, *do* successfully carry out their tricks – otherwise they tend to hurt themselves!

Also at the end of the bridge, on the left, you will see (just before the roundabout) a red brick building that used to be the **ROYAL WATERLOO HOSPITAL FOR CHILDREN AND WOMEN** 12. It had to close in 1976 amongst great controversy because a certain Dr William Sargant, a psychiatrist, had been conducting rather cruel experiments on depressed and anorexic women, locking them in rooms for weeks and administering electric shock therapy. It transpired that all sorts of disreputable characters such as terrorists and criminals were using his books as reference for some of their nefarious activities – and it was even suggested that his activities were supported by the Ministry of Defence! Like Papa in *Stranger Things*!

These days it's university halls of residence.

Just beyond this you can see the church of **ST JOHN THE EVANGELIST** 13, which is known as one of the 'Waterloo Churches'. This isn't because it's in Waterloo! In the 1820s the nation was still basking in the glory of its victory over Napoleon. Whilst riding this wave of triumph, Parliament felt that more churches were needed for Britain's expanding towns and cities, so Acts of Parliament were passed to build 612 'Waterloo Churches'.

This church is actually built on very muddy foundations – and at first the engineer, John Rennie, didn't know what to do. However, he remembered that an old Roman oak pile had been recovered from a fort in the City of London, having survived for hundreds of years despite being immersed in mud. You can still see it outside St Magnus the Martyr near London Bridge. Rennie decided this would be his solution and drove huge oak piles into the muddy riverbed, and then built the church on top of this watery foundation. Amazingly, its springy base rendered it even sturdier, to the extent that when bombs damaged the church during the war the walls just sprang back into place and could still be used when they restored the church. Other churches with firmer foundations had to rebuild their walls completely.

Idiots!!

Opposite you can see the rather grand entrance to **WATERLOO STATION** 14. Well, it used to look a bit grander before they built all the ugly office blocks around it! Despite what people think, it was not named after the battle of Waterloo but Waterloo Bridge. Opened in 1848, it was originally called Waterloo Bridge Station. The victory arch, which was completed in 1922 when the station was rebuilt, commemorates the First World War. Inside the station, above the concourse, hangs a four-faced clock (which you might recognise from the chase scene in the film *The Bourne Ultimatum*). If you have a rendezvous with someone and don't know where to meet, I would suggest 'under the clock at Waterloo' as a pretty convenient location.

Head into the underpass or cross the dangerous road to get to the station.

To the right of the station entrance, continue down York Road past the London Eye on your right and then turn left into Leake Street and through the tunnel. In the **LEAKE STREET ARCHES** 15 street artists can demonstrate their talents (or bums like me can go and try my best and scribble 'Joolz Woz Ere' on the walls). It started in 2008 after the famous street artist Banksy hosted The Festival of Cans. It's great for a bit of Instagrammery or a modelling shoot, but if you see a piece of art you like, be quick – because quite often it's painted over by the next day!

There are a few cool bars down here, too, which make me feel a bit like I'm in *Judge Dredd* or *Total Recall*…

At the other end of the tunnel you will emerge into Lower Marsh, where you can buy various types of street food from the stalls there at lunchtime. The name Lower Marsh refers to marshland that existed here in the Middle Ages.

Turn right and you'll come to Westminster Bridge Road. In front of you is a railway bridge, next to which stood the Canterbury Music Hall between 1852 and 1942, when the Nazis bombed it. It was the first purpose-built music hall/tavern and was known as 'the father of the music halls', capable of seating 700 people, one of whom was Charlie Chaplin when he used to come and watch his dad perform here. Rebuilt several times, at one point it had a retractable glass roof that could let out all the tobacco smoke. It had huge grand staircases and was the biggest theatre attached to a pub in all of London.

Turn left and continue until you see on your right **121 WESTMINSTER BRIDGE ROAD** 16, a splendid red brick building. The reason it looks rather lugubrious is that it used to be the first class entrance to the Necropolis

Railway. By 1852 London's cemeteries were so full that sometimes bodies would be dug up and thrown into the river, causing cholera outbreaks, and it became necessary to build a special 'city for the dead' in Brookwood, Surrey. Bodies would sometimes be stored in vaults under the Leake Street Arches while waiting to be transported by rail to Brookwood Cemetery via a first, second or third class service. The train only ran on days when there was a first class burial; you would go through the door here and up in a lift to take your place on the train with the coffins. Second class burials required extra payment if you wanted a permanent memorial – and if you didn't pay enough money your grave could be reused by another occupant!

A little further along you can see the **LINCOLN TOWER** 17, opened in 1876 in memory of Abraham Lincoln. If you have good eyesight you can see the Stars and Stripes motif on the steeple.

Now head left down Baylis Road.

Coming up on your right is Frazier Street, but just keep going straight. I only mention it because Greet House on Frazier Street is – as if you cared – the 'geometric centre of London'. That is to say, if you picked up London and then balanced it on a pin, you would have to put the pin here.

Yeah, well… Moving swiftly on, keep going straight and past the **Duke of Sussex** towards The Cut. You might wish to stop for a pint in the Duke of Sussex, which has a good outdoor drinking area. I've drunk there before and found them to be friendly owners!

The area is much changed since Victorian times, when the journalist George Sala described it in *Twice Round the Clock*:

PUB

The Duke of Sussex

It is the paradise of the lowest of costermongers, and often the saturnalia of the most emerited thieves. Women appear there in their most unlovely aspect: brazen, slovenly, dishevelled, brawling, muddled with beer or fractious with gin. The howling of beaten children and kicked dogs, the yells of ballad-singers, 'death and fire-hunters', and reciters of sham murders and elopements; the bawling recitations of professional denunciators of the Queen, the Royal family, and the ministry; the monotonous jodels of the itinerant hucksters; the fumes of the vilest tobacco, of stale corduroy suits, of oilskin caps, of mildewed umbrellas, of decaying vegetables, of escaping (and frequently surreptitiously tapped) gas, of deceased cats, of ancient fish, of cagmag meat, of dubious mutton pies, and of unwashed, soddened, unkempt, reckless humanity: all these make the night hideous and the heart sick. The New Cut is one of the most unpleasant samples of London that you could offer to a foreigner.

Further along is one of London's most famous theatres, the **OLD VIC** ⓲. Originally constructed in 1818 as the Royal Coburg Theatre, with the present building dating from 1871, it was named the Victoria Theatre in 1833 to cash in on connections with Victoria, Duchess of Kent, and her daughter,

Princess (soon to be Queen) Victoria, who visited it that year. In 1880 Emma Cons acquired the theatre and preferred to host lectures there instead of Shakespeare. She didn't approve of people drinking alcohol and watching plays (what a killjoy!) – but it wasn't all bad, as the lectures did result in the establishment of the nearby Morley College for adult education. Between 2003 and 2015 the Old Vic's artistic director was Kevin Spacey.

Look out for the **Fire Station** bar and restaurant opposite, on Waterloo Road, which looks rather charming. I do like it when they convert unused buildings into something useful that we can all use. It would be nicer as a fire station, of course, but at least they didn't turn it into luxury flats!

If we were hanging around longer, I might wander along The Cut to some of the bars and restaurants down there, or to the army surplus shop, which is still clinging on.

But on this occasion we're heading across to the Emma Cons Gardens and up Cornwall Road, under the railway arch, and then right into Roupell Street.

On your left you will see a plaque for **PHILIP AND PATTY ASTLEY** ⓳ who, in 1768, put on demonstrations of horsemanship here in a field known as Ha'penny Hatch, which led to Philip becoming known as the father of the modern circus. Stunts were performed in a circular arena as horsemen demonstrated swordplay and other acrobatics. Eventually he had to lease more land near Westminster Bridge and hire jugglers, clowns and stilt-walkers to occupy the time between acts. He eventually fixed the size of the open air arena at 13 metres (42 feet), which is the standard size for a circus still used today.

ROUPELL STREET ⑳ is named after John Roupell, a scrap metal merchant and property developer who built these houses on marshland in 1820. Originally the roads were named after members of his family, but they've changed most of them.

I suggest you take a drink at the **Kings Arms** next, because it still retains its classic pub charm and hasn't yet been ruined by new owners seeking to 'improve' it.

The street itself often pops up in TV productions such as *Doctor Who*, and many others, but my favourite thing about it is the presence of fire insurance plaques. I shan't tell you where they are, because it's more fun if you have to search for them yourself. There are a couple of them in this street, one of them being for the Sun Insurance Company, founded in 1710, which went on to become RSA (Royal and Sun Alliance). I wonder if the plaques came in useful in 1829 when a fire destroyed many of the houses here. If you didn't have a fire insurance plaque they wouldn't put out your fire. They'd just leave you to burn! Charming!

At the end of Roupell Street turn right into Hatfields, pass under the railway again, and then turn left along the railway arches. There are many bars and cafés along here, utilising the arches in a characterful way. If you are cool, young and firm-buttocked you might enjoy meeting friends here after work for the evening.

You will emerge beneath the railway bridge, near to what used to be the entrance of Blackfriars Station. Look out for the shrapnel damage on the walls caused during the war.

The big glass office block is the **PALESTRA** ㉑, which means 'wrestling arena' in Greek,

and is home to the Transport for London offices. This is where Rowland Hill's Surrey Chapel used to be in the 18th century. It was a chapel built in a round shape, so that the Devil couldn't hide in the corners!

In 1910 former middleweight boxing champion Dick Burge bought the chapel building and turned it into a boxing venue called The Ring, with the help of some local homeless people.

When Dick died of pneumonia in 1918 his wife, Bella (who was the first woman to attend a boxing match), took up the reins, popularising The Ring as a place for famous celebrities to go – even King Edward VIII attended. In later years Bella was featured on *This Is Your Life*, which some older readers may remember. She is one of the people with a plaque on the ground near the skateboarders earlier.

If you feel partial to another pint, opposite Palestra you will find the pub named after the boxing venue. **The Ring** actually used to have its own boxing gym (which has now moved to some nearby arches) and you will still see plenty of old photos and boxing memorabilia on the walls.

On the corner across Blackfriars Road from the pub, on top of a lamppost, you should see a **SCULPTURE OF A DOG LICKING A BOWL** ㉒. A blacksmith's shop stood here in Victorian times, with a dog and bowl sign above the door (the present-day sculpture is a replica). Charles Dickens knew it well; he had to walk past here on his way to the Marshalsea Prison where his dad was incarcerated.

My usual way home was over Blackfriars Bridge, and down that turning in the

*Blackfriars Road which has Rowland
Hill's chapel on one side, and the likeness
of a golden dog licking a golden pot over a
shop-door on the other.*

Look out also for the coal hole cover on the ground with the logo of the ironmongers who cast it. They would sell metal bowls and 'fire dogs' (parts of a fireplace).

Head along Union Street towards the railway viaduct. If you are on a pub crawl or fancy a tasty burger in a quirky pub, stop at the **Lord Nelson** on the corner of Gambia Street. I rather like it with its interesting decor.

Alternatively just turn left into Gambia Street and through a little garden to Dolben Street. Look out for the blue plaque commemorating **MARY WOLLSTONECRAFT 23**, early feminist and mother of Mary Shelley (author of *Frankenstein*), who lived here.

It was also in this street in 1835 that James Pratt, William Bonill and John Smith were arrested for buggery! William Bonill was transported to Australia, but James Pratt and John Smith became the last men in England to be hanged for sodomy. Poor old William

Bonill wasn't even there at the time, but his landlord (who had spied Pratt and Smith through the keyhole, the dirty old so and so!) stated that he frequently had male visitors who would arrive in twos. I guess that was enough to send him to Australia!

Now, only do this if you have time and if you've checked it's open, but just around the corner in Southwark Street, a little off our route but worth a visit, is **KIRKALDY'S TESTING WORKS 24**. It's a listed building which contains a museum displaying the original machinery of David Kirkaldy, a pioneer of testing standards during the industrial revolution. He created all sorts of machines to see how strong certain metals were and if you come here on the days when it's open you can see them pulling apart iron bars, pianos and tennis rackets, or anything you like!! Be sure to check their website, because it has limited opening hours.

If you didn't make it to the museum, just head back to Union Street and continue along it in the same direction as before, and then take a right down Pepper Street. I just like these streets with old buildings on them. Turn left into Copperfield Street, past some charming old houses.

Many of the streets around here have names pertaining to Charles Dickens – Copperfield Street, Little Dorrit Court, etc. – because it was near here that his dad was in Marshalsea Prison, next to today's Borough tube station. We're not going there on this walk, but you can always see the location on your way home, remembering to watch the Joolz Guides video about it first!

At the end of Copperfield Street is Great Guildford Street. Turn left, and then right into Doyce Street.

The **SIGN** 25 on the wall bids you to 'COMMIT NO NUISANCE', which basically means: don't pee against the wall!!! If you do need to pee, don't worry – because we are just getting to a lovely pub called the **Lord Clyde**, which you should be able to see ahead of you, across the junction of Southwark Bridge Road and Marshalsea Road, in Clennam Street. It's a listed building because it represents a good example of what pubs looked like at the turn of the 20th century. I always feel like I'm walking back into the 1970s when I enter; I can imagine the place filled with smoke and a big old cathode ray tube television in the corner showing the snooker.

Ah, well… Those were the days.

I'll take a pint of ale, please. Whatever's popular.

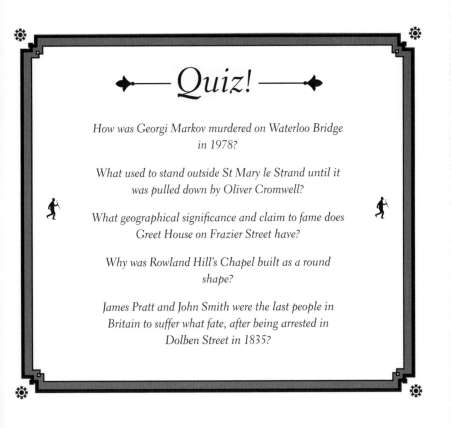

✦ — *Quiz!* — ✦

How was Georgi Markov murdered on Waterloo Bridge in 1978?

What used to stand outside St Mary le Strand until it was pulled down by Oliver Cromwell?

What geographical significance and claim to fame does Greet House on Frazier Street have?

Why was Rowland Hill's Chapel built as a round shape?

James Pratt and John Smith were the last people in Britain to suffer what fate, after being arrested in Dolben Street in 1835?

15

15 A RATHER SPLENDID WALK FROM SEVEN SISTERS TO TOTTENHAM

DISTANCE
5.6 km (3.5 miles)

TIME
2 hours 20 minutes

NEAREST STATION
Seven Sisters

Okay, I know what you're thinking. This doesn't look very pretty.

Well, it's true that Tottenham High Road isn't top of most people's tourism destinations – but Joolz Guides isn't just for tourists. We seek to point out that all areas of London have wonderful, interesting, beautiful and crazy little secrets.

For example, on the corner of Seven Sisters Road and Tottenham High Road there is a rather nice period building known as **WARD'S CORNER** ❶. This used to be an Edwardian furniture store, trading up until 1972. In recent times it has become a Latin American market, reflecting the great cultural diversity of the neighbourhood. At the time of writing they are embroiled in a battle to prevent the indoor market and the parade of shops from being turned into

luxury flats and gentrified outlets. It remains to be seen what the outcome will be.

The High Road used to be a Roman road to Lincoln called Ermine Street, around which Tottenham grew, with woodland to the west and marshland to the east. No one really knows what Tottenham means – it's thought it could refer to a number of things, including someone's name. The 'ham' bit definitely means what we would today call a 'hamlet' or 'small village', though.

As you head north you'll see Ashmount Road on your right, with a small green called **PAGE GREEN COMMON** ❷. If you're wondering why this area is called Seven Sisters, it's because of the seven trees that were planted here in a creepy circular *Blair Witch* style. I always imagine horror-film sacrifices being made here. Back in 1350, it is said, there were seven sisters who were about to embark on various journeys in separate directions and they decided to plant seven elm trees around a walnut tree.

The elms survived until 1833, spawning the name of the nearby Seven Sisters Road. Fast forward to 1997 and five families decided it was time to remember these old landmarks by planting new ones. These five families each had seven sisters, too. I don't know exactly where the original trees stood, but these modern ones are good enough for me. Come on, let's get out of here.

Across the main road towards the station, coming off the High Road, is West Green Road.

West Green Road is a useful local shopping street with many cafés, supermarkets and grocery stores. You'll find a range of African, Asian and Turkish shops, hair salons and restaurants. In fact, why not go and see my friends at **UNCLE JOHN'S BAKERY 3**? They were the first to bake Ghanaian sweet bread in London – and have cooked for the Prime Minister, too. I like their 'chin chins', which are very moreish. If you're feeling brave you could try their famous extra hot 'Shito' chilli sauce! (I don't think they find the name as amusing as I do, but that's probably because in one of the Ghanaian dialects it simply means 'pepper'.) Oh, and say 'tally ho' from me, too!

Turn off West Green Road up Portland Road (right just before the railway bridge if you're coming from the High Road, or left just after the railway bridge if you've been to Uncle John's Bakery).

At the end of Portland Road, the gated entrance to the Portland Place housing estate in front of you is all that survives of the **AUSTRO-BAVARIAN LAGER BEER BREWERY AND CRYSTAL ICE FACTORY 4**. Breweries creating ale were pretty commonplace in the 19th century – but this was the first dedicated lager beer brewery in the UK. Established in 1881, it was staffed by immigrant Germans and their English families who brewed the first 'Tottenham Lager'.

Some reports of it tasting a bit like garlic or curry caused them to change the name of the brewery to the Tottenham Lager Brewery, which eventually closed in 1903. (Curry-flavoured lager sounds okay to me!)

Return to the High Road via Pelham Road behind you.

Then turn left onto the High Road.

Continue northwards toward **TOTTENHAM GREEN 5**, passing on the right a highly regarded Nigerian tapas restaurant called Chuku's.

Tottenham Green is where the main village started, with six inns, various charitable institutions, alms houses and mansions springing up between 1500 and 1700. It remained a place for the upper middle class until 1870, when the railway was extended

to Tottenham. Workmen were offered cheaper fares on the train and this attracted more workers to the area.

To the right you can still see some nice old houses, giving some idea of how the area might have looked in the days when artist J.M.W. Turner used to come here to visit Benjamin Godfrey Windus (the great art collector, who was one of his patrons).

Luke Howard, father of meteorology and 'Namer of Clouds', also lived here. You can blame him for those boring geography lessons when you had to learn about nimbus, stratus and cirrostratus clouds!

I wonder if this is what led Turner's friend Mr Rose to recount:

'On one occasion I had the audacity to ask [Turner] if he painted his clouds from nature. One has heard of "calling up a look". The words had hardly passed my lips when I saw my gaucherie. I was afraid I had roused a thunderstorm; however, my lucky star predominated, for, after having eyed me for a few moments with a slight frown, he growled out, "How would you have me paint them?" Then seizing upon his fishing-rod, and turning upon his heel, he marched indignantly out of the house to the water's-edge.'

On the left you will see the old fire station, public baths and town hall. In 1965 Tottenham, Hornsey and Wood Green boroughs merged to become the London Borough of Haringey, at which point this town hall ceased to be a local seat of government.

Note also the memorial for Cynthia Jarrett, whose death sparked the Broadwater Farm riots. We won't be visiting the Broadwater Farm Estate on this walk, as it is a bit out of the way, but it is included in my video about the area. Through the magic of TV we managed to transport ourselves there but it might be a bridge too far on this walk.

Behind these buildings looms an industrial-looking Victorian chimney. I have a fascination for these chimneys and have always wanted to live near one. This used to be part of the old ice factory and lager brewery. These days it's used for something to do with air conditioning.

On the north side of Tottenham Green you will see what we in the tourism industry call 'ABC', or 'another bloody church'! Yes, consecrated in 1830, **HOLY TRINITY CHURCH 6** was the second to be built in Tottenham. Benjamin Godfrey Windus lived opposite and donated a lot of the fittings and carpets. Perhaps the most interesting thing is the memorial to Windus's wife, Mary, which was carved by Edward Hodges Baily (who also sculpted the statue of Nelson in Trafalgar Square).

Outside the church is an **OLD WELL 7**. It was sunk in 1791 by Thomas Smith, Lord of the Manor at Bruce Castle, where we will go later. Back then the 3,000 inhabitants of Tottenham would use a bucket and rope, before pumps became more popular. The present incarnation with its tiled roof dates from 1859.

From here I recommend a detour down Philip Lane. If not, skip the section in italics and we can continue up the High Road.

The bus depot on your right was built in 1913 and used to have one of the longest routes in London; the 171 ran from West Norwood to Bruce Grove!

I rather like Philip Lane for the houses along here. For example, on the right you first come to the Forster's Cottages. Josiah Forster was a Quaker and an abolitionist who had these built as alms houses for the elderly, particularly poor widows over the age of 50. I hate to admit it, but I am approaching that age and it always makes me feel old – but I suppose being 50 in those days was probably older than it is in today's money. Fifty is the new 40, after all!

Continuing along, there are some rather attractive houses on the right-hand side, with terracotta figurines on the roof ridges. One looks like a phantom of some sort and the other is a dragon.

On the corner of Lawrence Road there is a Turkish supermarket. The great thing about this area is that you get a really wide selection of food – and they aren't overpriced, either! This building used to be a pub but now sells all sorts of different types of honey and yoghurt (proper stuff that's good for your tummy). I rather like the bread they do here, too. Look out for the ghost sign, if it's still visible, high up on the side of the building.

Opposite the supermarket, on the corner of Kitchener Road, is the Diamond Off-Licence. This used to be the Williams Brothers Store, above which lived Dave Clark from the Dave Clark Five. They were pretty successful in the 1960s, with hits like 'Glad All Over' and 'Do You Love Me'. Dave Clark's music spawned what became known as the 'Tottenham Sound', although it's not much spoken of these days. They just sound a bit like the Beatles to me.

Further along Philip Lane, at the corner with Summerhill Road, is a terrace of old workers' cottages. At least, I assume they were workers' cottages because the area was popular with

workers in the 19th century and there is a charming plaque (looking rather decayed) with the motto LABOR VINCIT OMNIA – 'work conquers all'.

Okay, now go back to the old well to resume our walk along the High Road.

Looking up the High Road from the well you can see a monument known as the **HIGH CROSS** 8 . Originally there was a wooden wayside cross here (first recorded in 1409) but it was replaced by this one in the early 1600s by the Dean of Armagh, Owen Wood.

These days it has (confusingly) a weathervane on top of it instead of a cross, added during 'enhancements' in 1809. It would have originally had a cross much like the Eleanor crosses erected by Edward I in memory of his wife (such as Charing Cross). However, this is not one of the Eleanor crosses, even though it happens to be on the route from Lincoln, as hers were.

Wayside crosses were used as markers for pilgrims and walkers, often indicating dangerous places where you should keep your wits about you.

One dangerous occurrence that took place here in 1651 was a duel between Messrs John Nelham and John Whiston, who came at each other with 'pick staffs'. Perhaps they were inspired by the famous humorous poem from the 1400s called 'The Tournament of Tottenham', in which the protagonists fight a duel on old mares, armed to the teeth with farming equipment!

Nearby is a good place to stop for a pee… Well, it used to be a public lavatory and I daresay they still have a lavatory because it has been transformed into a rather charming

PUB

The High Cross

pub called the **High Cross**. There is more room inside than you would expect and there is outdoor seating, too.

Bottoms up!

But wait! This isn't the end of the walk. I just fancied a beer.

Let's keep going north and over to your left, down Drapers Road, you can see a yellow brick building called **OLD SCHOOL COURT** ❾. It used to be a school but is now a rather nice place to live! I have a friend who lives there who assures me they have very high ceilings. Terrific!

Okay, continue along the High Road and you will see a big old Victorian theatre on the left, opposite which is a **POLICE STATION** ❿, where the Tottenham Outrage began.

On the opposite corner of Chesnut Road there used to be a rubber factory. In 1909 Paul Helfeld and Jacob Lepidus, a couple of Latvian anarchists, held up the van carrying the wages of the workers there. Two policemen gave chase and gradually other members of the public joined in. One bloke was on a bicycle waving a cutlass, one housewife threw a potato and eventually a huge chase ensued,

which sounds like the closing credits of *The Benny Hill Show*. However, this was anything other than a comedy.

Having crossed the nearby River Lea, the miscreants commandeered a tram on Chingford Road, with the police chasing them on another tram. They then switched to a milk van, which they wrecked, finally switching to a greengrocer's horse and cart, before running across the marshes and getting cornered in an old barn. Both men ended up shooting themselves in the head, Lepidus dying straight away and Helfeld dying a few weeks later.

Four hundred rounds of gunfire were exchanged, during which a 10-year-old boy died, as did a policeman, whose plaque you can see on the side of the police station here. He has a charming gravestone in Abney Park Cemetery in Stoke Newington, with a policeman's helmet on it.

Crime doesn't pay, kids.

As you continue walking up the High Road, keep an eye out for many of the ghost signs on various buildings. I'm always fascinated by these signs – old pieces of advertising or publicity from Victorian times which you see painted onto walls, but have long since become redundant and disused. See, for example, the one for O'Meara Camping Ltd on St Loys Road, coming up on your left.

On the right-hand side of the High Road, opposite the O'Meara ghost sign, is Stoneleigh Road, where you will find a pretty cool pub called the **Beehive**, where they hold lots of unusual events such as life drawing classes and yoga... as well as serving a good pint!

Score yourself some **STREET FURNITURE CHALLENGE** points (see page 8) for the GR (King George V) post box on the corner!!

Continue up the High Road and eventually you will arrive at Bruce Grove Overground station, after which it's worth taking a brief detour left up Bruce Grove for 50 yards or so. On the right is Roller Nation, where you can go to a roller disco housed in what used to be the old cinema. Opposite this is **THE ONLY BLUE PLAQUE IN TOTTENHAM ⑪**, that of Luke Howard, whom we discussed earlier. He used to live on Tottenham Green but later moved here. I love the title 'Namer of Clouds'.

Back on the High Road, directly opposite Bruce Grove, there is an alleyway that smells of urine with lots of graffiti on the walls. If you are interested in street art you might want to visit the cheerful and charismatic fellow at VIP (Very Important Paint) on Stoneleigh Road. This is where street artists can purchase all sorts of special paint named after various parts of London. Sometimes the gate will be locked but he's still open. You just have to walk around via the next street, Factory Lane. He'll keep you entertained with all sorts of tales about all the street artists who have been in.

Further along the High Road you will come to an ALDI supermarket just before number 594. On the opposite side of the road, and indeed along the street, you will see many beautiful Georgian houses. These might look a little out of place but they demonstrate how the area once attracted the upper middle classes. In fact, it is gradually doing so once again as it becomes more gentrified. I think I even saw a Costa Coffee!

Behind number 594 you should be able to see the **FRIENDS MEETING HOUSE FOR QUAKERS ⑫**. This part of London, along with Stoke Newington, attracted many Quakers, abolitionists and religious dissenters. At this particular meeting house towards the end of the 19th century, Henry Chalkley (who was, rather pleasingly, a 'Quaker baker') created the Tottenham cake, which you can still buy today in various bakeries. It is like a sponge cube with pink icing on it; some people add hundreds and thousands. If you look carefully you might be able to see the mulberry tree in the garden, which provided the mulberries from which he created the pink icing. The cake was sold at a penny a cube. When Tottenham Hotspur Football Club won the FA cup in 1901 (the first non-league club to do so) it was given to children for free to celebrate.

On a personal note, I must protest about the dearth of Tottenham cake in Tottenham. I'm sure they must have it, but I've struggled to find it here and have to get mine in Camden! This also happened when I tried to buy Chelsea buns in Chelsea. Have you ever had a problem like this? I do hope I can find Scotch eggs in Scotland and Yorkshire pudding in Yorkshire!

By the way, Tottenham cake is not to be confused with Tottenham pudding. During the war Tottenham was heavily targeted and food shortages led to household waste being used to feed pigs and poultry. This was mashed together and named 'Tottenham pudding' by Queen Mary on a visit here.

At any point along the High Road you might wish to buy some Turkish *gözleme* if you're feeling peckish. There are some nice places to get this along here and they are much cheaper than in other parts of London!

Keep going, past the **Bluecoats**, which used to be a school (opened in 1735, although the present building dates from 1833), and continue past more period buildings, always remembering to look up to appreciate fully how the street might once have looked before the shop façades ruined the aesthetic. On the right you will pass the **OLD WHITBREAD BREWERY** ⓭ and on the left, just opposite, is a rather nice healthy organic grocery store and café.

Ahead of you is White Hart Lane and the stadium of **TOTTENHAM HOTSPUR FOOTBALL CLUB** ⓮.

Originally there was a cricket club here but a group of boys led by Bobby Buckle decided they needed something to do in the winter so, with the help of John Ripsher (who taught Bible Studies at the nearby All Hallows Church), Tottenham Hotspur Football Club was formed. Bobby Buckle became its first captain and goal-scorer.

They are called Hotspur after Harry Hotspur (Sir Henry Percy), whom you might know from Shakespeare's *Henry IV, Part I*. Born in 1364, he fought against the Scots and also, during the Hundred Years' War, against the French. Because he was known to be very willing and quick to attack, the Scots dubbed him 'Hot Spur'. The football team used to play on Tottenham Marshes (Northumberland Park), which was owned by descendants of Sir Henry Percy, and the emblem of the club is a cockerel standing on a football wearing a pair of spurs, which fighting cocks would often have (cockfighting being a popular sport in days gone by – it still is in some countries).

As well as being the first non-league club to win the FA Cup, Tottenham Hotspur were the first British club to win a tournament in Europe. Their glory days are mostly behind them now, but they hope to turn their fortunes around with this new stadium, which cost a billion pounds.

Unfortunately they were struck by delays, and the Covid-19 pandemic hit just as the stadium opened. It is one of the biggest in Europe and you can even do the 'Sky Walk', where you walk over the top for a great view of London and abseil down the side.

Famous Spurs supporters have included singers Adele and Bob Marley, cricketer Michael Holding, and Chas & Dave, who wrote such classics as 'Ossie's Dream' and 'When the Year Ends in 1', marking the fact that Spurs won trophies in 1901, 1921, 1951, 1961, 1971, 1981 and 1991.

Famous players to have graced the hallowed turf include Jimmy Greaves, Glen Hoddle, Ossie Ardiles, Paul Gascoigne, Jürgen Klinsmann and Harry Kane. Also Walter Tull, a remarkable man who became the first Black player to receive racial abuse, while playing in 1909. Born in Folkestone, Tull served in two football battalions of the Duke of Cambridge's Middlesex Regiment during the First World War. He fought at the Somme and became the first Black officer to lead white soldiers into battle, even though Black and mixed-heritage people were banned from being commissioned officers. In his case they made an exception.

WHITE HART LANE

Sadly he died in action and despite Tom Billingham, the Leicester City goalkeeper, taking heavy fire to try to retrieve his body, he remains in a foreign field somewhere, that is forever Folkestone.

Across the road you might want to take a pint in the **Beavertown Corner Pin** if you're interested in the local brews. (Beavertown have a brewery nearby, but not on this walk.)

In my video about Tottenham we finish just after the stadium on the left, at the **Bricklayers Arms**, a spacious pub popular on football days, with a big garden and lots of Spurs photos on the wall. Worth seeing if you're into football – and aren't an Arsenal fan! However, today we still have some things to see, so we're turning up Church Road, opposite the Corner Pin.

Keep walking for a few minutes, all the way to the end of Church Road, and then turn left into Church Lane. Ahead of you is **BRUCE CASTLE PARK ⑮**.

It will feel a bit like passing through to a different dimension as everything becomes very calm and serene.

In the middle of the park try to find the old oak tree. You can't really miss it, because it's 7 metres (23 feet) in circumference (I measured it). It was entered into the Tree of the Year competition by the Woodland Trust; apparently, it's one of the largest in Great Britain. It's had to have a few repairs down the years, though, as it's over 450 years old. In fact, Queen Elizabeth I would have seen it when she came to visit Bruce Castle in 1578 – and indeed it would have been a sapling when King Henry VIII came to visit his sister Margaret in 1516.

Beyond the oak tree is **BRUCE CASTLE ⑯**, which looks more like a large house, really – but it does have a splendid tower outside, possibly used for keeping falcons. It's named Bruce Castle after the Bruce family (as in Robert the Bruce from *Braveheart*), who owned the land on which it was built in the 16th century, and is where the lords of the manor used to live.

Amongst the many goings-on here down the years was the tragedy of the second Baron Coleraine's wife in the 17th century. Legend has it that because Coleraine was still so much in love with his ex-girlfriend, his wife

Constantia could take it no more and threw herself from the tower, clutching her baby to her breast. They say her ghost still haunts the grounds to this day.

During the 19th century Sir Rowland Hill, who invented the postage stamp, was the headmaster of a progressive school for boys here. Inside they hold exhibitions and events, and the building also houses the archives of much of Tottenham's history.

Head around the back of Bruce Castle and into Church Lane, where you will see ABC (another bloody church again)... except this one is superb. **ALL HALLOWS CHURCH 17** was founded in 1150, although the present building dates from the 14th century. It is the oldest building in Tottenham, standing on land donated by King David I of Scotland, whose sculpted head you can see adorning the side of the main entrance with his wife Margaret.

The church tower houses a peal of eight bells and you can learn campanology (that's the art of bellringing) at weekends. However,

my favourite bell is not one of the eight; it is the service bell, high up in the tower and smaller than the others.

The interesting thing about it is that if this bell had been rung in time in 1759, Canada would have been French rather than British. I know!!!! This was the garrison bell of Quebec. The French Army didn't realise that the British were climbing up the sides of the hill, so it wasn't rung in time. It was looted and eventually gifted to All Hallows Church.

The church also contains a lot of beautiful artwork, including a memorial featuring seven sisters carved by Britain's first great sculptor, Edward Marshall, and many other pieces which seem like they should be in an art gallery or a museum.

Outside there is a large cemetery, which you might wish to wander around. It is not part of the church's cemetery, though. In fact, it would have been built in Victorian times, when the church graveyards became too full. In Elizabethan times it would have cost two shillings for parishioners to be buried, but double that for foreigners – and even more, depending on how many times you wanted the bell tolled!

If you wander around the cemetery you might just have time for a game of Pooh Sticks on a little bridge over the remnants of the River Moselle, before heading back to the corner of Church Road and Church Lane (which we passed earlier). Here you will find a charming little pub called the **Antwerp Arms**, commanding splendid views of the park and claiming to be Tottenham's oldest working pub. After an attempt was made to knock it down in 2013, members of the community clubbed together and bought it so that we can enjoy a tipple here, at what they call 'the Annie'. There's even a photo of Chas & Dave on the wall!!

Bring ale, bring pie, and let us drink to Jimmy Greaves, Tottenham's top goal-scorer, who died on the day that I wrote this. He played in the 1966 World Cup but was left out of the final due to injury, thereby not receiving a winner's medal until 2009, when they changed the rules. He was regarded by many as England's greatest ever goal-scorer.

Cheers, Jimmy. Here's to you.

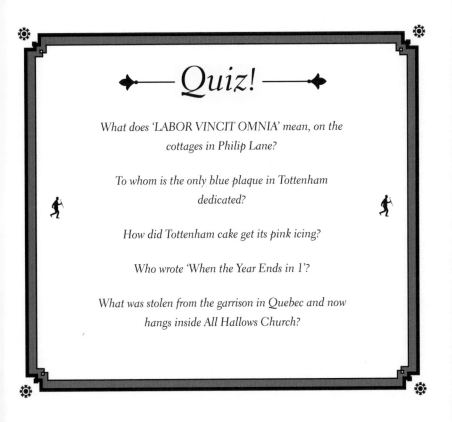

✦— *Quiz!* —✦

What does 'LABOR VINCIT OMNIA' mean, on the cottages in Philip Lane?

To whom is the only blue plaque in Tottenham dedicated?

How did Tottenham cake get its pink icing?

Who wrote 'When the Year Ends in 1'?

What was stolen from the garrison in Quebec and now hangs inside All Hallows Church?

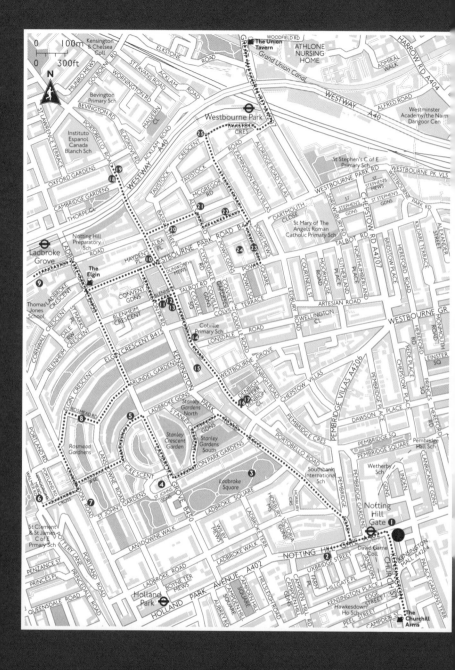

16

16 A JOLLY MARVELLOUS JAUNT AROUND NOTTING HILL

DISTANCE
7.7 km (4.8 miles)

TIME
3 hours 15 minutes

NEAREST STATION
Notting Hill Gate

Start by meeting your friends at the Churchill Arms on Kensington Church Street (not far from Notting Hill Gate tube).

This beautiful pub was built in 1750 and whilst you've been waiting for your mates to show up you will have noticed all the patriotic memorabilia inside pertaining to Winston Churchill (amongst other subjects). However, it was only named the Churchill Arms after the war. There is no evidence that Churchill himself ever drank here, although it is true that his grandparents were frequent visitors in the 19th century. To see it in all its glory it's best to visit in the summertime, when the whole exterior is covered in flowers. They spend £25,000 per year on the floral display and it's the only pub to have won at the Chelsea Flower Show! It's definitely a must for your Instagram account!

Once you've chinned your pint, come out and turn left up towards Notting Hill Gate.

It's hard to believe that a couple of hundred years ago this area was occupied by pig farmers and potteries. As much of the soil is clay, it was the perfect place to make tiles

PUB
The Churchill Arms

and pots. The pig farmers, meanwhile, had been kicked out of Marble Arch once that area had become more popular. Until the 1840s you would have been surrounded by coaching inns and workers' cottages.

Here at the junction of Notting Hill Gate and Kensington Church Street there used to be a toll gate. Hence the 'Gate'. 'Notting' most probably comes from some Saxon person's name (perhaps Cnotta), with 'ing' meaning a settlement of people.

Just across the road is the **MUSIC AND VIDEO EXCHANGE** ❶, where I bought most of my record collection! Many of my favourite albums by the likes of Bowie and Depeche Mode only cost me about 50p, but these days prices are a bit higher. I expect there are still a few Yes and Bread albums at reasonable prices, though. The quality of the vinyl in the bargain basement is actually not too bad! Definitely worth flicking through the rarer items, too. If you have any CDs or vinyl that you don't want, they will exchange it for you or even buy it.

Come out of the record shop and turn right (west). Further along the street on the left, after the junction, is the **CORONET THEATRE** ❷, which opened in 1898. One hundred years later it featured in *Notting Hill*, where Hugh Grant watches a film starring the love of his life, played by Julia Roberts.

Now walk back and turn left up Pembridge Road. Along the right-hand side there are more 'exchange' shops like the Music and Video Exchange, except that these range from retro vintage clothing to bric-à-brac and household items. One can easily while away a few hours looking for cool little bargains here and again, you can sell and exchange items of your own.

Usually, if you were just going to Portobello Road Market, you would continue along Pembridge Road and turn left at Portobello Road. There are more nice shops and pubs along there – but dammit, this is a walking tour, so let's take a left down Kensington Park Road.

Walk past the excellent green hut (one of the cabmen's shelters, which you can read about in the **STREET FURNITURE CHALLENGE**, page 13) and keep going until you reach a private garden on your left. This is **LADBROKE SQUARE GARDEN** ❸ – the largest private garden square in London. Notting Hill is riddled with these private gardens, which are only for special people who live in the surrounding houses. I'm not special enough to have ever been in one, but they look jolly nice.

In the 1820s James Ladbroke, the main landowner here, started developing the estate to make it more fashionable and appealing, with proper drainage systems and churches as a part of a model scheme. That's why so many streets and squares bear his name. Instead of having houses surrounding a square with a road going around it, he decided to give the houses access through the rear of the properties to these private garden squares, which makes them still very desirable today, keeping riff-raff like us out.

Keep going straight, past more private gardens and the Consulate of Ukraine, and when you reach the sandy-coloured St Peter's Church, turn left into Stanley Gardens.

George V post box alert!!!! (See the **STREET FURNITURE CHALLENGE** on page 8.) I've spotted a few old street signs around here, too.

Turn left and follow Stanley Crescent round to the end and turn right.

Why? Because the houses are jolly splendid and I wanted you to notice the number of crescents and curved roads there are in the area.

By now you should be standing in front of **ST JOHN'S CHURCH** ❹ on Ladbroke Grove, which was intended to be the mainstay of James Ladbroke's whole Garden City scheme.

(Score yourself more points by spotting the King Edward VII post box on the corner. That little abandoned fountain is jolly nice, too.)

The reason for the strange circular layout of the streets here is that in 1837 businessman John Whyte fenced off the whole area for a horseracing track known as the Hippodrome. (The term comes from ancient Greek, with '*hippos*' meaning 'horse' and '*dromos*' meaning 'racecourse'.)

Unfortunately the Hippodrome wasn't very successful. It kept getting flooded due to the clay soil, and the local pig farmers got very annoyed that the public right of way through the course got blocked off. So it closed after five years and if you look at a map you can really see how the houses and streets follow the shape of the racecourse.

Next we're going to visit Lansdowne Crescent. However, don't take the first turning into Lansdowne Crescent, which is next to the church. Instead, head along Ladbroke Grove and then take the next turning on the left, which will take us into the other end of the crescent.

At **22 LANSDOWNE CRESCENT** ❺ is the hotel where Jimi Hendrix died at the age of 27. Many people regard him as the greatest rock guitarist ever to have lived – the Beatles were astonished when they first saw him play. Paul McCartney regarded it as a great honour when Hendrix opened his set at the Saville Club with a rendition of 'Sgt. Pepper's Lonely Hearts Club Band', only a few days after they had released it themselves!

Hendrix had been suffering from a great amount of stress, due to a couple of legal fights – one was a paternity case and the other was a recording contract dispute – and he was taking a lot of drugs. His last live performance had been the previous night, when Eric Burdon, former lead singer of the Animals, had invited him to jam with him at Ronnie Scott's in Soho. Apparently, his performance was pretty subdued; he had originally meant to perform the night before that, but had been far too wrecked. On the morning of 18 September 1970 he was found dead, having choked on his vomit.

Carry on round the crescent and then turn right into Lansdowne Rise.

Walk to the end and do what is known in calculus as 'a point of inflection where $dy/dx = 0$' – or, as I like to say, a little shimmy left and then right at the end, into Clarendon Cross, which becomes Hippodrome Place.

Cute shops? Check.
Bijoux restaurants? Check.
More post boxes? Check.

HIPPODROME PLACE

I find it pleasing that all these street names survive, and many people wouldn't know why. But next time you're here with a friend you can impress them by telling them all about the etymology of the word 'hippodrome' and the racecourse!

You should emerge at the Earl of Zetland, which used to be a pub but has now sadly become offices. What a shame.

It's amazing to think that this whole area was occupied by poor pig farmers and potters in the 19th century. Just to the right, down Walmer Road, is a rather excellent surviving **KILN 6**! This is where they would have fired their tiles and bricks. That's why the street next to the Zetland is called Pottery Lane. Maybe your house was made out of tiles and bricks from this very kiln!!

By the way, fans of *Minder* might recognise some of the houses in Princedale Road, adjacent to Pottery Lane. I saw an episode once where Terry McCann was living in the building on the corner of Penzance Street and Princedale Road. (Well, I cared, anyway…) I just find it amazing to see how smart the buildings are these days, whereas in the 1970s and 1980s when *Minder* was filmed they all looked really run-down.

Now retrace your steps back to the point of inflection (where dy/dx = 0) at the junction of Clarendon Road and Clarendon Cross.

OM actual G!!! Look to your right!!!!

No, not the blue plaque on 50 Clarendon Road for **EMMELINE AND CHRISTABEL PANKHURST 7**.

I'm talking about the stink pipe opposite that!!! Yay!!!! (See the **STREET FURNITURE CHALLENGE**, page 12, for details.)

I'm not going there myself on this walk, but if you're a fan of the TV show *Absolutely Fabulous* you might want to turn right here to see 30 Clarendon Road, home to Edina Monsoon, sweetie darling, played by Jennifer Saunders.

But that's a slight detour, so let's turn left down Clarendon Road, then right into Elgin Crescent.

Are you a fan of the film *Notting Hill*? I keep going on about it, but I really like it, soppy though it is. You should watch it. If you don't cry then you have a heart of stone.

Just off Elgin Crescent is Rosmead Road and Rosmead Gardens, the site of the famous **'WHOOPSIDAISIES' GATE 8** where Hugh Grant tries, pathetically, to climb over with Julia Roberts. I don't know what would happen if you tried to climb over these days, but I expect someone would shout 'Oi!!!!!!' and you'd have to make good your escape.

Carry on past the gardens and turn left into Lansdowne Road, past yet more houses that I couldn't afford. (At time of writing, that is!!!! Hope springs eternal…) They were intended for middle and professional classes and many of them had mews stables, but the properties failed to attract their intended target. Therefore many of these grand houses around Notting Hill ended up being divided up into smaller flats. By the 1950s many of the flats were occupied by immigrants from the West Indies, which explains why, since 1966, the Notting Hill Carnival has taken place every summer.

These days living in Notting Hill is very expensive – well, these houses along here are, anyway!

Now turn left and walk all the way to the

The Churchill Arms

❶

❻

❾

❿

⓬

end of Ladbroke Grove before turning left into Lancaster Road (just before the railway bridge).

By the way, the cypher on the bollards here is 'RBKC': the Royal Borough of Kensington and Chelsea.

Along here on the left you will come to the **MUSEUM OF BRANDS** ❾. I love these strange little museums dotted all over London. I find them infinitely more fascinating than all the big famous ones.

Inside you will find all sorts of packaging, containers, toys, posters, games, packets of biscuits and laundry detergents that you haven't seen for years. They also have 'wind pills' for seasickness, items from the Great Exhibition of 1851 and much more. It can be quite alarming seeing things that you recognise from your childhood in a museum! It definitely makes you feel a bit old, but if you want a nostalgic look at brands from the last two centuries it's worth a look!

Right, okay. Time for a drink. All those hills are making my legs ache.

How about a quick pint at the **Elgin**!

Come out of the museum, back the way you came, turn right on Ladbroke Grove and it's there on your left, on the corner of Westbourne Park Road.

The Elgin is a beautiful 19th-century pub. Although it was popular with John Christie (the serial killer who lived at 10 Rillington Place nearby) I'm more attracted by the fact that during the 1970s Joe Strummer from The Clash used to come here, in the days when it attracted punks.

Splendid. I needed that! Now, let's carry on. Turn left out of the pub and up Westbourne Park Road.

By the way, the Egyptian decor on number 300 isn't original. It was added by the owner, who just happened to be into history.

Keep going past that.

Yes, yes, I know: more about the film *Notting Hill*… Well, at 280 Westbourne Park Road is **THE FAMOUS BLUE DOOR** ❿ to the house of Hugh Grant's character, where Rhys Ifans answers the door in his underpants. It used to be occupied by Richard Curtis, who wrote the film, but the current owners of the house don't seem to find it very amusing when people in their underpants ring the doorbell and take selfies. I hear they even sold the actual door and painted the new one a different colour, but when I visited it was still blue (though my underpants weren't).

Wait for it! Wait for it!!

We're not going up Portobello Road *yet*. Just quickly go back the way you came and turn left into Kensington Park Road, past more cafés and boutiques, and then left again into Blenheim Crescent.

Here you will see the original **BOOKSHOP** ⓫ on which Curtis based the shop in the film, though it wasn't filmed here – that's coming up…

What I really like is **THE SPICE SHOP** ⓬, a few doors along, with the cheerful yellow canopy.

In 1990 Birgit Erath was studying for a degree in business and needed some extra income, so she started selling spices on a stall in

PORTOBELLO ROAD

Portobello Road. By 1995 she had finished her degree and opened up The Spice Shop full time. It's the only shop of its kind in the UK, selling over 2,500 products. She is now revered as one of the foremost experts on blending spices and mixing and trading herbs, and has inspired many famous chefs.

Right… Deep breath: Portobello Road.

This is the sort of place where you can easily spend the whole day wandering up and down. Originally, in the 19th century, this was a country lane leading to Portobello Farm, where people would trade horses, no doubt influenced by the horse-racing track nearby. But after the railways arrived and the farm got built over with houses, Portobello Road developed into a much busier market, dealing in antiques, food and second-hand goods.

The best day to visit is Saturday.

From The Spice Shop turn right into Portobello Road, and walk past the **ELECTRIC CINEMA** **13**, opened in 1911. They don't make them like they used to! The interior is beautiful and retains the decor of the era.

In the 1940s John Christie, the notorious serial killer, is believed to have worked as a projectionist here! The cinema nearly got turned into an antiques market in the 1980s but thanks to 10,000 signatures, including

those of Anthony Hopkins and Audrey Hepburn, it survived!

You'll probably find plenty of things to distract you along Portobello Road, but let me carry on with my obsessions. At number 142 there is a souvenir shop with a sign above it: **'THE TRAVEL BOOKSHOP NOTTING HILL' 14**. Just in case there is any doubt, they also have a big picture of Julia Roberts in the window. Even though this isn't a bookshop, it is the location they used in the movie.

Keep going and you'll find that a lot of the stalls and shops at this end focus on antiques. My sister used to work in the clock centre along here and often took calls from people like Martin Scorsese trying to find the right clock for their film production.

In the old days you could get cheques cashed in a few of the places around here, which I always found a weird thing. These days people don't even know what a cheque is! My friend was trying to watch *Fawlty Towers* with his kids recently, but he said it was completely ruined for him because every two minutes the kids asked: 'Daddy, what's a cheque?', 'Daddy, what's a record player?' and so on.

Dotted all over the place you'll see various locations named after Admiral Vernon – pubs, streets, etc. He was the admiral who captured Puerto Bello, in Panama, during the pleasingly named War of Jenkins' Ear in 1739. Hence the name Portobello Road, commemorating his victory. One of Vernon's officers was Laurence Washington, half-brother of George Washington!

Further along on the right, opposite a row of hedges, is a tiny little turning into a mews called Vernon Yard. The offices at **2–4 VERNON YARD** are where Richard Branson started Virgin Records in 1972; he went on to sign the Sex Pistols, The Human League, Culture Club and Simple Minds, among others.

Continue a little further along Portobello Road until you come to Denbigh Close, with the charming antiques shop called **ALICE'S** on the corner. You might recognise this shop as 'Gruber's', where Paddington Bear gets his pop-up book for Aunt Lucy in the excellent film *Paddington*, which I recommend!! The shop itself is just as cluttered as it is in the film. If you want to buy an old cricket bat, a 1920s portmanteau or a hat-stand, this is your place! A few doors away, at **18 DENBIGH CLOSE** , is the house where Michael Caine's character Charlie Croker lives in *The Italian Job*. 'You're only supposed to blow the bloody doors off!'

These antiques are all very well and good, but personally I always preferred the other end of Portobello Road when I was a young punk (or so I thought). All the second-hand clothes and people selling things out of the back of their vans were at the north end.

So, head back the way you came to the other (north) end of Portobello Road, keep going, and eventually you'll go under a flyover. Further along from here is where the old Portobello Farm was. It's amazing to think how it's all changed in 200 years.

After the flyover at **NUMBER 293** , on the left, is a vintage clothing shop called Karen Vintage. It's nice that it's still a clothing shop, but it isn't the same one that was here in the 1960s when Mick Jagger and the Beatles used to visit; back then, the shop was called I Was Lord Kitchener's Valet.

They sold those military jackets which Jimi Hendrix famously wore and that the Beatles used for the *Sgt. Pepper* album.

That was all before my time but opposite, at **NUMBER 284** , was one of my favourite shops as a teenager: Planet Alice! It was opened by an ex-mortician called Christian Paris and his friend Clive Jackson (who was the Doctor from the band Doctor and the Medics), who also ran a psychedelic nightclub in Soho called Alice in Wonderland. In the shop at 284 Portobello Road you could buy all sorts of high psychedelia. I particularly liked the patchwork trousers they had, which inspired me to make a pair of my own. If you're wondering why I know so much about London, it's partly because I used to walk around the back streets of Soho endlessly hunting for bits of discarded fabric for my trousers!

Other clothes sold here were designed by Lee Starkey – Ringo Starr's daughter!

I never actually took drugs myself, but as a teenager I thought it was very cool to wear paisley shirts and purple satin trousers.

Now head back under the flyover again and turn left into Lancaster Road.

On the corner of Basing Street there's a lovely building that used to be an old church. For some time it was used as a storeroom for Madame Tussauds, before being converted by Chris Blackwell of Island Records into a music studio in 1969. Initially **ISLAND STUDIOS**, it later became **SARM WEST STUDIOS** .

So many cool artists recorded so many famous songs here that it makes me sad to tell you that they have recently turned the place into – you guessed it – luxury flats!!!

I mean, if I told you that they recorded the Band Aid single here in 1984… where Bob Geldof got all those famous stars along for his charity single, 'Do They Know It's Christmas': U2, Sting, Duran Duran, Adam Ant, George Michael and loads more!

Bob Marley recorded here… Dire Straits… The Clash… among many, many more… But most importantly, in my opinion, two of the greatest songs of all time were recorded here: 'Stairway to Heaven' by Led Zeppelin and 'Many Rivers to Cross' by Jimmy Cliff.

TUNES!!!!!!

Carry on along Lancaster Road until you reach All Saints Road and look at the curtain shop on the corner, at **20 ALL SAINTS ROAD 21**. Beatles fans might recognise this as the shop where Ringo Starr pops in to get a disguise in the film *A Hard Day's Night*.

Now walk south down All Saints Road and turn left into St Lukes Mews. It's amazing to think these pretty houses were once only good enough for horses! These mews streets are dotted all around Notting Hill and would originally have served as stables for the big properties nearby. (The other amazing thing is the confusing usage of apostrophes on the street signs around here. Some of them, like the Mews, have 'Lukes' and others, like the Road, have 'Luke's'. I mean, what was the point in my learning this stuff at school if they're just going to ignore it on street signs! I give up.)

Speaking of Bob Geldof, in 2000 his ex-wife Paula Yates died of a heroin overdose at **4 ST LUKES MEWS 22**, only three years after her then-boyfriend (Michael Hutchence from INXS) was found hanged in his hotel room. It was such a shock at the time because I'd remembered her presenting very cool TV

shows when I was growing up, including *The Tube* and *The Big Breakfast*. I wanted to work on those shows!! More tragedy followed in 2014 when one of her daughters, Peaches Geldof, also died of a heroin overdose. It makes me sad walking up this street.

At the end of St Lukes Mews turn right. Then turn right again and immediately left into Powis Terrace (another point of inflection).

In the 1950s and 1960s **NUMBERS 1–16 23** were owned by Peter Rachman, who bought up a large number of properties in Notting Hill at a time when many people from the West Indies were arriving in Britain to help with post-war regeneration. These poor people, who came after being invited by the British government, had to endure terrible prejudice and racism. Finding accommodation was difficult when many rooms had signs in the windows warning 'no blacks, no dogs, no Irish'. Rachman exploited these circumstances: although there was only room for 200 people in these flats, he managed to cram in over a thousand, extorting high rents from the tenants with threats from his hired thugs, who had scary dogs.

A short, bald man with thick, black-rimmed spectacles, Rachman looked a bit like a cross between Eric Morecambe and Captain Mainwaring from *Dad's Army*. After he died, aged 43, it emerged that he had been the lover of both Mandy Rice-Davies and Christine Keeler (of Profumo Affair fame) and that he also owned the famous mews house where they had stayed. Whatever those young women saw in millionaire Peter Rachman is beyond me…

These days there's even an expression, 'Rachmanism', which means to extort high rents with threats of violence. He sounds like a really nice, pleasant fellow!

At the end of the street turn right at the junction with Talbot Road, into Powis Square, and just behind Rachman's houses you'll see a lovely red brick Victorian place of worship, which is sometimes referred to as the 'Taj Mahal of North Kensington'. These days it's a community centre called the **TABERNACLE** **24**, overlooking Powis Square. Since the 1970s the Tabernacle has played host to many album launches and performances by the likes of the Rolling Stones, Pink Floyd, Damon Albarn, Brian Eno and both Joe Strummer and Paul Simonon from The Clash. In fact, it was after Strummer and Simonon were involved in uprisings and clashes with the police during the 1976 Notting Hill Carnival that The Clash released 'White Riot'. Perhaps most importantly, though, it was in Powis Square that Lemmy (later of Motörhead) made his debut as bass player and singer with the band Hawkwind!

Now retrace your steps, up Powis Terrace past the Rachman houses, and continue straight along St Luke's Road to the end. Talk amongst yourselves while I reminisce for a moment.

There's no need to visit it, but the next road over, Leamington Road Villas, is where a friend of ours, John, used to live. Actually, he wasn't really my friend; he was a friend of my brother's friend Stevie Stench, whose fault it is that I like all these bands.

I only mention it because it's amazing how coincidence turns out. I guess he would only have been about 20 years old at the time, but I was very scared of John as he was a leather-clad biker with long hair and I was only 16, so he was ancient to me. We used to go to his every Saturday and listen to 'Magnu' by Hawkwind and 'Stairway to Heaven' by Led Zeppelin. Then we'd go to Planet Alice… regular as clockwork, every week. If only I'd

known that 'Stairway' was recorded around the corner and that Lemmy played with Hawkwind right there! That would have blown my mind, man!

Oh well, I digress. Right, have you reached the end of St Luke's Road yet?

Do you see the modern white apartment building on the corner in front of you, **41 TAVISTOCK CRESCENT** **25**? I'm very sad they knocked the pub down that was here before, because in the film *Withnail and I* (which is one of the best cult classic British films of all time) it was where the two main characters have some drinks and have to run for their lives, after being confronted by a scary man who takes exception to the smell of essence of petunia on Paul McGann's shoes. The film shot Richard E. Grant to fame and probably remains his most memorable performance – although I liked him in *The Scarlet Pimpernel*, too! In *Withnail and I* the pub was called The Old Mother Black Cap.

> *I called him a ponce! And now I'm calling you one. PONCE!!*

The pair then run out of the pub and up the alley leading to the flyover.

In the distance beyond (if it's not obscured by the tree) you can see the much-loved-or-hated 1972 Trellick Tower, designed by Ernő Goldfinger in the brutalist style. Some people say that Ian Fleming hated Trellick Tower so much that he decided to name his famous James Bond villain after the architect, but I think in truth it was just after a disagreement between the two men. Either way, Bond's nemesis is named after the man who designed what many people feel is a very ugly tower block. I hear it's a lot nicer on the inside though, and let's face it, it's a listed building!

Anyway, we're not going up there. This might actually be a good place to finish, because if you turn right and follow Tavistock Crescent along to the end you should find Westbourne Park tube station, just around the corner on the Great Western Road.

However, after all that nostalgia I feel like I need a pint to contemplate old times. I say, there's a pub near here. Let's go for a Harold Pinter.

So at Westbourne Park tube station (where you'll see a Queen Victoria post box recessed into the wall!) I'm going to keep going, under the flyover and past the bus garage.

Just after you cross over the canal you'll find the **Union Tavern**, where there's a photo on the wall of Lemmy from Motörhead having a drink on the terrace. I think we should do the same while overlooking the canal. Here's to Lemmy. Chin chin.

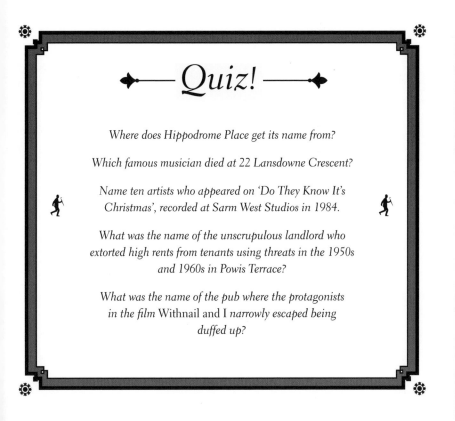

✦ — *Quiz!* — ✦

Where does Hippodrome Place get its name from?

Which famous musician died at 22 Lansdowne Crescent?

Name ten artists who appeared on 'Do They Know It's Christmas', recorded at Sarm West Studios in 1984.

What was the name of the unscrupulous landlord who extorted high rents from tenants using threats in the 1950s and 1960s in Powis Terrace?

What was the name of the pub where the protagonists in the film Withnail and I *narrowly escaped being duffed up?*

17

17 A PARTICULARLY SPIFFING WALK THROUGH KENSINGTON

DISTANCE
7.6 km (4.7 miles)

TIME
3 hours 10 minutes

NEAREST STATION
Queensway

What ho and well met! Gosh, it's hard to decide where to start these walks, but this seems a convenient spot.

Cross over the road and enter the park onto the **BROAD WALK ①**.

This is Kensington Gardens and it's jolly beautiful and big. I would usually recommend a walk around the park, but that will have to wait for another day. Today we're just walking through.

Back in the 16th century this whole area was used as hunting grounds for King Henry VIII, but in 1728 Queen Caroline, wife of King George II, asked for it to be turned into a beautiful garden. However, it wasn't until 1841 that they opened to the public. Mind you, they wouldn't let any old riffraff in.

You had to be properly dressed (whatever that meant!).

Soon on your right you should see the Princess Diana Memorial Playground. Walk towards it and look for the **ELFIN OAK ②** just on the edge of the playground. You should find it encased in a protective fence, because it's 900 years old! Around 1930 Ivor Innes decided that this old tree stump needed some residents – so he carved all these cute 'little people', saying that it had been the home of gnomes, elves, imps and fairies for hundreds of years. Within the bark you can see Huckleberry the gnome, Wookey the witch, Grumples, Groodles, Rumpledocks and Dinkie!

Now head back to the Broad Walk and I have a challenge for you.

You might not believe it, but Kensington Gardens has, for many years, been inhabited by fairies and J.M. Barrie knew this when he wrote *Peter Pan in Kensington Gardens* in 1906. We aren't visiting Peter Pan's statue on this walk because the park is too big, but if you have time definitely seek it out!

No, my challenge is for you to find **PETER PAN'S TOMBSTONES** ❸! You need to find two stones with 'PP' and 'WSM' written on them (see the box, right, for a clue as to where they are).

They aren't really tombstones – they're actually parish boundary markers (see the **STREET FURNITURE CHALLENGE**, page 11). Points!!!!! However, in the book Peter Pan goes around the park after the gates have closed at night time; rather depressingly, he finds all the dead babies that have fallen out of their prams without their mothers noticing, and then buries them!! (A bit odd for a children's story, but still…)

Two of them are supposedly buried here. Barrie writes:

> *I think that quite the most touching sight in the Gardens is the two tombstones of Walter Stephen Matthews and Phoebe Phelps.*

'PP' actually stands for 'Parish of Paddington' (not 'Phoebe Phelps') and 'WSM' is 'Westminster Saint Margaret' (not 'Walter Stephen Matthews'), indicating that you are on the boundary of the two different parishes. The '13' is supposed to indicate that poor Phoebe was 13 months old when Peter Pan found her. What a grim story. Not half as grim as what happened to the real boys who inspired the book, though! (See **Walk 6**.)

Look, you might not believe in fairies but I'm pretty sure they live here.

Now return to the Broad Walk and continue until you see **KENSINGTON PALACE** ❹. The statue of Queen Victoria you can see was actually sculpted by Victoria's daughter, Princess Louise. Victoria was born at Kensington Palace and grew up there before moving to Buckingham Palace.

You can go inside the palace, and personally I found it one of the better London attractions. (Usually I just like urine-stained

CHALLENGE
Peter Pan's Tombstones

As you walk up the Broad Walk, over to the left, about 20 yards from the path, next to a tree, try to find two stones with 'PP' and 'WSM' written on them.

alleyways and dingy pubs, so I don't talk much about the big main attractions, but I must say I enjoyed my visit!)

Originally, in 1605, Kensington Palace was just a mansion. It only became a palace when William of Orange and Queen Mary moved here in 1689. William didn't want to be near the Thames because of his asthma. Sadly, he fell off his horse after tripping over a molehill and they put him in bed to recover – but left the window open and he caught a chill and died. Careless.

These days it's where Prince William and Kate live. I beg your pardon: the Prince and Princess of Wales.

After Kensington Palace turn right and follow the path next to the palace called Studio Walk. Keep going straight through a little street where it all starts to feel a bit like you shouldn't be there but it's okay. Just walk through and you'll find yourself on **KENSINGTON PALACE GARDENS** **5**, one of the most expensive streets in the world.

Famous people who have lived here include Roman Abramovic, Bernie Ecclestone and the Sultan of Brunei. In fact, Bernie Ecclestone's wife, Slavica, didn't like it so they had to sell it to the Indian steel tycoon Lakshmi Mittal. Now they call that house the Taj Mittal! What a bunch of tacky horrible tasteless houses. Let's go.

Walk left (south) past a bunch of embassies toward the scary guys in the security huts and cross Kensington High Street. Turn right and then immediately left, down Kensington Court.

As the road narrows, look up to your left and beneath the window it says **ELECTRIC LIGHTING** **6**, which probably explains why Colonel Crompton lived here. He was an expert in installing electricity for Viennese theatres – but as far as I'm concerned, his greatest achievement was the invention of the electric toaster!!! Anyway, this big red brick housing development, which we are about to see more of, was the first in the world to have its own permanent electricity! There was a complicated system of tunnels dug for hydraulics with a boiler and a dynamo. Each house had its own battery charged every day by direct current.

Keep going straight. To your left you could take a look at the nice square with all the swanky houses around it. They are all part of this same Kensington Court, but I'm just going to go straight down to the junction of Kensington Court Place and Thackeray Street.

Back in Victorian times there was a man called Baron Albert Grant, who had a bit of cash to throw around and so he built a splendid 100-room marble palace here – but he ended up going bankrupt and they knocked it down, sending the staircase to Madame Tussauds (where you can still see it) and the lovely iron gates to Richmond Park.

Then in the 1880s Kensington Court was built, as a groovy new concept with coaches kept on the ground floor, horses' stables one floor above (accessed by a ramp), and coachmen's houses one floor above that (reached by stairs). You can see this curious arrangement here at **KENSINGTON COURT MEWS** **7** on your left, but of course nowadays they are used as garages and not stables.

Just next to the mews is the **OLD PUMP HOUSE** **8**. Jonathan Carr, the property developer who built these houses, wanted a cheap, quiet alternative to the usual steam-powered lifts, so this pump house pumped water all the way from the Thames. So, not only were the houses in this area the first to have their own electricity; it was the first time independent hydraulic power was used to power houses anywhere in the world!

You have to hand it to those Victorians.

Gosh, do you know, we're only a little way into the walk but there is a nice pub down here that I used to go to in my youth. If you're

PUB

The Builder's Arms

feeling a bit peckish or fancy a sharpener, just carry on down Kensington Court Place and pop into the **Builder's Arms** for one or two. A beautiful, bright 19th-century pub with decent food and they even allow dogs in.

Anyway, let's return to where we were at the Old Pump House and now turn down Thackeray Street, which leads to **KENSINGTON SQUARE** ❾. It's a jolly lovely old square, built in 1692, and has many listed buildings. Perhaps I'm just weird, but I'm obsessed with the cute green lampposts that you don't often see anywhere else. I love the ornate lettering on them saying 'RBKC' ('Royal Borough of Kensington and Chelsea'). Also look out for the old street sign from before 1917 and score some **points**!

Now turn right up Young Street and past **WILLIAM MAKEPEACE THACKERAY'S HOUSE** ❿, where he wrote *Vanity Fair*. If you're wondering why the plaque is brown rather than blue it's just because it is old. The first plaque of its kind was erected in 1867, and they were mostly brown because they were cheaper to produce than blue.

However, since 1965 they have stuck to blue apart from a few exceptions. You have to be dead to have a plaque like these. I wonder if I'll ever get one… The only plaque I've got is on my teeth! (Thank you, Mark, for that joke.)

Carry on to Kensington High Street and turn left. Then cross the road and stop outside **ST MARY ABBOTS CHURCH** ⓫. It was designed by George Gilbert Scott in 1872 and has the tallest spire in London. (The spire is the pointy bit on top of the church tower. Together with the tower they form the steeple.) George is not to be confused with his grandson, Giles Gilbert Scott, who designed the red telephone boxes!

By the way, if you look down Kensington High Street you'll see two big art deco buildings that used to be department stores: Barkers, just opposite you, and next to that is what used to be Derry and Toms. On the roof they have the beautiful Kensington Roof Gardens, which were open to the public from 1938 until 2018, but at time of writing are closed. I think there are plans to reopen them under new ownership, but it seems uncertain just when. I do hope you get to go up there because it's a beautiful 6,000 square metre garden with splendid views of London – and they even have (or used to have) resident flamingos, too!!

Anyway, as the roof gardens are closed I'm heading up Kensington Church Street.

Oh!!! On your right here, in Old Court Place, is a great place for some good traditional hearty English fayre, like sausage and mash, shepherd's pie, roast beef or game pie: Maggie Jones's! It's jolly nice and they have generous portions, too! You might need to book if you're going for Sunday lunch, though. Maggie Jones's opened in 1964 and was originally called Nan's Kitchen – but after it became a favourite hangout of Princess Margaret (Queen Elizabeth II's sister) and Lord Snowdon (Anthony Armstrong-Jones), they changed the name. Literally the place to eat like a princess!

Yum! That was really good!

Now continue up Kensington Church Street and turn left down Holland Street. Then turn left again into **KENSINGTON CHURCH WALK** 12.

Now, if you want to know where I get a lot of my vintage clothing and boating blazers from, it's here, at Hornets! They're very friendly and helpful and sell lots of bowler hats, top hats, dinner suits and all sorts of vintage second-hand clothing. I must pop down there again soon.

If you do go, remember to pop into Garnet, the vintage jewellery shop in the same street. The beautiful lady working there was very nice when appearing in my film and she has some lovely items. Down the years many famous customers have been through the doors. Princess Diana used to bring Princes William and Harry along here on their way to McDonald's, can you believe, and the boys used to enjoy running along the wall opposite. (I'd love to have been in McDonald's when Princess Diana swanned in and ordered a Big Mac!!)

Continue down the lane and when you see the church, turn into the gates as if to enter the church but look up to your right. This is the back of the **ST MARY ABBOTS PRIMARY SCHOOL** 13. Can you see the two rather smartly dressed figures on the wall wearing frock coats?

This indicates that when the school was originally opened, in 1712, it was a charity school. These Blue Coat Schools were first established in the 16th century and the uniform was blue because it was a very cheap colour dye!

Some of these schools did survive as actual schools, like this one – although it certainly isn't a charity school any more.

Now continue along Kensington Church Walk back onto Kensington High Street and turn right. Keep going and then turn right up Argyll Road and then second left onto **STAFFORD TERRACE** 14.

Many of these beautiful houses were built around the end of the 19th century for artists to live in. We will come to more shortly, but number 18 dates from the 1870s and was occupied by Edward Linley Sambourne, one of the chief illustrators of *Punch* magazine. Now it's another one of these cute little museums that I like. You can see just how he lived!

The decade of the 1870s was known as 'the aesthetic period' and Sambourne went out and bought all his own furniture and amazing *objets d'art*, which he assembled in a rather artistic, eclectic manner. The place is cluttered with them but I like features like the five-light gasolier – a chandelier that ran off gas. Above it you can see where the gas was extracted; all the houses in the street have a gas vent, which you might still want to see even if you don't go inside the house. The house hasn't changed since Sambourne lived there, so you can get a real idea of how they lived in those days. It is advisable to check ahead of your visit and maybe book a tour.

Now return to Kensington High Street and turn left towards High Street Kensington tube station. Just before you reach the station turn right down Wrights Lane.

Coming up on your right, on the corner of Cheniston Gardens, is The Muffin Man. Sorry, but I love the muffin man. My mum used to take me there when I was a child and we ate real English muffins while she'd sing, 'Come and meet the muffin man, run, run as fast as you can…'

I don't know that many places that offer English muffins these days. They aren't like those blueberry muffins you see in Starbucks! These are different. You should try one. They have all sorts of fancy combinations but I prefer butter and jam on mine, thank you very much, and a cup of Earl Grey tea. How civilised.

As you exit, turn right and follow Cheniston Gardens around the corner until it becomes Marloes Road (where my mum got married).

Continue straight for a bit and then, opposite number 59, there is a large gated property. The brick gate posts are the only surviving part of the original **KENSINGTON WORKHOUSE 15** which used to stand here. After workhouses got outlawed in 1930 it became a hospital, and was eventually knocked down in 1990. They were wretched places to be in Victorian times and only used as a desperate last resort. Whole families would sometimes have to earn their keep here with menial tasks such as darning wool, making rope or smashing rocks.

Meanwhile the authorities would try to discourage people from entering the workhouse by splitting families up and making them as miserable as possible. As a child I

never believed that the stories of Charles Dickens were based on reality, but those were indeed very hard times and he wasn't exaggerating about the extreme poverty and abject squalor. It must be weird to live here in these fancy houses, having to walk through the same gates that all those poor souls walked through. That's London, I guess…

Carry on walking along and opposite the **Devonshire Arms** (which looks like a perfectly good pub for a quick tipple) you'll see a **DRINKING FOUNTAIN 16**, which was set in the wall here in 1893 with a prayer for the poor people who had to endure the workhouse.

Now head up Stratford Road, past the Devonshire Arms and a charming row of shops and cafés, which make me feel like I've suddenly left central London.

On the right you'll see a gated drive called **STRATFORD STUDIOS 17**. If the gate is open you could cheekily take a peek at these artists' studios, built in the 1880s. All the artists were attracted to the area in the years following the Great Exhibition of 1851, which had been held in Hyde Park. If you carry on along Stratford Road you'll see another such gate at number 21a, with an old sign above the arch reading **SCARSDALE STUDIOS 18**. Here are yet more of these cute little homes which, along with Linley Sambourne's house, rather ruin the romance of the 'struggling artist'. When my friend Monica arrived from Spain she lived in a room in a flat in this street with several housemates, one of whom had a tiny room like Harry Potter's under the stairs. Now that's more like it! ¡Hola, Monica!

Carry on along this rather posh road of 'struggling artists' and at the end turn left at the church, then right into Logan Place.

It's a pretty grim-looking street for the area, I suppose, but keep going.

On the left, just before the end, is a long brick wall with a door saying **GARDEN LODGE** 19. This is the famous house where Freddie Mercury lived with his wife, Mary Austin. Well, his 'common-law wife', which means they decided to live together without all the ceremony and all that. He moved here in 1985 just before being diagnosed with HIV. Over the fence you can just about espy a bit of the house, where Mary Austin still lives while adoring fans still pay homage outside. Last time I went past there was a plastic sheet over the door, presumably to prevent all the fans from writing on it.

Keep going to the end of Logan Place and turn right. Then turn right again onto Pembroke Road and then left up Pembroke Villas.

Keep going straight. Goodness me, there are some lovely houses around here – and look at Pembroke Square, with a tennis court in it, on your right!

Well, I don't know if all this eating and drinking is getting too much for you, but there is a really nice pub up here on the right, called the **Scarsdale Tavern**. Do at least pop in for a look, even if you don't fancy a pint – although I'd recommend a little rest here. We've still got a little way to go.

Feeling a bit refreshed, let's continue up past the pub. You will see on your left yet another delightful square. If you aren't too tired you could take a quick turn around the square, which has more of those lovely lampposts. **EDWARDES SQUARE** 20 was built in the early 19th century. My favourite resident was Frankie Howerd (number 27). 'Oooooooh, matron!!!!' You know…from the

PUB

The Scarsdale Tavern

Carry On films. Roger Bannister also lived here, at number 16, but I don't know if he trained for his famous four-minute mile by running around the square like *Chariots of Fire*. I expect he must have done so a couple of times, though, surely!!

Okay, time waits for no man, so let's continue up to Kensington High Street.

Now turn right and you'll soon come to the **DESIGN MUSEUM** 21, founded by Sir Terence Conran, the famous designer and restaurateur. It's a very stylish space, where you can see graphic and architectural design that you might recognise from your youth! It's always a bit alarming seeing things like BBC Micro computers and Walkmans in museums, when they seem pretty modern inventions to me!

Now exit the museum and turn right up Kensington High Street and then turn right up Melbury Road. Then turn left into Holland Park Road.

At number 12 is **LEIGHTON HOUSE** 22, another one of these lovely preserved museum/houses of yet another local artist. Again, it's definitely worth a visit, as Frederic, Lord Leighton, one of the most celebrated

Victorian artists, decorated it with splendid themes inspired by his travels.

Inside Lord Leighton's 'palace of art' you'll find rooms decorated with 16th-century tiles from Damascus and a very grand staircase, which I love. Lovers of art will find a great deal of masterpieces to peruse, but – philistine that I am – I'm fascinated by the fact that The Stranglers filmed the video for 'Golden Brown' here, and it's also where Spandau Ballet filmed 'Gold'.

'Always believe in your soul…' Classic.

Come out and turn left. Then turn left again, up Melbury Road.

Follow the road round just past Ilchester Place and as you go you will see more blue plaques dotted around, for various artists who didn't want to be associated with the traditional white stuccoed properties – so they had these fabulous red-brick houses built.

Immediately after Ilchester Place, on the right, is number 31, **WOODLAND HOUSE** **23**, with a plaque for Sir Luke Fildes, who painted King Edward VII here. When the king sat for the painting he said that the room was 'the most beautiful in London', and I can believe it, too. It has some huge windows, so the rooms must be very bright and cheerful. In fact, there were 48 rooms here last time I counted! That should be enough for pop singer Robbie Williams, who lives here! He bought it off Michael Winner (who directed the film *Death Wish*) after he died here in 2013.

And just next door, at number 29, is the **TOWER HOUSE** **24**, where Jimmy Page

(from Led Zeppelin) lives. David Bowie wanted to buy it, but Jimmy Page beat him to it. He is very protective over the fixtures and fittings, as it is a listed building designed by William Burges, who also designed Castell Coch in Wales (which it kind of resembles, actually).

Last I heard, Jimmy Page was involved in some sort of neighbourly dispute because Robbie Williams wanted to dig a basement and the vibrations were damaging Jimmy Page's old walls. Perhaps 48 rooms weren't enough, after all.

I also like the fact that Richard Harris lived here before Jimmy Page. He played Dumbledore in the first two *Harry Potter* films. It looks like the sort of place where Dumbledore would live!!

Now go back and turn left up Ilchester Place. You will soon enter Holland Park.

Keep going straight until you reach some arches, and pause a moment. I want to turn left under the arches, but first we need to go right and look at what remains of **HOLLAND HOUSE** **25**.

Originally, when it was built in 1605, it was called Cope's Castle, and Holland Park is what used to be its grounds.

Walter Cope was the Chamberlain of the Exchequer under King James I of England; the house later passed to Earl Holland, the first Baron Kensington, who had his head chopped off by Oliver Cromwell. They say his ghost walks around with his head under his arm (which became all the rage for ghosts after Anne Boleyn first started doing it).

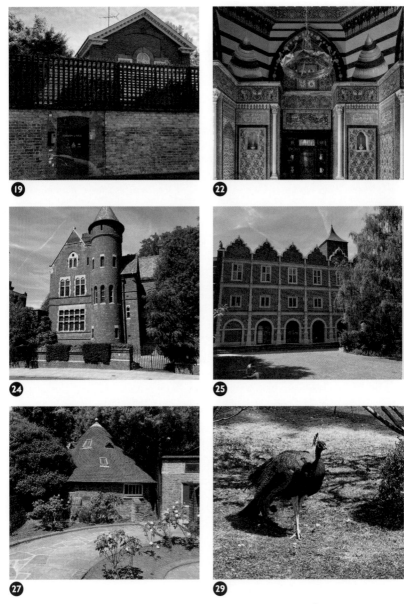

Continuing to the right (with the arches on your left) you will see an area to your left where they put on operas during the summer. It's a lovely experience in the open air. I once saw *Cavalleria Rusticana* and *Pagliacci* there (probably my favourite operas)!

A little further along on the left you will see that the stage area sits in front of what remains of the lovely original house. These days it's one of the most beautifully located youth hostels I've ever seen, and is all that survives of the 17th-century mansion. The Luftwaffe flattened a lot of this area – although quite what they were aiming at, I don't know. If you see any of the guests of the hostel, try asking them if they've seen the ghost! Not only did his head get chopped off, but his house got flattened too. No wonder he's restless.

Later, in the early 19th century, Holland House was used as a literary salon where Charles Dickens, Benjamin Disraeli and Lord Byron used to hang out. In fact, it was here that Byron met Lady Caroline Lamb for the first time. She called him 'Mad, bad and dangerous to know' during their short-lived love affair. My mother never tires of telling me about how Lady Caroline Lamb sent her pubic hair to Byron in the post and had cut it a bit too carelessly, so there was still some blood and skin attached.

That's pure romance, folks.

Now walk back past the opera area to the arches and go under the one at the end, through a sort of tunnel.

You should find yourself in a pretty garden with a fountain and some frescoes on the wall depicting the grounds in times gone by. Looking out at the fountain you'll see to the left is the **ORANGERY** 26, where fruit trees could be protected during the winter. They have exhibitions and stuff in there these days. Over to the right, the cute little building with a turreted roof isn't actually where the witch from Hansel and Gretel lives; it's the **ICE HOUSE** 27 where they kept ice.

It's really very pleasant here on a sunny day. Ahead of you past the fountain is the serene **DUTCH GARDEN** 28 where you can even play chess on the giant chess board. I like to sit here and read my book sometimes, daydreaming about being Lord Byron or some posh aristocrat of a bygone age.

Beyond all this (you'll have to follow the signposts) try to seek out the **KYOTO GARDEN** 29, which was donated in 1992 after a Japanese festival was held. It's a little slice of Japan here in London and you can see nice water features and fish ponds and cute bridges. Keep an eye out for the peacocks ruling the roost! They're all over the place and not only restricted to the Kyoto Garden. When it's the mating season they get frisky and roam all over the place, sometimes hopping into the neighbours' gardens!

I think you'll find that only the males are peacocks. The females are peahens. The males are the more flamboyant, with their bright blue and green feathers, which look amazing when spread out.

If you have time, and are feeling at one with nature, you should explore the woody bit beyond the Kyoto Garden. I actually prefer parks that are a bit overgrown and less ordered, so this is where I like to wander lonely as a cloud, while philosophising and thinking about the meaning of life.

Goodness, this has been a long day. Let's head out of the park via the exit just to the east of Holland House, by the hostel. Watch out for the bicycles! Then turn left up the path and follow the edge of the park until you see some tennis courts. Then turn right into Campden Hill.

Don't worry – we're nearly at the pub.

Walk to the end of Campden Hill and then turn left into Campden Hill Road.

Soon, on your right, on the corner of Peel Street, you'll find the **Windsor Castle**,

which was a coaching inn where mail coaches and stage coaches could replace their tired horses with fresh ones from the stables. They say that when it was built back in the 1820s you could see the actual Windsor Castle from the upstairs rooms. Fat chance these days, though. It has very cute little snugs and corners if you like that sort of thing, along with good food and a beer garden.

I need a pint. Tally ho.

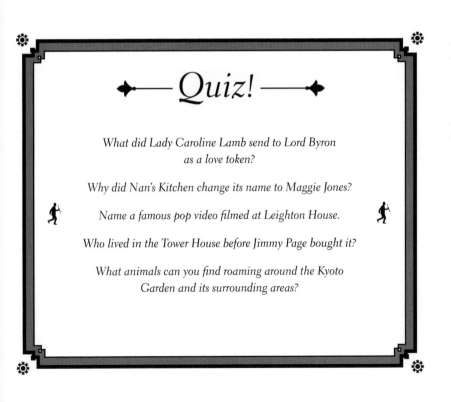

— Quiz! —

What did Lady Caroline Lamb send to Lord Byron as a love token?

Why did Nan's Kitchen change its name to Maggie Jones?

Name a famous pop video filmed at Leighton House.

Who lived in the Tower House before Jimmy Page bought it?

What animals can you find roaming around the Kyoto Garden and its surrounding areas?

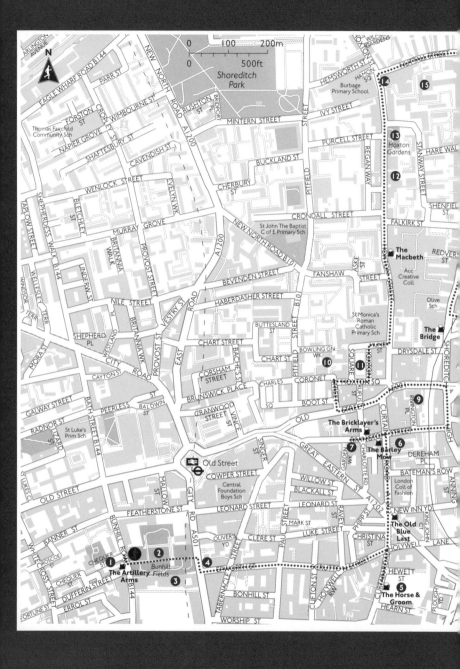

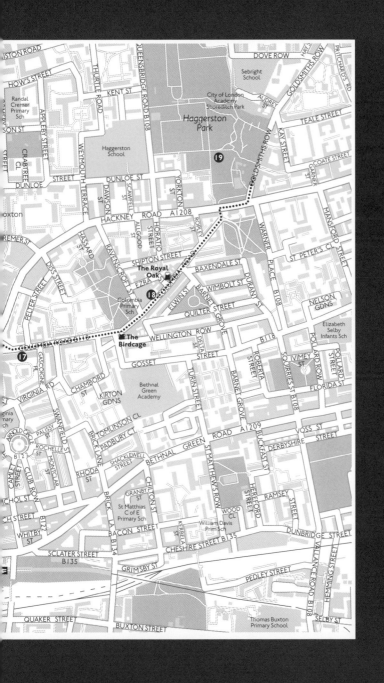

ISTON ROAD
HOW'S STREET
SON ST
STREET
DUNLOE
oxton
REMERS
THURTLE ROAD
APPLEBY STREET
Randal Cremer Primary Sch
CRABTREE CL
WEYMOUTH TERRACE
KENT ST
Haggerston School
DUNLOE ST
SCAWELL ST
DAWSON ST
ALLGOOD STREET
HORATIO STREET
HASSARD STREET
RAVENSCROFT ST
SHIPTON STREET
DISS STREET
PELLER STREET
QUEENSBRIDGE ROAD B108
YORKTON ST
HACKNEY ROAD A1208
ROPLEY ST
The Royal Oak
18
EZRA ST
Colombia Primary Sch
The Birdcage
17
GASCOIGNE PL
CHAMBORD ST
VIRGINIA RD
SWANFIELD ST
ARNOLD CIRCLE
B121
ROCHELLE S
PALISSY ST
CAMLET ST
CUB ROW
CH STREET
B122
WHITBY ST
ginia mary ch
NICHOL ST
SCLATER STREET B135
BRICK LANE
MONTCLARE
RHODA ST
QUAKER STREET
KIRTON GDNS
COLUMBIA ROAD
ELWIN ST
WELLINGTON ROW
GOSSET STREET
Bethnal Green Academy
TOMLINSON CL
PADBURY CL
SHACKLEWELL STREET
BETHNAL GREEN ROAD A1209
BRICK LANE B134
CHILTON ST
GRANBY ST
St Matthias C of E Primary Sch
BACON STREET
CHESHIRE STREET B135
GRIMSBY ST
BUXTON STREET
SHIPTON STREET
BAXENDALE ST
WIMBOLT ST
BARNET GROVE
QUILTER STREET
DELIA ST
STREET
TURIN STREET
BARNET GROVE
ROBERTA STREET
KERBELA ST
William Davis Prim Sch
WOOD CL
PEDLEY STREET
Sebright School
DOVE ROW
City of London Academy Shoreditch Park
AUDREY ST
TEALE STREET
Haggerston Park
19
GOLDSMITHS ROW
GOLDSMITHS ROW
KAY STREET
WARNER PLACE
GARNER ST
COATE STREET
MANSFORD STREET
ST PETER'S CL
DURANT ST
B108
B118
SQUIRRIES ST
IVIMEY ST
POLLARD ROW
POLLARD STREET
FLORIDA ST
NELSON GDNS
Elizabeth Selby Infants Sch
ST MATTHEW'S ROW
BUCKFAST ST
DERBYSHIRE STREET
HEREFORD STREET
RAMSEY STREET
VOSS ST
STREET
DUNBRIDGE STREET
VALLANCE ROAD B108
HEMMING STREET
SELBY ST
Thomas Buxton Primary School
GOLDSPRIES ROW
PRICHARD'S RD
HAY

18

18 A FIRST-RATE SUNDAY WALK THROUGH HOXTON AND COLUMBIA ROAD

DISTANCE
5.1 km (3.2 miles)

TIME
2 hours 10 minutes

NEAREST STATION
Old Street

Oh, if you want to see the flower market in all its glory you should really do this walk on a Sunday morning (the flower market only takes place on Sundays, and is usually in operation between 8.00 a.m. and 2.00 p.m.) – but then again, some of the shops might not be open on a Sunday.

Spiffing. Well, I think a good place to meet is the **Artillery Arms**, on the corner of Bunhill Row and Dufferin Street. Come out of Old Street tube station and walk west down Old Street, before turning left at Bunhill Row. Soon you'll reach the Artillery Arms.

Nice pub. A couple of the patrons were fans of Joolz Guides when I last visited!

Come out of the pub onto Bunhill Row, turn left and stop at the next street. About 10 yards up Chequer Street, look at the ground where it changes colour and you can score some points (see the **STREET FURNITURE CHALLENGE**, page 11) for a very rare example of **WOODEN PAVING** ❶. London used to have a lot more, but much of it was used after the war to burn in people's fireplaces for warmth. I'm so pleased that this bit survived!

Now walk back towards the pub and turn left into **BUNHILL FIELDS BURIAL GROUND** ❷.

In 1549 they demolished a charnel house (a place for storing people's bones) at St Paul's Cathedral and ended up depositing over 1,000 cartloads of bones here and covering them with soil. This formed a hill which became known as the 'bone hill', hence 'Bunhill'.

Then in 1665 it was used as a plague pit, which explains why over 120,000 bodies have been buried here, in quite a small area.

As the ground was never consecrated by the Church of England, Bunhill Fields became popular with nonconformists and other people not connected with the Anglican Church. There are also some famous names here. Daniel Defoe (who wrote *Robinson Crusoe*), John Bunyan (*The Pilgrim's Progress*) and William Blake are all buried in Bunhill Fields.

You must know William Blake, one of England's most famous artists and poets. He wrote the poem which we have come to know as the words of the hymn 'Jerusalem'; 'O Rose thou art sick'; 'Tyger Tyger, burning bright'; etc. Splendid fellow, even if he couldn't spell 'tiger'. He also did all those scary paintings of dragons and Satan arousing rebel angels.

I just like coming here to feed the squirrels.

Come out of the opposite exit, onto City Road.

The building to your right as you exit, which looks like a castle, is actually the **HONOURABLE ARTILLERY COMPANY MUSEUM** ❸. The Honourable Artillery Company is the oldest regiment in the British Army, founded in 1537 by Henry VIII. Unfortunately you can only go for a tour of the museum by special appointment. You wouldn't think it, but there's a whole cricket pitch behind that building.

A cool place that you *can* visit is to your left, across the road: the **MUSEUM OF METHODISM** ❹.

The museum occupies an excellent example of an 18th-century townhouse, which hasn't changed since it was built in 1779, when John Wesley, the father of Methodism, lived

here. In the 18th century the Church had strict opinions on how the Bible should be taught, and to whom; but Wesley wanted to spread the word far and wide, so he travelled 250,000 miles on his horse to teach religion to the poor and illiterate, as well as others.

He was also a bit of a quack, writing pamphlets on medicine and creating special machines, which you can see inside the museum. One of them administered electric shocks to treat migraines – although he was careful to test them on his flock before trying them on himself!!!

Don't forget to visit the toilet to the right of the chapel. It's one of the best preserved Victorian public lavatories in London!

Come out and turn left into City Road and then left again into Epworth Street. Keep going straight.

This whole section behind the Museum of Methodism is a network of streets that once contained old warehouses. These are now full of offices for very cool trendy young people who work in fields like tech and social media, among other things. A cool place to explore and hang out later, if you want. There are a few good pubs and places where office workers buy their food.

We're continuing straight ahead, though, and soon Epworth Street becomes Scrutton Street. (Not *Scruttock* Street – your *scruttock* is the bit between your scrotum and your buttocks.)

When you reach Curtain Road turn right and stop at the **STAGE** ❺, a set of buildings on Curtain Road between Hewett Street and Hearn Street which dwarf the cute little pub in the middle called the **Horse & Groom**.

The Horse & Groom is another place to go if you're younger and cooler than me. They have dance music, craft beers, decent grub and good-looking people. What is also interesting is that this was probably the entrance to the Curtain Theatre, which stood here in the 17th century.

In the 1570s the Mayor of London banned playhouses, so little theatres started to pop up outside the walls of the City of London, where the strict rules didn't apply. This was the second theatre in the district (we'll see

PUB

The Horse & Groom

the first in a moment) and these playhouses outside the City were where Shakespeare made his name. He probably premiered some of his plays at the Curtain, including *Romeo and Juliet*, with his jolly band of actors, the Lord Chamberlain's Men.

If you go inside the visitor centre within the Stage complex you can see the remains of the actual theatre. It's pretty cool.

Another famous playwright, Ben Jonson, had great success here in 1598 with his play *Every Man in His Humour*, also performed by the Lord Chamberlain's Men. It sounds like

Jonson was quite a badass!! After writing one play called *The Isle of Dogs* he was banged up in prison for 'leude and mutynous behaviour' because it was so offensive. One of the actors in the production, Gabriel Spenser, was also locked up; a year after they got out, Jonson killed Spenser in a duel near Hoxton Square. Jonson only managed to avoid the death penalty by proving he could read Latin, thereby claiming the right to be tried in an ecclesiastical court, by quoting a verse from the Bible!!

All a bit ridiculous, really. Anyway, they soon did away with that loophole and branded Jonson's thumbs to stop him trying it again!

Come out of the Stage (or the pub, if you're still there) and turn right, going north up Curtain Road.

Soon the buildings start looking nice again and, goodness me, another beautiful Victorian pub with its lovely brewery sign on top: the **Old Blue Last**.

Just across New Inn Yard, at the time of writing, is a Foxtons estate agent, with a plaque on the wall stating that this is where London's (and, in fact, England's) first purpose-built theatre stood in the 1570s. Until then, travelling actors just performed in pubs and other public spaces. This first theatre, founded by James Burbage (who lived around the corner), was known simply as 'the Theatre'. Burbage's son Richard was the lead actor and a good friend of Shakespeare's – in fact, many of the famous roles were written knowing that Richard Burbage would be the first to perform them. When the lease ran out after James Burbage's death, Richard and his brother got into a dispute with the landlord and were worried that they'd lose the theatre, so, under cover of darkness one winter's night in 1598, they got some mates to dismantle and remove the entire theatre; they subsequently transported the beams and everything over the river, where they built the famous Globe Theatre.

Continue up Curtain Road and on your right you'll see a little mews called **STRONGROOM** ❻. There's a cool little bar here with an outdoor drinking space (where traffic doesn't whistle past your head) and also a studio that has been used by many recording artists, including Björk, So Solid Crew and S Club 7 (I know you're a fan). Most importantly, it's where the Spice Girls recorded 'Wannabe'! I believe the building is under threat from developers, so I hope it's still there when you come!

On the other side of Curtain Road is the **Barley Mow**. If you have time you could pop in for a pint, or turn left to explore a bit of Rivington Street. The Barley Mow and the **Bricklayer's Arms** are both pretty trendy pubs. Further along on the left, at number 32, is a lovely Edwardian building which used to be an **ELECTRICITY SUBSTATION** ❼ to power trams. It was a restaurant last time I went inside, but it's been shut since the Covid-19 lockdowns, and at the time of writing it appears to have closed permanently.

Return along Rivington Street the way you came, crossing back over Curtain Road, and then turn left up Shoreditch High Street.

Did I mention how achingly trendy this area is? There are loads of bars and cafés and places to buy food. Ideally you should be a millennial with a long beard and a tattoo, eating street food and working in a tech startup. But you don't have to be!!

On the right is **ST LEONARD'S CHURCH** ❽. Maybe you sang about it as a child in the nursery-rhyme 'Oranges and Lemons':

When will you pay me?
Say the bells at Old Bailey.
When I grow rich,
Say the bells at Shoreditch.

There has been a church on this site since medieval times, but the present building dates from the 1730s. It is known as an actors' church because of the number of actors buried here. After all, this was the first theatreland in London!

Richard and James Burbage are both buried here, as is Gabriel Spenser, who was killed by Ben Jonson.

It was also from St Leonard's that the funeral of Mary Jane Kelly, Jack the Ripper's final victim, departed en route to St Patrick's Cemetery in Leyton.

Now, if you're hungry, this area is great for Vietnamese food. There are numerous restaurants straight ahead, up Kingsland Road, and they don't have to look snazzy to be good, either!

Anyway, we're turning left, into Old Street.

On the left is **SHOREDITCH TOWN HALL** ❾, or at least, it used to be. The building, opened in 1866, is in the grand Italianate

OLD STREET

style, with lovely statues carved into it high up. One is holding a torch and two more are flanking the Shoreditch borough motto, 'More Light, More Power', which refers to the local council's intention to generate its own power for local industries – as we saw with the electricity substation. This is where the inquest was held for the aforementioned murder of Mary Jane Kelly.

I miss town halls being in huge impressive buildings like this. These days it's an arts venue and community space, and it certainly has a magnificent assembly hall, perfect for concerts. But if you need to do some sort of council-related admin you probably have to go somewhere far less inspiring in a soulless prefab down a urine-stained back street, take a ticket and wait for three hours.

People my age might remember them holding the Whirl-Y-Gig club there in the 1990s – although most people who attended the Whirl-Y-Gig don't tend to remember much of it!

Carry on along Old Street past a few more bars and turn right up Coronet Street.

At the end of the street the red brick building is the **NATIONAL CENTRE FOR CIRCUS ARTS ⑩**, previously known as Circus Space, where you can learn trampolining, flying trapeze, juggling, tumbling and how to ride a unicycle. The actual building, built in 1896, is further evidence of the borough generating its own power. Look above the door (over to the left) where you will see the slogan *E PULVERE LUX ET VIS* ('Out of the dust, light and power'). This was the Shoreditch Electricity Generating Station and Refuse Destructor, where they collected all the local rubbish and burned it to provide electricity. No wonder London had such thick smog!

Go back a few steps whence you came and turn left off Coronet Street into **HOXTON SQUARE ⑪**. The name 'Hoxton' comes from 'Hogesdon', indicating a farm or enclosure belonging to someone named Hoch, or Hocq. The farm and surrounding land stood here back in Shakespeare's time before they built all the houses. It was in these fields that Ben Jonson had his duel with the aforementioned Gabriel Spenser.

The house at number 32 dates from the 1680s, while the rest is more modern, though still characterful – see, for example, the old furniture workshops which you can identify by the large doors for access even at higher levels. There are yet more bars and restaurants here, which are worth checking out if you're on a night out. Look also for the plaque on number 1 for James Parkinson, who first documented what became known as Parkinson's Disease.

Leave the square by the north-east corner, past the school, and enter Mundy Street.

Then turn left into Hoxton Street.

When you get to Fanshaw Street, look to your left for more of those typical Victorian workers' buildings with the pulley supports and big doors for access.

Continuing along Hoxton Street, you'll walk past the **Macbeth**, yet another pub where Charles Dickens used to drink, according to their website. (The fellow certainly got around, but why not!) If you're into live music you'll like it here. Past acts have included Franz Ferdinand, Pete Doherty and Johnny Marr.

We are now approaching the Hoxton Street Market. You might recognise this from the

Verve's video for 'Bitter Sweet Symphony', where Richard Ashcroft walks along bumping into everyone.

One of my favourite shops is at number 159: Hoxton Street Monster Supplies!

Over 200 years ago a monster called Igor came to London and found there weren't any shops to serve the monster community, so he opened this up – although it was only about 10 years ago that a curse was put on the shop and it became visible to humans. If you need some slime lollipops, pickled eyeballs or damsel's hair, this is the place to come. The bottom two shelves are for humans and monsters who believe in getting along with humans; but if you want anything from the top shelf you have to provide a valid death certificate.

They also have the monster postal service, whereby six lonely monsters have written to the shop wanting more communication with humans. Kids of any age (especially my age) can strike up a correspondence with any of their favourite monsters by replying to their letters. I'll take one jar of the thickest human snot, please. Thank you kindly, madam.

A bit further along on the right is **HOXTON HALL** ⓬. Music hall was a huge part of entertainment in the late 19th century. Without TV or radio, people would flock to the music halls to see their favourite performers, such as Marie Lloyd ('My old man said, Follow the van, and don't dilly dally on the way') and George Leybourne (see **Walk 9**). Only two Victorian music halls survive in London and this is one of them, dating from 1863. If you can look inside you'll really feel like you're in *The Picture of Dorian Gray* or something. Film production companies love the place and you can still see shows here.

You can even rent it for private events. I must get my friend Tom Carradine to do one of his Cockney singalongs here. It's just the place!

Anyone for pie and eels? If you're feeling peckish and want a traditional Cockney East End dish, try F. Cooke's Pie and Mash, a little further along on the right. Together with the funeral directors next door, these shops give an idea of what shops looked like 100 years ago.

Now, if you're feeling adventurous, you could try the jellied eels (steamed are also available); or you might feel safer with pie and mash with liquor. The liquor is made with flour, water and parsley and some other special secret ingredient. The Cooke family business has run these shops in the East End since the 1860s – it was typically cheap food for poorer Londoners. The East End was home to many poor people because the prevailing winds always carried all the pollution from people's chimneys from west to east, making the air in the East End less pleasant than other parts of London.

If you're wondering why there's sawdust on the floor, it's supposed to be because people used to spit bones out onto the floor. Maybe you still do! That said, one chap told me it's for when there's a fight, to soak up the blood!

After your slap-up feast, carry on up Hoxton Street. Soon you'll see a little public garden on your right. It looks pretty unremarkable at first glance – but look again at the **CLOCK** ⓭. It's like someone removed the tower from the top of a building. Well, that's because they did! It originally adorned the Eastern Fever Hospital in Homerton but now is precariously balanced on a metal frame! Like someone sliced off the top of a building and just dumped it here. I love stuff like that.

Now continue up the street until you see the big 'Hoxton Street Market' banner across the road.

On your right before the banner is a very sad sight indeed: yet another closed pub, the Unicorn. Look up high at the splendid pub sign, which has been here since the early 19th century. More and more London pubs are closing and you probably wonder why I always go to so many. I just think they are a wonderful part of British culture that we mustn't let die out.

The next building along is another that evokes Charles Dickens and Victorian poverty. The **ST LEONARD OFFICES FOR THE RELIEF OF THE POOR** 14 was connected with the Shoreditch Workhouse, which was just behind it; this building was more for administration.

Turn right into Nuttall Street and you will reach what is now **ST LEONARD'S HOSPITAL** 15 on your right. Originally it was the workhouse infirmary and you can see how forbidding and lugubrious the building looks. So *Oliver Twist*!

At the end of Nuttall Street, turn right into Kingsland Road, around another typical red brick Victorian church. Soon you will pass the front of the hospital, which was originally the main entrance to the workhouse – through which thousands of miserable people with very few prospects in life entered. The Poor Law of 1834 meant that you could get no relief unless you worked, so this was the fate of thousands of unmarried mothers, disabled people, the elderly, orphans and abandoned children.

Carry on walking and score yourself some points for spotting the abandoned fountain near the phone box on the left-hand side. Or do you? Hmm… This one doesn't actually specify that it was placed there by the Metropolitan Drinking Fountain and Cattle Trough Association – so should I award points? Oh, go on, then.

It's a pity so many phone boxes are in such disrepair, but they just aren't used these days (except by drug dealers and people who need the toilet). However, they generally can't be removed because they are listed.

Another listed building is the **MUSEUM OF THE HOME** 16, which was previously known as the Geffrye Museum, on your left behind the iron railings. At least, I assume the railings are iron. They should be, because Robert Geffrye was Master of the Worshipful Company of Ironmongers and also Lord Mayor of London. These buildings were originally alms houses, established in 1714 with money left in Geffrye's will. Until 1910 they were used to house poor people, but since 1914 the site has functioned as a museum. The museum contains various rooms decorated in the styles of different eras, leading up to the present day. It's also a lovely place to sit and read this book in the grounds!

These smaller museums are really wonderful and London has so many of them.

It's amazing to think you are now walking along an old Roman road, which was

KINGSLAND ROAD

known then as Ermine Street. Presumably this is the route along which King Edward I (Edward Longshanks from *Braveheart*!) accompanied his dead wife's coffin in 1290, following the route to Westminster Abbey from Lincoln. Edward had a big ornate stone cross erected at each point where they had stopped to rest during the journey. There were twelve 'Eleanor Crosses' in all, the last one being Charing Cross; but I don't see any around here.

Carry on past more Vietnamese restaurants and try to spot the post box with the insignia of King George VI. It must be something about the area, but this seems to be in need of a lick of paint, like the phone boxes. Pity, as I really like the George VI post boxes; but the lack of colour does make it harder to spot, so more points!

By the way, further along, under the bridge, there is a pretty nice little bar called the **Bridge**. It's another one of these cluttered bars with lots of velvet and characterful paraphernalia.

Turn left under the railway bridge into Waterson Street. Straight ahead at the end there's a green grassy area where it meets Columbia Road.

Just beyond that are the **LEOPOLD BUILDINGS** ⑰, which were constructed in 1872 as a part of Sydney Waterlow's Improved Industrial Dwellings Company. (Sydney Waterlow is the one who donated Waterlow Park in Highgate. Must have been a nice bloke.) I think they're rather splendid and would love to live in one of those. What's amazing is that the builder, Matthew Allen, didn't see any need for architects and just decided to do it himself. I think he did a grand job. I wish he could do my bathroom!

PUB

The Royal Oak

Continue along Columbia Road until you see the **Birdcage**. By all means pop in for a drink, but we're not finishing here. If you're here on a Sunday you will be at the start of the massive **COLUMBIA ROAD FLOWER MARKET** ⑱, which really is a beautiful experience, especially in the summertime. Coming down here really cheers me up!

As far back as the 18th century, immigrant Huguenots were selling flowers here – and they also sold caged birds (hence the name of the pub).

It can get very busy here, and you'll probably want to spend a good while milling around and taking in the atmosphere. There's more than just flowers, too. Try to visit some of the shops on the road, if you can get past the crowds.

I'd also turn into Ezra Street a little further along on the left. A charming street of Victorian shop fronts and warehouses. I found a nice oyster-shucking shack hidden in a small alcove here, but the bloke running it might have gone by now. There are so many things to see that you really will need to spend a while here.

And look at that pub on the corner of Ezra Street, the **Royal Oak**! What a great original sign! Frankly, this would be a great place to finish – but just in case you feel inclined for a bit more walking, you could continue to the end of Columbia Road.

At the end, turn right into Hackney Road. Over the road there's a grassy patch, but if you look opposite that, at 324 Hackney Road, you can still see the figure of a black horse from the days when this was the Nag's Head pub. I'm glad the horse is still there, but I do wish they'd stop closing down pubs.

Speaking of horses, turn left off Hackney Road into Goldsmiths Row.

Here you'll find **HACKNEY CITY FARM 19**,

which is really rather lovely (but it's closed on Mondays, except for bank holidays).

You can see horses, chickens, piggy-wig-wigs and goats and stuff. It really feels like you've stepped out of the city and straight into the countryside. Remember to wash your hands, though!!!

Okay, okay, it was a bit of a walk… But I bet now you're really ready for that pint.

See you back at the Royal Oak. Last one there's a rotten egg.

Tally ho!

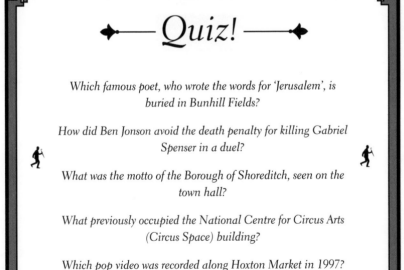

Quiz!

Which famous poet, who wrote the words for 'Jerusalem', is buried in Bunhill Fields?

How did Ben Jonson avoid the death penalty for killing Gabriel Spenser in a duel?

What was the motto of the Borough of Shoreditch, seen on the town hall?

What previously occupied the National Centre for Circus Arts (Circus Space) building?

Which pop video was recorded along Hoxton Market in 1997?

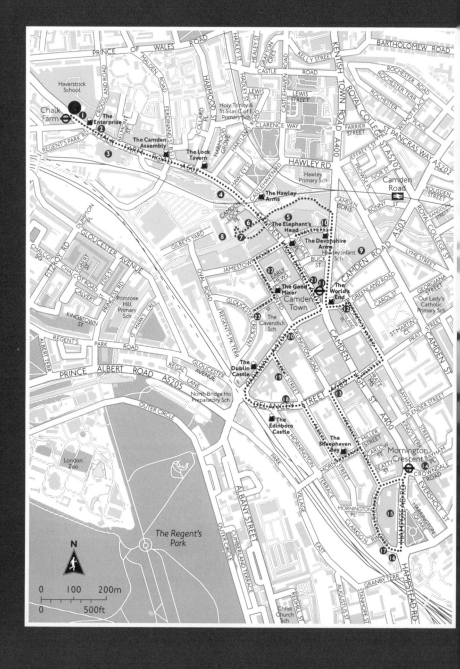

19 A BADASS ROCK 'N' ROLL TOUR OF CAMDEN

DISTANCE
5.6 km (3.5 miles)

TIME
2 hours 20 minutes

⇌ ⊖

NEAREST STATIONS
Chalk Farm & Camden

Rock 'n' roll. Peace out, man!

Now, we'll start at Chalk Farm Station, where (as you might recall from **Walk 8**) Madness took the photo for the cover of *Absolutely*. Indeed, from here you can either follow the Primrose Hill walk or this Camden walk; but frankly, both are quite close, so you could actually do one after the other.

We are going to follow Chalk Farm Road towards Camden Town – but first, look across towards the **Enterprise**. Just next door to the left is a new block of flats called **MARINE ICES APARTMENTS ❶**. When I was young we used to go here very often for ice creams, when it was one of London's only actual ice cream parlours. They had a whole ice cream section where you could sit and have a Knickerbocker Glory, Bomba, Peach Melba or Banana Split; or you could sit in

the restaurant section to have pizza or pasta. Such a pity it's gone.

Anyway, as a reference to the institution that was Marine Ices, the developers agreed to have an ice cream cone painted on the side of the building.

Further along is **MARATHON ❷**. You might wonder why I'm mentioning a kebab shop in this guide. This place is legendary amongst locals as a place to go after the pubs close. I've spent many a late night over the years, kebab in one hand, can of lager in the other, watching the live music in the back room. They've had their problems with the council over the years and their late licence intermittently gets revoked – but hopefully by the time this book comes out it will be back. I wonder if the French rockabilly Daniel Jeanrenaud (I call him 'French Elvis') and the old saxophone players will be back, too. The amazing thing is that you can meet people from all walks of life here, from a high court judge to a penniless hobo, all of whom have one thing in common: they simply desire a drink and kebab after the pubs close.

On the other side of the road you can't miss the **ROUNDHOUSE** ❸, built in 1846 as a railway shed with a turntable in it, where locomotives could revolve. Unfortunately, it only lasted 10 years before trains got too big for it and it had to be used as a warehouse. By the time of the Second World War it had been abandoned – but it became a music venue in the 1960s. It was here that Pink Floyd made their debut in 1966 and it's also said that punk rock was born here when the Ramones supported the Stranglers in 1976. It's where Led Zeppelin played their first London gig, too. A whole string of famous bands have appeared at the Roundhouse, but for me the most important was when David Bowie performed here with the Spiders from Mars. It was the first time he made them all wear make-up and sparkly jumpsuits. Mick Ronson and Woody Woodmansey, who were tough Yorkshiremen, refused at first, saying, 'We're not bloody wearing that!' But after they saw the amount of attention they were getting from the women in the crowd, they were begging Bowie to hand over the mascara for subsequent gigs! It's still a popular music venue today.

On the roof you can see a statue by Antony Gormley (famous for the Angel of the North) and you can also score points by spotting the cattle trough outside, by the bus stop (see the **STREET FURNITURE CHALLENGE**, page 6).

Just opposite is a closed-down bar that was most recently called Joe's, and before

PUB

The Lock Tavern

that the Engine Room, but was previously Belmont, where Lemmy from Motörhead was often seen propping up the fruit machine in the 1980s.

Keep going and you will pass another popular live indie music venue and pub called the **Camden Assembly** (but I remember it as the Monarch). This whole stretch is constantly changing, though they've definitely spruced it up a bit in the last few years, and there are many bars and cafés. You will also soon pass the **Lock Tavern** – another cool pub that gets lively in the evenings. There's a nice roof terrace and garden too. It's bigger than it looks!

The best time to visit Camden is the weekend when the market is at its most bustling.

Coming up on the right is the **STABLES MARKET** ❹, named after the stables that existed here when the whole area was dominated by the Camden Goods Depot. Actually, they have changed the sign, so it now reads 'Camden Market', but it's the entrance on the right opposite Hartland Road.

STABLES MARKET

This is a warren of passages and tunnels with shops and stalls of all different kinds, especially popular with young people with piercings and tattoos.

In the 1980s the market was a lot more rough around the edges and less orderly, and it had punks everywhere. Speaking of punks, as you enter just walk diagonally to your left and you'll see some stairs going up the side of the building. It was on these steps that The Clash took the photo for the cover of their self-titled debut album. Had you turned right on entering the market you would have also come to a statue of Amy Winehouse, which is quite good for your Instagram.

You'll probably see statues of horses and workmen all around the market, reminding you of the time when the area would be teeming with transport activity. Goods arriving from the London and Birmingham Railway would be lugged by horses onto carts or barges, to be taken off to the docks or other parts of London. The poor horses worked very hard, so there had to be a horse hospital here, too, where they could get new shoes and recuperate. The last horse was taken out of service in 1967, and in 1975 it turned into a market.

I suspect you will want to spend quite some time hanging out in the market and exploring all the nooks and crannies and trying all the various food, so I'll pick you up again from Chalk Farm Road, just outside the entrance of the Stables Market where we came in.

Continue along Chalk Farm Road towards the railway bridge. Just before it, to your left down Castlehaven Road, is the **Hawley Arms**, where Amy Winehouse was known to drink. Apparently she was partial to a drink called a Rickstasy, which is three parts vodka,

one part banana liqueur, one part Southern Comfort and one part Baileys. Anyway, I tried one and it was bloomin' disgusting. But the pub is another cool, trendy and lively place with several floors and a roof terrace.

Now continue under the railway bridge on Chalk Farm Road as it becomes Camden High Street and stop on the bridge over the canal. There will probably be one of the last remaining punks here with a sign reading: 'Help punk get drunk'. I guess you could take a photo with him or just get a nice selfie with the railway bridge in the background, emblazoned with the words 'CAMDEN LOCK'.

By the way, along this section of road there are a couple of chances to score points by spotting some wooden brick paving. Just before and after the canal bridge there are manhole covers that look as though they were retained after the pavement was re-paved. If you look carefully, you will see that the brickwork within the round covers doesn't match the surrounding pavement – it is actually made out of wooden bricks!

Over to the left they have just finished renovating this part of the market after major fire damage (the 'Great Fire of Camden' obliterated the area in 2008, and there was another significant fire in 2017). I remember seeing gigs right here beneath the railway bridge at the Caernarvon Castle pub in the 1980s, although that closed down before the fire. There are lots more food places to explore here, along with some shops. If you've got some jeans that you want customised for a very reasonable price, try Koo Style! They did mine and I was happy!

From here you can also see, on the other side of the canal, a building with little egg cups on top. When I was young and we only had four TV channels it was a pretty cool thing when they started showing early morning TV; this was the studio for the breakfast show produced by TV-am. After 1992 it became the **MTV STUDIOS** ❺.

Continue to the end of the little bridge and then turn right onto the canal. Then cross back over the iron footbridge across the lock.

Can you see the building with 'T. E. Dingwall' on it? That was the name of the original owner in the 19th century, and the sign has remained here. Dingwalls, now renamed as **POWERHAUS CAMDEN** ❻, was a popular gig venue for several decades, and the scene of a legendary weekend in punk history during the 1970s. The night after the Ramones played at the Roundhouse they did a gig here, supported by the Stranglers. The Sex Pistols, The Damned and The Clash were all present in the crowd. A fight broke out between Stranglers guitarist Jean-Jacques Burnel and members of the Pistols, The Clash and the Ramones, resulting in the Stranglers' guitarist being ostracised by the music press.

… and there I was at about three o'clock in the morning looking for 1000 brown M&Ms to fill a brandy glass, or Ozzy wouldn't go on stage that night! (Just kidding… but all these stories remind me of Del Preston in *Wayne's World 2*.)

The Regent's Canal, completed in 1820, stretched from Paddington to Limehouse as an extension to the Grand Junction Canal (which led all the way up to Birmingham). Barges filled with goods such as coal and timber would be towed along here by horses. Look at the handrails on the iron bridge and also on the wall at the end of the bridge. You can still see the deep **GROOVES** ❼ created by years of the tow rope rubbing against here.

The big red brick building overhanging the other buildings is the **INTERCHANGE WAREHOUSE** ❽, where freight was transferred between barges and trains. Can you see the little ingress underneath the other iron bridge? It's known as 'Dead Dog Hole' because of all the dead animals (and sometimes people) who have washed up here over the years. These days the building is used as TV studios and other stuff which I'm not allowed into.

The big block of flats that looks like a car park opposite the Interchange Warehouse on the south side of the canal used to be the Gilbey's Gin warehouse. I only mention it because it's nice that my friend Mark Holdsworth has opened his own gin distillery just inside the market, behind Dingwalls, called HALF HITCH Gin. It's pleasing to know that gin is still made here! You can go and learn to make gin right there or just buy some. It's rather fun.

It's tricky plotting a route through Camden. You'll have to go back on yourself a lot.

I'm assuming you'll be here all afternoon, walking up and down the High Street, so you don't have to follow this route in this particular order!

Find your way onto the canal and walk east past the MTV (egg cup) building. In fact, you could continue along the canal for a lovely stroll up to King's Cross and Islington, but that's for another day. We're getting out at the next bridge.

Exit the canal and turn right on Kentish Town Road.

Across the road are some modern space-age-looking flats, which probably looked a lot nicer when they were first built. They're not my cup of tea, but their creator, Nicholas Grimshaw, did win a design award for them.

They're part of the big **SAINSBURY'S COMPLEX** **9**, which was built behind here on the site of the old ABC building. Older readers might remember the Aerated Bread Company, which developed a special way of making bread and had many popular tea rooms dotted around London. They often pop up in novels, including *Dracula* and those by Agatha Christie and P.G. Wodehouse, with people 'taking tea at the ABC'.

On the right, at the corner of Hawley Crescent, there's a red brick building with an elephant above the door. This was the **CAMDEN BREWERY** **10** from 1859 until the 1920s – they were famous for their Elephant Pale Ale. Look out for the cute little elephant heads on the railings, too! Some people think that the elephants are a reference to the Marquess of Camden, who had an elephant on his coat of arms. There's even the **Elephant's Head** at the corner of Hawley Crescent and Camden

High Street, which was also part of the Camden brewery.

Opposite the brewery is the **Devonshire Arms**, which has been a goth pub since the 1980s and still attracts people wearing a lot of black leather. You can see local bands here, too, but I particularly like the smoke extractor fan on the ceiling. Obviously it isn't used any more, but it's a reminder of the days when you could smoke in pubs and you came home reeking of cigarettes. One advantage of smoking in pubs was that *all* you could smell in those days was smoke. Now you can smell all the BO and urinal cubes emanating out of the toilets…

Carry on along Kentish Town Road and just before Camden Town tube station is **THE BRITISH BOOT COMPANY** **11**, which some people will remember as Holts, when I were a lad. The shop dates back to 1851, when they were known for selling hobnail boots. More recently it became famous for being one of the original Dr. Martens stockists (they've been selling them here since 1958). Buying your first pair of DMs felt like a real rite of passage, and many of my friends remember their first time coming here. In the 1980s it became a hangout for skinheads and punks – and a bloke in the pub told me that the band Madness used to live upstairs and wrote the song 'Our House' about this flat. I can't confirm or deny, but it does feature in a few of their pop videos and they definitely bought shoes here.

Having reached the tube station, cross the road to the **World's End**, which has another popular venue for bands downstairs, called the Underworld. Needless to say, all these pubs get very busy, especially on weekends, and Camden is a great place for a night out if you're younger or hipper than me.

PUB

The World's End

There's been a pub here since at least 1691, when it stood in fields, allowing weary travellers to rest on their way from London to Hampstead or Highgate. It became known as the Old Mother Red Cap because of a supposed witch called Jenny Bingham, or 'the Shrew of Kentish Town', who used to sit outside all day in her red bonnet.

The man who got her pregnant when she was only 16 was hanged for stealing sheep; then another lover disappeared mysteriously; her parents were hanged for witchcraft; and another of her lovers was found burnt to a cinder in the oven! She was charged with the murder, but – amazingly – let off because it was discovered that he would often sleep in the oven to escape her nagging tongue! Anyway, people were scared of her and thought she had mystical powers, so they'd go by, shouting abuse at her. I'd love to have the number of her lawyer!

Just after the pub turn left down Greenland Road and then right into Bayham Street.

The first house on your right, **NUMBER 141** ⑫, is where Charles Dickens used to live when he was young, in the 1820s. The original house has been knocked down and replaced, but it's interesting because it's probably what he had in mind when describing Bob Cratchit's house in *A Christmas Carol*. The Cratchits lived in Camden Town and on the other side of the road you can see some houses from that period – so that's the sort of house he lived in, but I bet they go for a pretty penny today!

Walk along Bayham Street as far as Pratt Street and turn right.

Charles Pratt was the first Earl of Camden, in case you're wondering. You should notice some nice old street signs around here. The ones which only show 'NW', instead of 'NW1', are usually pre-1917, unless they're replicas.

We've come round the back of the High Street because it's a bit too busy for me. So now go straight over the High Street and up Delancey Street.

On the left, just before you reach Arlington Road, is the **CAMDEN COFFEE SHOP** ⑬, which is still hanging in there, defying the developers. The Greek owner has been there since the 1970s, but the shop dates from 1947 and is the oldest one in London that still roasts coffee beans in the shop. The aroma of coffee always pervades the whole street and you can see all the smoke billowing out. He even uses the old-fashioned scales, too. It's like going back in time.

Now turn left into Arlington Road and walk to the end. You will reach a big white building.

Ooh… What a nice old pre-1965 road sign!

Turn left on Mornington Crescent and you will see Mornington Crescent tube station in front of you, with **KOKO** just beyond.

I remember KOKO (originally opened as a theatre in 1900) being called the Camden Palace. In the 1970s and 1980s it was called the Music Machine, hosting numerous new wave and punk bands. Famously, this was the last place that Bon Scott from AC/DC was seen drinking before ending up in the Dublin Castle (which we'll come to) and dying later that night of alcohol poisoning.

It was also the last place that *The Goon Show*, with Spike Milligan, Harry Secombe and Peter Sellers, was ever recorded by the BBC; and Monty Python's Flying Circus recorded their first album here.

Speaking of BBC radio shows, if you want an example of the very strange British sense of humour, try listening to BBC Radio 4's *I'm Sorry I Haven't a Clue*, featuring a game called Mornington Crescent. The rules seem to be a complete mystery and the contestants just name London tube stations in turn until someone finally names Mornington Crescent – at which point the game finishes and everyone bursts out laughing. Totally inexplicable!

Inside the tube station there is a plaque commemorating Willie Rushton, who was a frequent contestant!

This is also where the KGB used to meet double agents like Guy Burgess. The code would be to approach the agent and ask for directions to the fictional 'Harvard Square' station. I always thought those code words from James Bond films were nonsense, but apparently they actually used them!

Now cross the road towards the big white building opposite, called **GREATER LONDON HOUSE** 15.

Back in the 1920s, after they had just dug up the Pharaoh Tutankhamun, there was quite an obsession for Egyptian things in London. The Carreras Black Cat Cigarette Factory decided to decorate their building with Egyptian themes, to suggest that smoking their cigarettes was the equivalent to the luxuries of ancient Egypt. For the opening ceremony they even had a big chariot race outside the front.

Walk past the big cats outside the front door and then stop at the corner, where you score points for seeing the horse drinking trough.

Across the road there is a brown plaque on the wall, indicating that **GEORGE CRUIKSHANK** 16 lived there. He was a friend of Charles Dickens and illustrated some of his stories.

Just next door, on the main road, used to be Wellington House Academy before it was knocked down. This was the school that Charles Dickens attended after managing to escape from his job working in a shoe-blacking factory as a child. He had to work in the factory because his dad was in debtor's prison – but once he managed to get into this school he met his sadistic headmaster, William Jones, who inspired Mr Creakle in *David Copperfield*. Dickens later recalled in a speech:

> *I don't like the sort of school to which I once went myself – the respected proprietor of which was by far the most ignorant man I have ever had the pleasure to know; one of the worst-tempered men perhaps that ever lived, whose business it was to make*

as much out of us and put as little into us as possible, and who sold us at a figure which I remember we used to delight to estimate, as amounting to exactly £2 4s. 6d. per head.

Now walk up Mornington Crescent to your right and past the plaque for **WALTER SICKERT** 🔟, who some people thought was Jack the Ripper. One of the reasons he was accused of this was that he painted *Jack the Ripper's Bedroom* and his landlady had claimed that one of the occupants of his room had been Jack the Ripper. Later on, when another prostitute was murdered in Camden, he also produced a series of paintings of the Camden Town Murders, but I'm pretty sure he wasn't Jack the Ripper!

Follow the crescent round and check out the old bollard from 1823 on the corner of Mornington Place.

Continue and turn left into Arlington Road, which we came along before. Then turn left into Mornington Street.

If you want a drink in a proper local pub, stop here at the **Sheephaven Bay**. I don't know if he'll be there when you read this, but the manager, Pat, is one of the most convivial fellows and excellent quizmasters I've encountered. You used to get free sausage, chips and beans after the pub quiz and there are plenty of TV screens if you want to watch sports. I hope he's still doing the quiz!

After the Sheephaven Bay turn right on Albert Street and keep going until you get back onto Delancey Street.

Watch out for the ghost signs written on the brickwork on the opposite corner. Points, yay!!

Turn left on Delancey Street, walking past **DYLAN THOMAS'S OLD HOUSE** 🔟 at number 54 and you'll see the **Edinboro Castle**. Remember in **Walk 8** I was saying how the navvies building the railways would often fight, so they built pubs to segregate them between English, Irish, Scottish and Welsh? The Edinboro Castle was built for the Scots… supposedly. And don't ask me why they've misspelt 'Edinburgh'. Probably some hilarious joke.

Follow Delancey Street round until it meets Parkway. Goodness, there are so many options. A nice walk in Regent's Park if you turn left? Primrose Hill straight ahead? No – this is a Camden walk, so let's turn right down Parkway.

Soon on the left you'll see Rock 'n' Roll Rescue. I do like this shop because a lot of the money goes to charity and some of it goes to saving bees! You can find some interesting second-hand stuff in here, too. There are T-shirts, 7-inch singles, posters, and down the back they've got old guitars and drums etc. I once found one of Depeche Mode's actual keyboards in there, which they used on tour, and it still had their music programmed into it!

Next door is the **Dublin Castle** – this pub was supposedly built for the Irish navvies that I mentioned.

In 1979 Madness managed to wangle a gig here after pretending to be a jazz band, when they were called the Camden Invaders. They were so good that the landlord gave them a weekly residence, which helped cement its reputation as a hip rock venue – and it has since played host to countless bands, including Blur and Arctic Monkeys. Amy Winehouse (of course)

PUB

The Dublin Castle

performed here and was even known to pull pints behind the bar.

Continue down Parkway and turn right briefly into Albert Street. These are lovely houses now, although in the 1960s the one at **NUMBER 127 ⑲** was a bit run-down and was full of actors who studied at the Central School of Speech and Drama in Swiss Cottage. This is where actor and future film director Bruce Robinson lived with his eccentric friend Vivian MacKerrell, who was an out-of-work actor. The crazy antics in the house were the inspiration behind Robinson's film *Withnail and I* (an absolute cult classic). In fact, it was in this house that MacKerrell drank lighter fluid, just like Withnail did in the film.

Bloody fool… You should never mix your drinks!

Now go back and carry on down Parkway, past yet more cafés.

One Shot Coffee do a particularly nice chocolate and almond croissant/pastry thingy, and I also like the Italian delicatessen at number 30 (which is run by a lady who

knows her mortadella from her prosciutto di Parma). The restaurant next door is also pretty decent and reasonably priced. I go there when I want a quick bowl of pasta.

Opposite here is what is currently a Gail's Bakery, but look at the signage above the door: **'TALKING PARROTS' and 'MONKEYS' ⑳**. I remember when this was a pet shop and my dad used to take me in to see the spiders and snakes. It was the first time I saw a parrot talk.

As you cross the road towards the Odeon cinema, glance to your right and mourn the loss of yet another pub. You can still see the sign for the Camden Stores above what is now a curry restaurant. Keep an eye out also for any street signs which show 'Borough of St Pancras' instead of 'the London Borough of Camden', because these are from before 1965, when Holborn, Hampstead and St Pancras got amalgamated into one London Borough.

When you reach Camden High Street again, turn left, passing the tube station on your right-hand side.

Soon after the tube station, on the right, is the **ELECTRIC BALLROOM ㉑**, one of the most iconic music venues in Camden. It started life as an Irish ballroom in the 1930s and has had many incarnations, but when it opened as the Electric Ballroom in the 1970s the first band to play there was called the Greedies, or the Greedy Bastards, whose members included Paul Cook and Steve Jones (of Sex Pistols fame), Gary Moore, and the guys from Thin Lizzy. Sid Vicious was at this gig and it inspired him to form a band called the Vicious White Kids, and to do a one-off show called Sid Sods Off to raise money for his trip to America with his girlfriend, Nancy. While he was in New York he was accused of killing Nancy and he overdosed on drugs, never to return.

In fact, by sheer coincidence, just opposite here (where Urban Outfitters now stands, next to Holland & Barrett) used to be the Camden Plaza cinema – where I saw the film *Sid and Nancy*. (I blagged my way in, pretending to be 18!)

Keep going up towards the canal again and there's loads more shops and stuff to explore. When you get to Jamestown Road (you'll see the Elephant's Head pub I mentioned earlier), turn left. Then turn left again into Arlington Road.

The huge red brick building is **ARLINGTON HOUSE** **22**, a hostel for homeless people. It used to be known as a 'doss house' and is one of the houses set up in 1905 by Lord Rowton to help house the poor. Most of the Rowton Houses have been turned into luxury flats now, but this is the last one that still operates with its intended purpose.

There's a very sad song by Madness called 'One Better Day' where they mention it: 'Arlington House, address: no fixed abode'.

It was in one of the Rowton Houses that George Orwell stayed in *Down and Out in Paris and London*. He described them as being of a very high standard, except for the strict rules about playing cards and cooking. There is one that looks just like Arlington House in Whitechapel, where Joseph Stalin stayed!

I think standards must have improved since the 1970s, when I remember some extremely poor, destitute people hanging around here. I used to be very scared of them but my sister always said she wanted to be one. (She was only about eight, to be fair.)

Carry on until you come to the **Good Mixer**.

Yes, yes, wait for it! We're not going in yet. There's just a little bit to the right here. Turn into Inverness Street and you'll come to the stunning Gloucester Crescent. The first house on your left, number 23, is where playwright **ALAN BENNETT** used to live **23**. It was here that an old lady called Mary Shepherd parked her van on the street and lived in it. He felt sorry for her because she got lots of hassle from pedestrians, so he let her 'temporarily' park on his land – but she ended up staying for 15 years! Afterwards he wrote *The Lady in the Van*, which was adapted into a pretty good film. He doesn't live there any more, but you do see him wandering around the neighbourhood in his overcoat sometimes.

Right, time for that drink.

Head back the way you came and let's go into the Good Mixer. It's one of those pubs that doesn't really look like a pub from the outside, so I was always slightly suspicious of it. But it's an achingly cool place to hang out. In the 1990s all the Britpop bands used to come here – Blur, Oasis and so on… And yes, naturally, Amy Winehouse was known to pop in for a game of pool!!

Bottoms up. Make mine a Camden Hells.

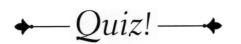

Where did David Bowie first make the members of the Spiders
From Mars wear make-up and crazy costumes?

What are the ingredients of a Rickstasy, the cocktail favoured by
Amy Winehouse at the Hawley Arms?

Why wasn't 'the Shrew of Kentish Town' prosecuted for the
murder of her husband, who was found burnt to a cinder?

What was the previous name of the band Madness?

What was the name Sid Vicious's one-off show to raise money to
go to America?

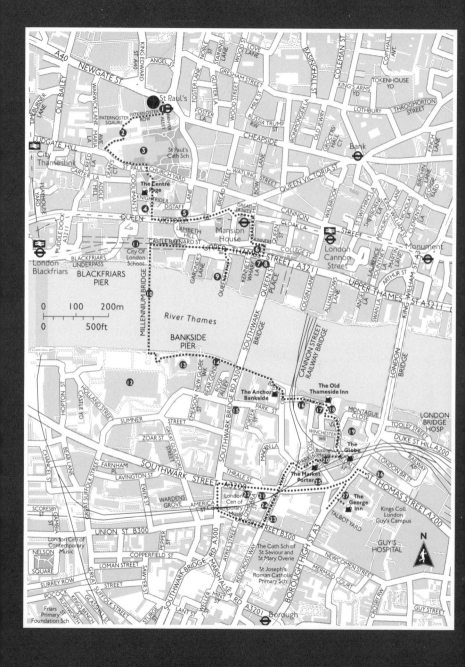